PRINCIPLES

FOR THE GATHERING
OF BELIEVERS UNDER
THE HEADSHIP OF
JESUS CHRIST

PRINCIPLES FOR THE GATHERING OF BELIEVERS
UNDER THE HEADSHIP OF JESUS CHRIST

First Edition: June 2013
Second Edition: September 2013

ISBN-13: 978-1489557315
ISBN-10: 1489557318

For more information visit: *GospelFellowships.net*

Acknowledgements

EVERY NEW Testament Epistle is full of acknowledgments[1] of believers who were in different cities and those who were laboring hard in the Lord. The names of those who have had a part in this volume are too numerous to mention. To all those who labored in editing, revising, suggesting and offering your counsel we are indebted. Above every human help we recognize the Lord's hand in this volume from the start to finish. The messages in this book were birthed out of a genuine burden[2] of the Lord and we pray this burden has been conveyed with as little interference from the human vessels[3] as possible.

We dedicate this work to *our Lord Jesus Christ* and His kingdom work. For from Him and to Him and for Him are all things.[4] *Amen.*

---

[1] Romans 16
[2] 2 Corinthians 11:28, Ephesians 5:27
[3] 2 Corinthians 4:7
[4] Romans 11:36

"I WILL BUILD MY CHURCH,
AND THE GATES OF HADES
WILL NOT OVERCOME IT."

The Words of Jesus Christ our
Lord and *soon coming King.*[5]

---

[5] Matthew 16:18

Table of Contents

Foreword 11
Preface 13
Introduction Letter 17

PRINCIPLES FROM THE BOOK OF ACTS

Principle 1 - Solely Looking to the Person of Jesus Christ 23
Principle 2 - Where 2 or 3 are Gathered Together 27
Principle 3 - God's People Scattered in Sects 31
Principle 4 - God Directed Churches Needed 35
Principle 5 - The Book of Acts Our Example 39
Principle 6 - Not Depending On or Needing Buildings 43
Principle 7 - The People of God Are the Church 47
Principle 8 - Taking a Stand For the Testimony of the Church ...51
Principle 9 - The Early Apostles Didn't Seek After Money 55
Principle 10 - Preaching the Good News 59
Principle 11 - Leading is Serving in Humility 63
Principle 12 - Jesus Christ: The Head of the Church 67
Principle 13 - A Growing Vibrant Movement 71
Principle 14 - Making Disciples Not Just Converts 75
Principle 15 - Not Pleasing Men but God Alone 77
Principle 16 - The Church Was Birthed in Prayer 79
Principle 17 - The Spirit is Essential 83
Principle 18 - The Satanic Counterfeit 85

Principle 19 - Dependence on the Spirit of Jesus.........................89
Principle 20 - Holy Spirit Normal Christianity.......................93
Principle 21 - Hungering After the True Holy Spirit Baptism 97
Principle 22 - God Uses the Weak by His Spirit.......................99
Principle 23 - Cults, False Gospels and Division 103
Principle 24 - Christ the Unity of the Body 105
Principle 25 - Not Judging Others...107
Principle 26 - Having a Right Doctrine but Wrong Spirit..........111
Principle 27 - The Priority of Love..115
Principle 28 - Examine Yourself and Correction in Love............119
Principle 29 - Being Rich in Mercy..123
Principle 30 - Reading the Entirety of Scriptures 125
Principle 31 - Godly Disciplines for Assemblies........................129
Principle 32 - Godliness Through the Act of Submission 131
Principle 33 - The Obedience of Believers Baptism....................135
Principle 34 - The Body of Christ: An Army of Evangelists........137
Principle 35 - The Lord's Supper: The Death of Christ 141

PRINCIPLES FROM THE UNDERGROUND CHURCH IN CHINA

Principle 36 - Dependence on the Moving of the Holy Spirit....147
Principle 37 - Jesus Christ As Lord and Head 151
Principle 38 - The Spirit of Martyrdom 155
Principle 39 - God Actually Answers Prayer...............................159
Principle 40 - The Body of Christ Is the Church........................161
Principle 41 - The Back To Jerusalem Movement.......................165
Principle 42 - The True Mission of the Church..........................167

PRINCIPLES FROM THE UNDERGROUND CHURCH IN NORTH KOREA

Principle 43 - North Korea's Leader, an Image of Antichrist.......173
Principle 44 - A Cost to Be Part of the Church..........................177
Principle 45 - Five Challenging Reminders.................................181
Principle 46 - Meeting in Home Churches 185
Principle 47 - The Lord's Day Can Be Everyday!........................189
Principle 48 - We Are a Body of Christ Together.........................193
Principle 49 - Sharing and Memorization of Scripture...............197
Principle 50 - Not Merely Listening...201

Principle 51 - Measuring True Christian Growth 203
Principle 52 - The Practice of Teaching Children 207
Principle 53 - Raising Up Many Leaders in the Body................211
Principle 54 - Remembering the Poor 213
Principle 55 - Witnessing and Missions Work by Faith 217

PRINCIPLES FROM THE UNDERGROUND CHURCH IN IRAN

Principle 56 - Explosive Growth in an Antichrist State 223
Principle 57 - Sharing the Faith Constantly in All Situations 229
Principle 58 - New Converts Every Church Meeting 233
Principle 59 - Networking Small Groups of Believers................237
Principle 60 - Martyrs Esteemed in the Church 241
Epilogue: The Call to Gather as Fellowships 245

Appendix I - PREPARING THE BODY OF CHRIST FOR PERSECUTION

Preparing for Persecution; To be a Christian by brother Edgar ...251
The Coming Tsunami of Persecution by brother Greg................261
A Plain Vision for Coming Persecution by brother Brian...........269

Appendix II - SELECT TEACHINGS FOR GOSPEL FELLOWSHIPS

Chinese House Churches Interview by brother Denny 299
God's New Thing by brother David 307
Submission and Leadership by brother Zac...............................323
Baptism of the Holy Spirit by brother Denny 335
Without the Holy Spirit of God by brother Chadwick 351
Loving Your Brothers and Sisters by brother Edgar 359

Appendix III - GOSPEL FELLOWSHIPS ADDITIONAL RESOURCES

Statement of Faith for Gospel Fellowships 369
Chronological Bible Reading of Scriptures................................379
Gospel Fellowships Hymnal..391
Gospel Fellowships Readings 451

Foreword

THERE IS only one house that will stand in the coming storm, and only one people who will not be swept away in a flood of last-day deception. There is only one temple that God will fill with His indescribable glory, and only one lighthouse that will forever shine as a pure testimony of God's saving grace. There is only one kingdom that can never be shaken, and only one ark that will be spared in the sudden outpouring of God's righteous judgment. There is only one Bride for the Bridegroom; there is only one, called to the marriage supper of the Lamb.

This one and only is the beloved Church of the Lord Jesus Christ. She is the apple of His eye. This is His body and this is His Bride. This is what Christ has promised to build.

"I tell you that you are Peter, and on this rock I will build My Church, and the gates of Hades will not overcome it."[6]

The book you are now reading is a clarion call to return to the Lordship of Jesus Christ and to join Him in building the Church He started on the day of Pentecost when He sent the promise of His Holy Spirit. This book is not an authority; nor are the brothers who wrote it. They are simply humble men who have a burning passion for the Glory of God and the exaltation of Jesus Christ alone! I believe you will find the principles here to be thoroughly Biblical, intensely practical, and very helpful to any who wish to gather as a true Church under the Lordship of Jesus Christ. The messages are

---

[6] Matthew 16:18

prophetic, and the examples of our brothers and sisters who make up the persecuted Church in China, Iran, and North Korea are sobering and convicting.

The false church, Babylon, will one day fall under the Mighty hand of God's awful judgment never to rise again, and all of heaven will shout, "Alleluia!"[7] Therefore, God says, "'Come out of her, My people,' so that you will not share in her sins, so that you will not receive any of her plagues."[8]

The time is now. Count the cost. You will be persecuted, tested, and tried. You will be misunderstood, hated by the world, and sometimes hated even by the members of your own household.[9] There will be tears, heartache, tribulation, suffering and pain. But, you will be living for the One who is worthy of all, and whose eternal kingdom cannot be shaken nor ever fade away. You will have the privilege of serving the King of kings and the Lord of all lords. Moreover, you will one day have the awesome indescribable experience of seeing His glorious face and hearing Him call you by name as His own.

May God stir up the burning hearts of a Remnant who love Jesus Christ more than their own lives![10] May the Lord bring them together as one so that the fire burns hotter and the light shines even brighter! May Christ have a true and holy testimony on the earth where He has called you to gather with other saints today! May the whole earth be filled with the knowledge of the glory of The Lord, even as the waters cover the sea![11] May we be found ready when He suddenly returns for His Bride!

Looking to Jesus, the Author and Finisher of our faith,[12]

- *brother Brian*

---

[7] Revelation 19:1
[8] Revelation 18:4
[9] Matthew 10:34-36
[10] Revelation 12:11
[11] Habakkuk 2:14
[12] Hebrews 12:2

Preface

THIS VOLUME has been developed out of a burden to see vital gatherings of God's people established in these last days.[13] The time of pressure and persecution that is coming worldwide will be such that it will demand the unity of the true body of Christ. For in the Gospel of Matthew it is declared by our Lord: "Then you will be handed over to be persecuted and put to death, and you will be hated by all nations because of Me."[14] This truth of persecution is Biblical and repeated often in the Scriptures.[15]

Some specific goals for writing this book are:

1.) To assist true believers and Biblical churches in preparing for coming persecution by assembling in smaller groups.[16]

2.) To encourage true believers to leave churches that no longer teach the whole Word of God and to gather as believers under the Headship of Jesus Christ.

3.) To provide a manual of Biblical principles and guidelines for gatherings of believers.

4.) To unify believers who have been separated by various denominational issues, within a gathering under the Headship of Christ.

---

[13] Hebrews 1:2
[14] Matthew 24:9
[15] 2 Timothy 3:12, John 15:18, Luke 6:22, Revelation 6:9-11
[16] To gather in smaller groups where servant leadership can be fostered and where believers can grow in maturity in their Christian walk is essential for coming persecution.

God is desiring to bring great glory to His Son through the body of Christ (*gatherings of true believers*) on the earth. The Scriptures declare that the "Gospel of the kingdom will be preached in the whole world as a testimony to all nations, and then the end will come."[17] This preaching and spreading of the Gospel will be done not by the ingenuity of men, but by the working of the Spirit of God. God is raising many servant leaders to shepherd His Church in these end times. Yet, most will not be men of renown or of prestige. God is raising up many obscure godly servants—who share the Spirit of the True Shepherd—to call for the gathering of His body in our day.

The vision of the book is for gatherings of believers in local areas under the Headship of Jesus Christ, to assemble even with just 2-3 other believers. The name the Lord gave us for this burden is *Gospel Fellowships*.[18] You are free to use that term to associate what God is doing in your area in response to this book.

We do not consider ourselves, or this book, to be an authority, but rather seek to provide simple guidelines to help those who will hear the voice of God and gather with like-minded believers to accomplish God's eternal purpose in the earth.

Many brethren have given their time and consideration in making this book more readable and a reflection of the mind of the Lord. We truly believe this effort has been a collective effort of the body of Christ and a concern of many, not just of a few brothers and sisters in the body. Therefore, we pray that this book can be received by many more in the body of Christ.

The appendices contain, among other resources, some longer transcribed sermons of consequence preached in the last decade that reflect the Lord's heart towards the gathering of believers. There are over 1000 footnotes in this volume—mostly Scripture references. The references are not exhaustive, but they are more than sufficient to be a help to believers. We encourage you strongly to look up many of these verses as you go through the *Principles* book.

May God Himself unify the people of God by His Spirit for encouragement and strengthening in these last days.

---

[17] Matthew 24:14

[18] This name does not need to be used to denote your gathering. To learn further how this name *Gospel Fellowships* came about read the *Statement of Faith* section in *Appendix III*.

Holy Father, we desire to see Your Son glorified and lifted up in our midst. We are everyday humbled to be children of Yours and to be a part of Your body, the Church. We are tired of seeing what men can do in Your Name, and our burden is to see You do a fresh work of Your Spirit to allow many more to become disciples of Jesus Christ. Please Lord, breathe upon Your servants, give us renewed commitment to carry the cross and follow You in the narrow way that leads to life. May we be full of Your love by the Holy Spirit for others and look for a wonderful end times expansion of Your kingdom into the entire world. We ask that You would do these things and much more for the glory of Your holy Son, Jesus Christ. Amen.

Introduction Letter

DEAR SAINTS scattered abroad,[19]

Greetings in the precious Name of our Lord Jesus Christ. To all who are reading this book, called to be saints and beloved of God, grace to you and peace from God our Father and the Lord Jesus Christ.

With such powerful modern movements of the Spirit such as the house Church Movement in China,[20] the underground Church in North Korea, and the underground Church in Iran, we need to reevaluate the fruitfulness of the body of Christ in our countries. There is a great need to see such a move of God's Holy Spirit in many of the churches in the world. As the Church, we believe that there is a need to again learn godly discipline, prayer and discipleship from these suffering brothers and sisters, especially in countries where no strong persecution is yet taking place. The Lord is in deep pain.[21] He is mocked and He is blasphemed.[22] The Lord wants us to return to Him.[23] As we compare our lives to the Christians in China, in North Korea, in the Middle east, in other persecuted countries and even Christians in the Book of Acts, there is little similarity.

---

[19] Paul in Ephesians 1:1 and other verses declares all Christians *saints* or *holy people* so this letter is addressed to all believers in Jesus Christ.

[20] Referring to the unregistered underground rural house Churches

[21] James 4:4

[22] 1 John 2:15

[23] Revelation 3:19

In 2 Timothy it says: "In fact, everyone who wants to live a godly life in Christ Jesus will be persecuted."[24] Western Christianity as an example, more often than not, finds Christians living so much like the fallen world around them[25] that there is no need to persecute them. Only 3-5% of Christians witness in North America. The salt has lost its flavor. The light is barely flickering. May God, by His Spirit, use this book to turn the hearts of His people back to Him, for He is willing to pardon us.[26] May we return to Christlikeness,[27] responding in obedience and love to God's Word, and receive power from the Holy Spirit, to become bold witnesses for Him. May the Lord use this book to prepare us and make us worthy[28] of the persecution that will come globally.

We don't need more large church buildings; we need the kind of true fellowship of the Body that these persecuted believers experience. We have a desperate need to see an expression of the Church where Jesus Christ is allowed to be the Head, and where there are servant leaders who share His heart to shepherd His body. In this day there is a tendency and a temptation to rely more on technology, websites, and money than the Holy Spirit of God. We truly have "acquired wealth and do not need a thing."[29] Yet we desperately need God's empowering to be His disciples and witnesses to a lost and dying world.

With over 40,000 registered denominations worldwide, the true members of the body of Christ are scattered abroad and divided into many different groups, sometimes over nonessential doctrines. God clearly calls this division in the Church *carnality* in the Book of Corinthians.[30] We are in need of a unified gathering of brothers and sisters to meet under Christ's Lordship and to obey Christ's call for the discipleship and evangelization of the world.[31]

However, not all unity is right unity. For there are many movements with apostate believers who desire unity apart from truth.

---

[24] 2 Timothy 3:12
[25] Philippians 3:18-20
[26] 1 John 1:9
[27] 1 John 2:6
[28] Ephesians 4:1
[29] Revelation 3:17
[30] 1 Corinthians 3
[31] Matthew 28:18-20

These movements declare we should not judge or preach truths that might be offensive to some. They say that we are one with all believers in Christ—even cults, sects and other religions such as Catholicism. This calls for the wisdom of the saints to seek only unity with all true believers in Jesus Christ. The fruit of the Spirit[32] and regard for Holy Scripture should be a primary test for true fellowship in Christ.

We must respond with the love of 1 Corinthians chapter 13 to accept brothers that we can disagree with on some nonessential doctrinal points but with whom we can have fellowship as part of the body of Christ. There are even true believers who hold to teachings that can be wrong and we can have fellowship with these believers and still not accept their teachings. This calls for the maturity and discernment of the believers who are able to in meekness and love guide believers into the fullness of the true faith.[33]

Jesus Christ is coming back for a unified Church. A holy Church. An uncompromising Church.[34] A Church that is full of love for each other and for the lost world. May we begin to be an expression of such a Church for the Lamb that was slain. He deserves the reward of His sufferings.

Please consider using these following principles in your house fellowships, gatherings, and churches as the Lord leads. Also—as you are led of the Lord—consider assembling with others in your local area, even with just 2-3 other believers in the Lord.

"Let us be awake and sober,"[35] as we "look forward to the day of God and speed its coming."[36] May all of us seek Him anew for the power of His resurrection and to be found worthy[37] to be invited to the marriage supper of the Lamb of God.[38]

- brother Greg, brother Edgar (on behalf of other brothers and sisters in the Lord.)

---

[32] Galatians 5:22-23
[33] 2 Timothy 2:25
[34] Ephesians 5:27
[35] 1 Thessalonians 5:6
[36] 2 Peter 3:12
[37] Luke 21:36, Philippians 1:27
[38] Revelation 19:9

Principles 1 to 35

Principles from the
Book of Acts

Principle 1

Solely Looking to the Person of Jesus Christ

WE NEED the kind of humility that was expressed in the early Church as recorded in the Book of Acts. This kind of humility is today manifested in many underground and persecuted Churches across the world because they have dealt the death blow to pride and independence.[39]   These persecuted believers have become solely dependent on Jesus Christ as the Head to lead them and guide their meeting as Churches.[40] A brother stated this truth, in another way: "Christ should be the gathering center of His people. We should be drawn by His presence, not by a man. When believers see this and act upon it, the local Assembly need not be shaken by the departure of any man. An Assembly where Christians gather to Christ has strength, stability and solidarity."[41]

When we come together to hear a famous speaker or elevate one specific teaching, this in many ways does not glorify or speak of Jesus Christ as Head of that Assembly. It is a good thing that orally in every meeting and through song Jesus Christ is honored, glorified and proclaimed Head of the Church. This constant referring to His

---

[39] Acts 2:44
[40] Colossians 1:18
[41] William MacDonald (1917-2007)

person will ensure that this burden is kept in the forefront of every gathering of believers.[42] "The sign of a New Covenant Church is that people meet with Jesus every single time we gather in His name."[43]

When we come together for fellowship we are prone to bring many preconceived notions of how a meeting should operate. We tend to rate our experience based on how good the worship made us feel, or how affected we were by a particular sermon—all too easily forgetting that it isn't about us at all. It is about Him. If we come to meet with the living God and to experience Him rather than looking to men, we would be much more edified and that would result in our glorifying Him even more. The famous pastor in Scotland known as the prophet of Dundee[44] once wrote: "For every time you look to men, *look ten times to Christ.*" This constant looking back to Christ will keep us from judging others, and will allow us not to be discouraged even when we see problems with others in the body.

In chapter ten of Mark's Gospel we find Jesus Himself teaching the early Church leaders how to lead a group of believers:

"Jesus called them together and said, 'You know that those who are regarded as rulers of the Gentiles lord it over them, and their high officials exercise authority over them. Not so with you. Instead, whoever wants to become great among you must be your servant, and whoever wants to be first must be slave of all.'"[45]

Sadly, some Pastors and church leaders today *lord* over their congregations.[46] They exercise human power, control and pride. The Lord taught His disciples and He reminds His Church today: If you lead a gathering of believers, act in humility, be a servant and even a slave. In another text Jesus said: "Instead, the greatest among you should be like the youngest, and the one who rules like the one who serves."[47] In Jewish society this was a radical statement. The older had the right to the best seat. The older would speak while the younger

---

[42] Colossians 1:28
[43] Zac Poonen
[44] Robert Murray M'Cheyne (1813-1843)
[45] Mark 10:42-44
[46] 1 Peter 5:3, Matthew 24:48-50
[47] Luke 22:26

had to listen. The Lord Jesus was telling the future leaders in the body of Christ: Act in humility, listen often and serve others.[48]

We need shepherds who desire that the Lord Jesus Christ have the preeminence and not themselves. The challenge comes to us from the Lord: "How long will you waver between two opinions?"[49] We must seek to have our Assembly meetings like the New Testament and not like popular modern churches.

Jesus Christ is the Alpha, He is the first of everything.[50] Therefore He should be the first in our fellowships. His Name should be honored first, His death and resurrection proclaimed,[51] and His person praised. For it is His Gospel, His Church, His Glory, His Scriptures and His kingdom that we proclaim. He spoke the world into being.[52] He rules God's creation.[53] It is His Spirit that He gives us. For He is the only Son of God.[54] "For from Him and through Him and for Him are all things. To Him be the glory forever! *Amen.*"[55]

---

[48] Philippians 2:7
[49] 1 Kings 18:21
[50] Revelation 1:17
[51] Philippians 1:14
[52] Colossians 1:16
[53] Revelation 3:14
[54] Revelation 2:18
[55] Romans 11:36

Principle 2

Where 2 or 3 are Gathered Together

THE GENESIS of a Church in Scripture is seen in this simple statement of our Lord: "For where two or three gather in My Name, there am I with them."[56]

A gathering of believers where the Lord Jesus is present is the Church, even if there are only two or three believers there. When believers gather in smaller groups it allows the Lord's people to meet more frequently during the week, even daily, as the early Church did.[57] This provides the confidence and expectation to meet with other wholehearted disciples of Jesus Christ, to meet with the Lord Jesus who is in the midst, to receive direction from the Lord and to benefit from mutual encouragement[58] and prayers.

The meeting of the Church does require thought and guidance from the Lord as 1 Corinthians tells us: "Everything should be done in a fitting and orderly way."[59] Matters to be considered include the establishment of leadership [60] by the Holy Spirit, and the keeping of

---

[56] Matthew 18:20
[57] Acts 2:46
[58] 1 Corinthians 5:4
[59] 1 Corinthians 14:40
[60] Titus 1:5, Matthew 10:1

traditions[61] that were practiced in the early Churches. Two important practices as revealed in the Word of God are Baptism[62] and the Lord's Supper.[63] As we submit our minds and wills to the Word of God then He will establish the Church He desires through us.

What a beautiful simplicity to see the body of Christ meeting under the Headship of Jesus where the presence of the Lord manifests Himself.[64] There is something special when you meet a brother or sister for the first time and after spending some time talking there is that fellowship of kindred minds in the Spirit of the Lord. Yet the meeting of the Church that Jesus Christ recognizes is more than just meeting to talk or even discuss the things of the Lord. It is a time given to invoke the Holy Name of God in reverence and to verbally proclaim His goodness, promises and character. It is a time where we come together to exalt the Son of God, Jesus Christ, and worship Him in words of heartfelt gratitude in His holy presence.

There are many examples of people who were flippant in the presence of God in the Old Testament who were killed or judged because of this.[65] As believers in Christ in the New Covenant we have access to God through the blood of Christ freely, yet we should carry with us the fear of the Lord and reverence as we meet together as God's people. This does not mean there cannot be happiness but rather it becomes a holy joy, a holy rejoicing, a holy thanksgiving.

The Anabaptists were a group of godly brothers from many different backgrounds that met in small groups during the time of Martin Luther and the reformation. From early Anabaptist literature[66] we learn that they were instructed to meet together in small groups 3-4 times a week. They also understood that any fellowship they would have with each other resulted directly from their fellowship with Christ, thus keeping the reality of an individual vibrant relationship with Christ an integral building block of any Assembly or gathering of the saints.

---

[61] Acts 2:42
[62] Acts 2:38
[63] 1 Corinthians 11:28
[64] 1 Corinthians 5:4
[65] 2 Samuel 6:6-7, 1 Samuel 6:19-20
[66] Schleitheim Brotherly Union (1527)

Those who gather together as the body of Christ must be gathered by the Lord. Many are too busy and rushed to really hear the voice of God speaking to them.[67] It is time to wait upon the Lord and allow Him to direct us where He would take us. It is very important at the end of the age to be found directly in the will of God.[68] Our Lord Jesus gives us a very sobering account of five foolish and five wise virgins.[69] It should be our goal to find like-minded fellowship with believers in Jesus Christ who are trimming their wicks and filling their vessels with oil.[70]

Many lament the lack of true godly fellowship but only find it in a few other saints in the Lord. Thus may we be freed to realize that when we meet in this way, even as 2-3 believers in a room, we are the Church. As God grows and adds to the number, then giftings and callings will manifest. These giftings allow for a fuller expression of the Church[71] which brings honor to the Head of the Church, Jesus Christ.

---

[67] John 10:4, Hebrews 3:7
[68] 1 John 2:17, 1 Peter 4:2
[69] Matthew 25:1-13
[70] Matthew 25:3-4
[71] Ephesians 4:15-16

Principle 3

God's People Scattered in Sects

WE SEE the beginning of a movement where God is waking up many of His sheep to hear His voice in the midst of the noise and rustle of the denominational confusion. God never intended His Church to be divided,[72] confused and led back and forward with every wind of doctrine. "Then we will no longer be infants, tossed back and forth by the waves, and blown here and there by every wind of teaching and by the cunning and craftiness of people in their deceitful scheming."[73]

In the current setting of tens of thousands of sects and groups we believe the Lord has His people in almost every one of them. One brother speaking of his personal journey with the Lord felt that the Lord told him to "Leave Mount Ism's and go to Mount Zion." With such counsel we agree that the work of God would be much purer and a more brightly shining light in this current world system if saints left the *Ism's* they were a part of and joined in unity, under the Headship of Jesus Christ. This does not necessarily mean a physical leaving of a church or denomination, but rather the departing from

---

[72] 1 Corinthians 1:10
[73] Ephesians 4:14

these divisions in the hearts of God's people. Jesus prayed in John 17 that they all may be one.[74]

There is a Biblical simplicity and truth that the true Church is always unified as one in God's eyes. The Church today is in many ways unified in purpose spiritually, but unity rarely manifests physically in a locality. Yet it is the will of God for the local gathering of the body of Christ to be unified spiritually in a physical setting. The Chinese underground Church is a great example to us. They have eight major branches but are unified with respect to all major doctrines. God has allowed for different sects and groups to form with unique recoveries of truth in each generation. Yet in the end of the age each group must desire the true unity of the body of Christ.

In the end times God is calling for all believers to have the same mind as Jesus Christ in seeing the Church as one, for in heaven there will be only one Church and it is a called-out Assembly that glorifies God and walks in holiness.[75] So we must look past all labels and denominations and see each true believer as God sees them. In 2 Timothy the Scriptures clearly show how God sees those who are His: "Nevertheless, God's solid foundation stands firm, sealed with this inscription: 'The Lord knows those who are His,' and, 'everyone who confesses the Name of the Lord must turn away from wickedness.'"[76] So we also see those in different sects and groups who are departing from sin and the ways of the world and we can have fellowship with them as we are on this similar pilgrim way.[77]

If we would have spiritual eyes to see the body of Christ as the Lord sees from heaven we would be shocked to see believers shining in *white*[78] from all different denominations and sects. Though there is a precious gem of truth to be admired in each denominational group in that they perhaps have more light on a certain doctrine than others, the burden of the Lord for the end times Church is to have a unified body that shares all these truths in balance. The fullness of Christ is God's ultimate end for each local body, a Bride without spot

---

[74] John 17: 21
[75] 1 Peter 1:15-16, 1 Peter 1:22
[76] 2 Timothy 2:19
[77] 1 Peter 2:11
[78] Revelation 3:5

or blemish, or wrinkle.[79] It should be every believer's goal to be a part of a maturing gathering of believers[80] where all grow up into full maturity. In the same way, it is every believer's individual aim to become *perfect* even as our Father in heaven is perfect.[81] The Lord will have a Bride, His holy people,[82] gathered in the end times under one banner: The Lord Jesus Christ.

There are many shining examples in Church history of those brothers and sisters who did not conform to patterns of men and doctrines of men but sought to be under the banner and Headship of Jesus Christ. One brother who was leading many saints into this reality said of his calling from God: "I was to bring people off from all the world's religions, which are in vain."[83] Few believers today see that such things are vanity, because to promote a denomination in itself is vain; it is promoting the kingdom of man, which is spiritual Babylon. God can free us from all such things and release His body to build His kingdom as one Body.

A longing prayer of a godly saint from the past speaks of the need for a *God birthed* and *God sustained* work in gathering His body together: "I want to see something that God builds. I want to find some people so hungry for God that every night they want to pray and make intercession. We've tried every scheme and every fancy thing to try and work something up. But what we need is for somebody to come down. Some person! Not a new theology, a Person!"[84]

May God assemble His children together for His glory alone. So that the Person of Jesus Christ can be magnified and adored.

---

[79] Ephesians 5:27
[80] John 17:23
[81] Matthew 5:48
[82] Revelation 19:8, 2 Corinthians 1:1
[83] George Fox (1624-1691)
[84] Leonard Ravenhill (1907-1994)

Principle 4

God Directed Churches Needed

WE CAN take heed to the admonition given by the Psalmist: "Unless the Lord builds the house, the builders labor in vain."[85] If we attempt to start a Church gathering without the calling of the Lord, the entire endeavor can be in vain. If the Church model is not built solely upon the Word of God then we can end up building our own church[86] and not the Lord's. To have a desire to escape a religious atmosphere in order to have a less formal meeting where people are free to 'just be themselves'—without reverence for God or submission to authority —is not the Church. We are deceived if we think we can redefine the body of Christ to be a place where there is no leadership, no holy presence of God, no conviction of the Spirit, no crying out to God in prayer. We live in a world where comfort, happiness and financial prosperity are the goals, but we know that, "friendship with the world is hatred towards God."[87] We must look not to the culture around us for our example, but to our Lord and to the example of the early followers of Christ.

---

[85] Psalm 127:1-2
[86] 3 John 9, Philippians 2:21
[87] James 4:4

Another helpful thing for us to do, is to look outside ourselves to countries where there are true organic models of New Testament Christianity being formed by the Holy Spirit. We think of the house Church movement in China, the underground Church in North Korea, and many others who are forced to rely solely on the Holy Spirit to guide their meetings. Such believers are not looking to find a model of Church that fits them or feels right for them, rather God is leading them to be His Church. Many of us reading this volume live in Western countries where not only the secular culture, but the church itself, has become saturated with a busy worldly mentality. The work of the Church cannot be done with the world's ways or methods. There must be a divorcing of this system of men when we are seeking to be involved with the Lord in the building of His Church on this earth. Clever ideas never build the heavenly Jerusalem but just build Babylon on the earth. We are to be led by the Spirit of God submitting to what the Lord wants according to His Word. If our heart cry is, "Not my will, but Yours be done,"[88] when looking to establish a more Biblical meeting of the Church, we should come to the Scriptures and ask, *God, what does Your Church look like?* He is faithful to show and guide.

We should nurture the type of mindset the Apostle Paul had when he declared to the Church in Corinth that we are only servants doing God's will. "Who then is Paul, and who is Apollos, but ministers through whom you believed, as the Lord gave to each one?"[89]

A servant has one purpose only and that is to please his Master and receive directions from Him.[90] Thus we must hear the Holy Spirit of God directing us when setting out to start a fellowship gathering and we must remember the Spirit of God will never lead contrary to the revealed Word of God.[91] So we should be careful not to follow any method of man[92] but rather endeavor to be led of God's Spirit back to the Word of God.

---

[88] Luke 22:42
[89] 1 Corinthians 3:5
[90] Colossians 3:22
[91] John 16:13
[92] Galatians 1:1

As God directs in the formation of the body of Christ, and as we follow the whole counsel of the Word of God, sharing our faith freely, the Lord will add to the Church daily.[93] We simply need to follow His directions by the Holy Spirit of God. The New Testament writings with divine direction from the Holy Spirit will guide you. Holy reliance on His Word and obedience to the direction of God will build your gathering into the Church God desires.

---

[93] Acts 2:47

Principle 5

The Book of Acts Our Example

ALMOST EVERY denomination and Christian movement has begun with a desire to get back to the model and example found in the Book of Acts.[94] Those that are Biblically building the Church and being led of the Lord are invariably drawn back to this Apostolic example which God has preserved for us. We have heard many reasons why different Christian movements practice a specific doctrine and why they promote a certain teaching. Yet, when we carefully study the Book of Acts we find that many practices in modern evangelical churches are not found in this record of the apostolic Church.[95]

It can be a good practice to read through the Book of Acts noting the practices of the Church. With careful reading there are hundreds of practices we can find in the Book of Acts so we can emulate early believers. When comparing this list with the typical modern evangelical church we sadly note few similarities.

Besides obtaining theology from the Book of Acts in the Bible, we must also use all of God's Word to avoid error of interpretation.

---

[94] Originally rendered: *Acts Of The Apostles*
[95] We encourage ever believer to read the *Book of Acts* afresh. To learn principles, traditions and the way this ancient Church operated under the direction of the Holy Spirit of God.

The Book of Acts together with the Gospels of Matthew, Mark, Luke and John provide the foundational knowledge for discipleship and Church work, the deeper spiritual realities of which are later expounded in the Epistles. There can be dangers when getting all of our theology from the Book of Acts alone. It is important to read the Book of Acts in light of the other Books of the Bible and especially the New Testament writings, to determine all foundational principles of the Church. It can also be noted that the Church was birthed in persecution which seemingly makes the Book of Acts not palatable for those who are not living under such pressures. Yet, we should note that the Church Scripturally is shown to always be hated by the world[96] and not to fit in with the fashion and ways of the world system.[97] Lastly, the end times Church will clearly be marked with tremendous persecution which makes the Book of Acts a vital record for us on how to react as God's children during such times. We must also read through the Epistles and learn of the Spirit on how Assemblies in the Lord can grow to full maturity, especially as it relates to the end times.

A Chinese underground Church leader noted: "God is only interested in His work, not our work. He oversees and empowers those things that originate in His heart."[98] Thus, "Is it found in the Book?", should be one of the main questions we ask ourselves when part of a forming fellowship. If the direction, goals, vision, means and plans of a Church are not found within the Book of Acts and Scriptures one has to ask "Is it God's will?" The early Christians did not question God's ability to reach foreign cultures (*Gentile idol worshipping peoples*), rather they trusted the Lord daily to build His Church and took orders from the Spirit of God. Thus, the Church grew and many became obedient to the faith.[99] God's Word was glorified in many regions that had never heard the Good News.[100]

We should also be very open to God's leading in different local areas and not prescribe one style or method of meeting to be exactly

---

[96] 1 John 3:13
[97] 1 John 2:15-17
[98] Brother Yun
[99] Acts 6:7
[100] Acts 13:49

replicated. Though there are principles and commands[101] that all gatherings should exactly keep the same.[102] Yet there were differences in the way believers met, which one can see in the Book of Acts and Epistles. Some examples can be meetings where one brother teaches,[103] meetings where all share,[104] gatherings where there are prophets,[105] gatherings were there are strong teachers.[106] Also in some places the believers met daily in areas,[107] in others they met each day for a teaching, in others prayer meetings,[108] in others unbelievers were present,[109] and in others they practiced the Lord's Supper.[110] Thus we see a wonderful variety of meetings and we should not demand all Assemblies to meet and form in one fashion. We can rejoice with all types of gathering. Perhaps one gathering of believers has one mature brother that teaches mostly compared to another Assembly where every meeting all are encouraged to prophesy. There should be no standard especially in times of persecution. God's Spirit will lead in many different ways. In the underground Church in China primarily one brother will teach yet many are sent out as missionaries. It would be more fruitful in many countries to see this happen then simply a meeting where all get to share something but no missionaries are sent out. Such a meeting can just end in spiritual selfishness and self-importance rather then self-denial and humility.

As we look to the example of the early Church we can be encouraged that by faith they overcame many struggles. So we should not lose heart when we desire to emulate them in word and deed. The only true way of Church growth is to depend on the same principles and truths in the Book of Acts which the early believers had. What a blessed assurance we can have, for we have sure commands and principles that the Lord has left for us in the record of Scripture, especially the Acts of the Apostles.

---

[101] 1 Timothy 4:11, Titus 2:15
[102] 1 Corinthians 7:17, 1 Corinthians 14:33
[103] Acts 20:9
[104] 1 Corinthians 14:31
[105] Acts 13:1
[106] Acts 18:27
[107] Acts 2:46
[108] Acts 12:12
[109] 1 Corinthians 14:24-25
[110] Acts 20:7

Being a part of the Church work that is growing is not an easy task. Even though it is God's work it still requires time, devotion, and suffering. Yet, as we allow the Lord to build His kingdom on this earth through our lives there is great reward and joy. Individual sacrifice becomes corporate surrender to the will of God and reaps the fruit of everlasting life.

"If we would reform the Church, we must make use of the Holy Scriptures and especially of Acts where it is clearly to be found how things were in the beginning what is right and what is wrong, what is praiseworthy and acceptable to God and to the Lord Jesus Christ. The Scriptures knows no others than those who acknowledge Christ as their Head and willingly yield themselves to be ruled by the Holy Spirit who adorns them with spiritual gifts and knowledge."[111]

May we come back to this apostolic simplicity to trust the Lord to build His Church and look to the Book of Acts as our example.

---

[111] Kaspar Schwenckfeld von Ossig (1489-1561)

Principle 6

Not Depending On or Needing Buildings

ONE OF the things you do not find in the Book of Acts is the reliance on church buildings. Yet in almost every Christian circle and denomination, there is an emphasis upon building the church, not that "the body of Christ may be built up"[112] but rather the building of an actual structure that we refer to commonly as the *church*. There is a great benefit at times in having a building where the Lord's people can meet in and use for the ministry of the Gospel. Yet, when we look at the Book of Acts, we find no visible record that the Church built buildings. Though they met in some physical locations such as Solomon's Colonnade[113] and the hall of Tyrannus for even two years! [114] Yet, this was not the common practice of how saints met across the rest of God's Churches. Even when looking carefully in Church history it is hard to find evidence of a building being used until 300 AD when pagan temples were being converted into churches under the reign of Constantine.

---

[112] "*To equip His people for works of service, so that the body of Christ may be built up.*" (Ephesians 4:12). "*You also, like living stones, are being built into a spiritual house to be a holy priesthood, offering spiritual sacrifices acceptable to God through Jesus Christ.*" (1 Peter 2:5).
[113] Acts 5:12
[114] Acts 19:9-10

The clear indication is that the early Church met in believers' homes and other venues such as caves, rivers and the catacombs in Rome, which were underground tunnels. When persecution came, as it did constantly in the record of the Acts of the Apostles, they were able to minimize the effects on the Church by relocating meetings to other secret locations in the city or towns and villages nearby. "The Church was always low-keyed, there were places where there were tens of thousands of believers, like Ephesus, and they had no building at all."[115] Even as Church history progressed and an institutional system that became the Catholic church took the stage, many true believers in sects and groups met in homes. To be more concise, many met in caverns, caves, and beside river banks outside cities. Such were the meeting places of many who were severely opposed for the testimony of Jesus Christ which they held. The forbidding of believers meeting together has been the reality of the Church since its inception.

Therefore, there is a great benefit to realize and even practice the independence of the Church from owning and relying on one specific building. The saints should have flexible meeting places.[116] Whether such places change from time to time should be a decision made by each Assembly. There should be openness to seasons of using different structures such as renting an old church building or meeting in an open public venue. Yet, historically it seems the most readily accessible and available option was to meet in homes with smaller gatherings. This type of meeting caters more to disciple-making,[117] and helping the needs of individual fellow-believers.

Sadly in our day the chief obligation and goal of a new church plant is to get to a place where they can build or buy a building. We need to reevaluate that desire as times of persecution are and will be increasing.[118] May we put our emphasis and goal back to what the early Church did, which was to spread the message of the Gospel and to help the poor. Some will be called to have a building but it seems —especially under persecution—that the Church will thrive and exist well without owning any church buildings.

---

[115] Brother Andrew
[116] Acts 2:46
[117] 2 Timothy 2:2
[118] Revelation 2:10

History is full of wonderful testimonies from the true Church where believers have shared their burdens from the Lord towards the Headship of Jesus Christ. Here is one such testimony from the 1500s: "At another time it was opened in me, 'that God who made the world did not dwell in temples made with hands.' This at first seemed strange, because both priests and people used to call their temples or churches, dreadful places, holy ground, and the temples of God. But the Lord showed me clearly, that He did not dwell in these temples which men had commanded and built, but in people's hearts. Both Stephen and the apostle Paul bore testimony, that He did not dwell in temples made with hands, not even in the one temple of Jerusalem which He had once commanded to be built, since He put an end to the typical dispensation; but that His people were His temple, and He dwelt in them."[119] Buildings can be good places to be recognized as a meeting place of God's people but the danger is that we consider the place itself sacred apart from whether or not God is present. The presence of God separates what is truly of Him and what is not.[120] May it be so that we do not reverence the building but the actual presence of the Lord that comes when we gather as His body.[121]

---

[119] George Fox (1624-1691)
[120] Psalm 51:11, Genesis 4:16
[121] 1 Corinthians 3:16

Principle 7

The People of God Are the Church

CONSIDERING CHURCH history and the moving of God's Spirit in many groups that stood for the truth, a house Church or small gathering of believers is not so radical. Rather, gathering in this way is a preferred Biblical approach, especially when the Church is under persecution. If it was important to have specific church buildings to represent God and spread the Gospel, would God not have commanded them in Scripture? Although we find detailed instructions for the tabernacle in the Old Testament[122] we find quite a different emphasis in the New Testament.[123] We see this truth prophetically spoken by Stephen just before he was martyred: "However, the Most High does not live in houses made by human hands. As the prophet says: 'Heaven is My throne, and the earth is My footstool. What kind of house will you build for Me? Says the Lord. Or where will My resting place be? Has not My hand made all these things?' You stiff-necked people! Your hearts and ears are still uncircumcised. You are just like your ancestors: You always resist the Holy Spirit!"[124]

---

[122] Exodus 36
[123] 2 Corinthians 3:6
[124] Acts 7:48-51

He spoke those words in the Sanhedrin which met inside the temple. God was doing a new thing where He lived in the hearts of His people and not in temples.[125] Thus wherever the Lord's people would meet did not matter, for the presence of the Lord was with His people.

Contrary to the Biblical pattern, to this day God's people put emphasis on the buildings which they call "the church," but they fail to realize that they themselves—not a building—are the body of Christ.

It can also be noted that some house Church movements lack vision and direction where the Headship of Christ and the guidance of the Holy Spirit are disregarded. Some house Churches in non-persecuted countries are formed by disgruntled people who did not submit to authority or correction in their previous church experiences. Other emotions such as pride and recognition also play a part where individuals are seeking acceptance for a doctrine or teaching they themselves have developed. These attitudes are also evident in main-line denominations. Such misguided doctrines and people must be opposed and dealt with in love. In some cases, these are doctrines of devils[126] seeking to destroy and divide the body of Christ which are diversions from the truth of the Word of God.

While we present a case for meeting in smaller groups without a physical building, it is of course true that the body of Christ can function in church buildings. We see this in some godly churches where the leaders continue to preach the Word of God without wavering and where they emphasize that the people of God are the Church, the temple of the living God. The temple in Jerusalem was destroyed, and God has moved His holy temple inside true believers, for it says in Scripture: "Don't you know that you yourselves are God's temple and that God's Spirit dwells in your midst?"[127] Scripture tells us also that God the Father inhabits this temple inside of us, as it says in 2 Corinthians: "What agreement is there between the temple of God and idols? For we are the temple of the living God. As God has said: 'I will live with them and walk among them, and I

---

[125] 1 Corinthians 3:16
[126] 1 Timothy 4:1
[127] 1 Corinthians 3:16

will be their God, and they will be My people.'"[128] The Holy Spirit and God the Father dwell in us,[129] and Scripture tells us that the Lord Jesus Christ inhabits us also: "I have been crucified with Christ and I no longer live, but Christ lives in me. The life I now live in the body, I live by faith in the Son of God, who loved me and gave Himself for me."[130]

Stephen stated that God's throne is in heaven. Other passages describe God in His heavenly throne room with the Lord Jesus Christ at His right hand. The Scriptures quoted above are also correct because God the Father, God the Son and God the Holy Spirit are omnipresent. They are able to be present everywhere at the same time. They are present in the heavenly throne room and they are present in the temple of God, not made of hands, inside the inner man of every true believer. We can now worship Him in Spirit and in truth[131] without any physical buildings, for we have become the temple of the living God.

In the end times there will be great pressure from antichrist spirits to have people assemble in places called churches which are not Churches at all.[132] The true body of Christ—who are able to discern between truth and error[133]—will not worship and gather in such an unholy atmosphere. Thus home meetings, even worldwide, will be outlawed. For anyone to meet as a religious group outside of "some" government allowed churches will be illegal. So in light of this and the examples in the Book of Acts[134] there is a healthy, historical and Biblical precedent for the meeting of God's people in homes as the primary meeting place rather than buildings called churches.

[128] 2 Corinthians 6:16
[129] John 14:23, Ephesians 3:16-19
[130] Galatians 2:20
[131] John 4:23-24
[132] Revelation 2:9, Revelation 3:9
[133] 1 John 4:1
[134] Acts 20:20, Romans 16:3-5, Colossians 4:15

Principle 8

Taking a Stand For the Testimony of the Church

"IN THE various crises that have occurred in the history of the church, men have come to the front who have manifested a holy recklessness that astonished their fellows. When Luther nailed his theses to the door of the cathedral at Wittenburg,[135] cautious men were astonished at his audacity. When John Wesley ignored all church restrictions[136] and religious propriety and preached in the fields and byways, men declared his reputation was ruined. So it has been in all ages. When the religious condition of the times called for men who were willing to sacrifice all for Christ, the demand created the supply, and there have always been found a few who have been willing to be regarded reckless for the Lord. An utter recklessness concerning men's opinions and other consequences is the only attitude[137] that can meet the exigencies of the present times."[138]

---

[135] Wittenberg, Germany (1517)

[136] There is a time when there needs to be a holy boldness from the simplest of saints to follow God rather than men and question even the most practiced tradition.

[137] Though we need to fear the Lord alone and not care for the opinions of men, if men disagree strongly with us we must show the character of Christ in meekness and love. If we have to separate, we should do so in the most honorable way possible, not speaking evil of others.

[138] Frank Bartleman (1871-1936)

There is coming a time and perhaps it is already here where many in the body of Christ in countries with little or no persecution will have to take a stand for truth in these end times. There will be such a strong apostasy[139] that will overtake many churches, denominations and groups that the true body of Christ will be called out by God to meet together under the Headship of Jesus Christ. These gatherings will be led by servant leaders who know the true Shepherd[140] and will lead the flock of God into holiness and purity.[141] There could be a time coming soon when even the weakest, simple believer in Jesus Christ will have to take a courageous stand for truth and God's Word. Are you willing to stand amongst all those in Hebrews 11 that stood for faith and righteousness? Are you willing to stand with the millions of Martyrs before the throne of God?

May it be so that God would raise up many to stand up and be counted with those in history who had such a love for Jesus the Son of God that they sacrificed their homes, their possessions, their jobs, their friends, their lives, their all.[142] These believers in Hebrews 11 suffered much, being scattered from home to home, cave to cave, den to den. Like the prophets of old "they were put to death by stoning; they were sawed in two; they were killed by the sword. They went about in sheepskins and goatskins, destitute, persecuted and mistreated—the world was not worthy of them. They wandered in deserts and mountains, living in caves and in holes in the ground."[143]

The world was not worthy of them and will not be worthy of us if we follow steadfastly in their example and ways. Nothing less than a full recovery of the Church in the Book of Acts is the crying need of these last days. May we simply be found willing in the day of His power.[144]

God is calling many of His saints to take a radical stand for truth and seek to be the Bride of Christ in view of the soon coming of the Lord.[145] This will mean bearing the reproach of Christ, not only from

---

139 2 Thessalonians 2:1-3, Matthew 24:12
140 John 10:14
141 Ephesians 5:27, Ephesians 1:4
142 Hebrews 10:32-35
143 Hebrews 11:37-38
144 Psalm 110:3
145 1 John 2:28

the lost world, but also from a believing Christendom that has not submitted to God's Spirit in these last days. "So Jesus also suffered outside the city gate to make the people holy through His own blood. Let us, then, go to Him outside the camp, bearing the disgrace He bore. For here we do not have an enduring city, but we are looking for the city that is to come. Through Jesus, therefore, let us continually offer to God a sacrifice of praise—the fruit of lips that openly profess His Name. And do not forget to do good and to share with others, for with such sacrifices God is pleased."[146]

Such a following of the Lord in this day will seem strange to most, yet it is out of a desire to be only involved with what the Lord is involved with. If the Gospel of Jesus Christ and His Holy Spirit's power are absent from the modern church, then such a church cannot be the Bride of Christ. "Oh how He longs to hear those voices of repentance and intercession asking Him—and saying to Him, Lord, if you don't go with us, we aren't interested in going anywhere. We're not interested in church anymore if You Yourself are not present."[147] When the Lord comes in the midst of His Church in full splendor we will see the glory of the Book of Acts again.

May we be of those that are fully pleasing[148] to the Lord in these last days as we step out to follow the Lord "outside the camp."[149]

---

[146] Hebrews 13:12-16
[147] Allan Halton
[148] Revelation 14:4, Colossians 1:10, Ephesians 5:10
[149] Hebrews 13:13

Principle 9

The Early Apostles Didn't Seek After Money

CHRISTIANITY IS not about money, it's about people. Sadly modern Christendom has been overwhelmed with the salesman who sells Christ as ware and treats the holy things as a way to profit financially.[150] It does not take much discernment for the worldly person to see the counterfeit preacher on TV who makes money look like their god.[151] Yet, sadly, believers who are asleep spiritually, and have not been seeking the Lord, are given over to this delusion which is coming upon them in masses.[152] False teachers abound and the saints are sleeping. There needs to be a clarion cry across all nations that God is not for sale and is against those who love money and equate righteousness with financial gain and profit.[153]

The abuse of seeking after money even in the position of elder or preacher[154] is something that goes back all the way to the Old Testament. Characters such as Balaam and others sought ministry

---

[150] 2 Corinthians 2:17, 1 Timothy 6:10
[151] Matthew 6:24
[152] 2 Peter 2:1, 2 Timothy 4:3-4, Deuteronomy 13:1-3
[153] 1 Timothy 6:5
[154] 1 Timothy 3:3

endeavors for their greediness to gain financially.[155] The Scriptures speak of the error[156] of Balaam, the way[157] of Balaam and the doctrine[158] of Balaam. He was hired and sought to do his priestly work for monetary gain even teaching things contrary to the Word of God.[159] Such hirelings sadly abound in Christendom today.

All true coworkers in the Lord never seek for money[160] but for God's anointing to serve other people. Many in our day state that we need large sums of money to do the work of God and this is false.[161] God never said that the work to disciple the nations required large amounts of money but rather it requires sacrifice[162] which in some cases ends in martyrdom for the Gospel witness.

In the early Church sacrificial giving was a way of life. As stated in Acts: "They sold property and possessions to give to anyone who had need."[163] Jesus did not stop the poor widow from giving her last money. He knew that His Father would provide for her. The early Church took up special collections for the poor and saints in need. Tithing was not practiced in the early Church but Christians gave to each other to support those in need. They also supported the Apostles and the brother of Jesus who were in ministry. First Corinthians chapter 13 teaches us that if we do anything without love then it is worthless.[164] If we give in order to get something from God it is worthless. If we give under duress when we really did not want to give, it is worthless.

In the days of Eli the priest, his two sons were greedy for gain and used *fleshhooks* to take back the best sacrifice meat for themselves.[165] "This was happening in the house of God. Robbing God of His portion. What a sin. The same thing is happening today among God's servants in God's house. The love for money, love for

---

[155] 2 Peter 2:15
[156] Jude 1:11
[157] 2 Peter 2:15
[158] Revelation 2:14
[159] Numbers 22
[160] Acts 20:33
[161] Acts 3:6
[162] Acts 9:16
[163] Acts 2:45
[164] 1 Corinthians 13:2-3
[165] 1 Samuel 2:12-16

power, love for fame and Name. These are the three great fleshhook teeth today among God's people and God's servants. Doing much for money's sake never satisfied. Telling false stories for more money. What a shame. Making God a beggar."[166]

In many countries we find that there are preachers and evangelists demanding payment and a certain status of living.[167] We find in the New Testament something opposite, where Paul the Apostle willingly suffered and lived with less so as to serve them as an Apostle: "Was it a sin for me to lower myself in order to elevate you by preaching the Gospel of God to you free of charge?"[168]

In the New Covenant, giving should not be by compulsion of any law or commandment like it was under the Old, but rather men should yield to the compulsion and urging of the Spirit according to God's natural order.

Though there has been such an abuse of pastors seeking to be greedy after money yet that does not nullify God's desire to provide for those who truly minister in the Gospel. It is a Gospel principle that a worker is worthy of his hire.[169] Therefore, those who serve as full-time workers are to trust the Lord and thus the Lord's people will give to them as they are led of the Spirit. Such giving should be done privately to the individual and should not be demanded. Yet there should be an expectation of giving if one is truly sowing and ministering the Gospel as a full-time worker called of the Lord. God's design for providing natural things in exchange for spiritual things goes back to the priests and Levites.[170]

If there is a certain need that arises in the local fellowship—or for another cause—an offering[171] can be set aside but this is not something that needs to happen weekly; rather it is something that might be done on a *needs* basis as the body of Christ is led by the Spirit. There were collections made by the Apostles from time to time for great needs in the body of Christ such as in this case for believers in Jerusalem: "On the first day of every week, each one of you should

---

[166] Bakht Singh (1903-2000)
[167] 1 Timothy 6:8
[168] 2 Corinthians 11:7
[169] 1 Timothy 5:18
[170] Joshua 13:33, Numbers 18:21
[171] 2 Corinthians 9:5

set aside a sum of money in keeping with your income, saving it up, so that when I come no collections will have to be made."[172] So there cannot be a law about giving and each Assembly of the Lord's people needs to be led of the Spirit in these matters. Servant leaders in small gatherings of believers should not seek to receive money from believers. Only those who God clearly calls as full-time workers should expect the Spirit to provide—through the saints—the needed resources. Keeping themselves free from the love of money and seeking to be content with the Lord's provision in their lives.[173] Such freedom in the body to give as the Spirit leads will result in greater giving[174] to the actual work of God and to things that truly build the kingdom of God such as giving to the poor[175] and to those who truly serve in the Gospel.

---

[172] 1 Corinthians 16:2
[173] Hebrews 13:5
[174] 2 Corinthians 9:6-7
[175] Galatians 2:10

Principle 10

Preaching the Good News

ALL CHRISTIAN service is based on the finished work of Christ.[176] The early Apostles did not go around preaching a Gospel of works[177] or a message of believers needing to do so much[178] to enter heaven but rather all godly living[179] was out of appreciation of the mercy of God. "Therefore, I urge you, brothers and sisters, in view of God's mercy, to offer your bodies as a living sacrifice, holy and pleasing to God—this is your true and proper worship."[180]

They had the Good News message of the resurrection of Christ and the hope of trusting in Him for eternal life. This message of God's love is open to all humanity[181] and is not to be a message of condemnation.[182] The finished work of Christ is something that was preached by the Apostles through everything they did. When they partook of the Lord's Supper it celebrated the resurrection and sacrifice of Christ. When they baptized individuals it spoke of the work of Christ in redeeming us from death to life. All doctrines were centered in the Good News of our redemption through the cross of

---

[176] Galatians 6:14, Romans 6:6-7
[177] Galatians 1:6-7, Galatians 3:1-3
[178] Romans 9:16
[179] Titus 3:8, Ephesians 2:10
[180] Romans 12:1
[181] John 3:16, 2 Peter 3:9
[182] John 3:17

Christ Jesus. "In him we have redemption through His blood, the forgiveness of sins, in accordance with the riches of God's grace."[183]

God has made us who were sinners to become saints not just in word but in actual experience. Such is our standing now that we become holy because of the blood of Christ and His redeeming work. Our heart is made new as we grow into His likeness.[184] Yet from this vantage point of being a redeemed saint of God we should never look down on or despise others who are still in the filth of sin being outside of Christ, for it is from hence we came![185] Thus the true work of Christ in us allows us to love all others because God in Christ loves all: "Who gave Himself as a ransom for all people. This has now been witnessed to at the proper time."[186]

Though there is a narrow road[187] that we walk with the Lord—in sanctification and growing into His likeness—we must never forget that it is the Good News of the Gospel that saves us and keeps us in daily communion with our Lord.[188] One little girl wrote the words on her arm *"Don't forget Me"* as if Christ had written them on her arm; this reminded her of who He is and what He has done for her. Every time she looked at her arm she communed with the Lord. This is a wonderful example to all the Lord's people of the need to continually remember our precious Lord who bought us at such a great price.[189]

The preaching of the Good News must be under the power and direction of the Holy Spirit. In Acts 1 it tells us: "But you will receive power when the Holy Spirit comes on you; and you will be My witnesses in Jerusalem, and in all Judea and Samaria, and to the ends of the earth."[190] Without the work of the Holy Spirit in us we have no witness and no power to do the work of God. The Good News itself is power.[191] This message must be preached in purity and simplicity; it doesn't need any wisdom of words or craftiness of

---

[183] Ephesians 1:7
[184] Romans 8:29
[185] Titus 3:3-4, 1 Corinthians 6:11, Ephesians 2:11-12
[186] 1 Timothy 2:6
[187] Matthew 7:14
[188] 1 John 1:7
[189] 1 Corinthians 6:20
[190] Acts 1:8
[191] Romans 1:16

speech. It doesn't need any enticing cultural relevance or sensitivity to the hearers. The simple proclaimed Good News stands all on its own. "Our Gospel came to you not simply with words but also with power, with the Holy Spirit and deep conviction."[192] God has chosen the act of preaching the Gospel as a means to offer salvation to all.[193]

"Gross moral darkness is none but our hopeful light of Christ's return. As the darkness intensifies we must shine the Gospel more intently. Abounding lawlessness must produce two characteristics in the hearts of the redeemed, relentless evangelism and hastening Christ's return."[194] One of the greatest reasons to preach the Good News is the soon coming of Jesus Christ back to the earth. This Gospel must be preached to the ends of the world before His coming[195] in the midst of growing lawlessness and wickedness and the reign of the antichrist in the world.

Our Lord gave the great commission to preach His Gospel to the ends of the world. Such preaching is also given by His authority[196] so we must have great boldness to proclaim the Gospel. If your goal is anything less than "all nations"[197] then we are not obeying some of the last Words given by our Lord Jesus Christ to His Church. Lastly, we have the wonderful assurance and blessing of our Lord's presence with us as we do His work: "Surely I am with you always, to the very end of the age."[198] Hallelujah!

---

192 1 Thessalonians 1:5
193 1 Corinthians 1:21
194 Derek Melton
195 Matthew 24:14
196 Matthew 28:18
197 Matthew 28:19
198 Matthew 28:20

Principle 11

Leading is Serving in Humility

THOUGH THERE is leadership in the Book of Acts, the examples we find are of those who *serve* the body of Christ. A gathering of believers is still an Assembly even if there is no defined servant leader. As the fellowship grows in the Lord, the Spirit will gift certain men as shepherds.[199] The 12 Apostles were servants to widows giving them bread daily for a season,[200] until they realized they needed to fully devote themselves to studying the Scriptures and giving themselves to prayer.[201] They delegated the function of physically serving the widows but expanded their service to the congregation to give them spiritual food. Though a shepherd in the body of Christ has concerns

---

[199] *"It seems quite clear that a pastor (the Greek noun is poimain, meaning shepherd, found only once in the New Testament) is equivalent to an elder (the Greek noun presbuteros, found numerous times in the New Testament), and is also equivalent to an overseer (the Greek noun episkopos, translated bishop in the KJV). Paul, for example, instructed the Ephesian elders (presbuteros), whom he said the Holy Spirit had made overseers (episkopos), to shepherd (the Greek verb poimaino) the Flock of God (see Acts 20:28). He also used the terms elders (presbuteros) and overseers (episkopos) synonymously in Titus 1:5-7. Peter, too, exhorted the elders (presbuteros) to shepherd (poimaino) the Flock (see 1 Peter 5:1-2)."* - David Servant

[200] Acts 6:2

[201] Acts 6:4

to watch over the Flock,[202] in the Word and prayer,[203] and teaching the body, he must do all in the spirit of servanthood to help others.

To serve others is the example our Lord Jesus gave us when He who was the *teacher* and *rabbi* took the form of a servant[204] and washed the feet of His disciples.[205] When a leader desires honor for his own self; when he wants esteem from men, when he exercises control for gain and power, he is not a leader in the body of Christ. Paul didn't even exercise authority over Apollos to come to Corinth even though Paul "greatly desired him to come." Paul allowed the Holy Spirit to guide Apollos in his personal walk when he said, "He was quite unwilling to go now, but he will go when he has the opportunity."[206] Overseers also are not to desire preeminence.[207] In fact, where there are such desires of greatness Jesus gives clear teachings on not taking titles[208] and not lording over others in the body of Christ.[209] Concluding with this powerful statement for those who would be leaders in His kingdom: "The greatest among you will be your servant. For those who exalt themselves will be humbled, and those who humble themselves will be exalted."[210]

We need to be humble or the Lord will not use us in His greater work. God does not use those who are full of themselves but rather who are unqualified and emptied of their desires and opinions. The greatest brothers God will use in local areas are those who do not feel qualified to lead and are simply servants. Such unqualified ones will be some of the shepherds—God is raising up—that will fully rely on Jesus Christ and not their own abilities. God does not entrust Himself to those who are ambitious for position, power or prominence in the work of the Gospel.

The Apostle Paul was complaining to the Corinthian Church that they had allowed themselves to be taken advantage of by self-centered humanistic leaders. "In fact, you even put up with anyone who

---

[202] Acts 20:28
[203] 1 Timothy 5:17
[204] Philippians 2:7
[205] John 13:4-5
[206] 1 Corinthians 16:12
[207] 3 John 1:9
[208] Matthew 23:8-10
[209] Mark 10:42-45, 1 Corinthians 16:15-16
[210] Matthew 23:11-12

enslaves you or exploits you or takes advantage of you or puts on airs or slaps you in the face."[211] Such leaders had private agendas even in the Name of God and even with very spiritual motives and teachings. God will not share His glory with others especially in the end times work of the body of Christ.

When a leader starts to control what people do in their private life, he is then not allowing the Holy Spirit of God His proper role of convicting and guiding people in their personal walk with the Lord. When shepherds demand, speak harshly, yell or accuse the Lord's people in anyway[212] there is a great likelihood that individual is not a true shepherd from the Lord. Servant leaders in the body of Christ simply want to see the entire body come to fullness in Christ. They are called of the Lord to protect the flock as the Lord grows each member by His Spirit. "Have confidence in your leaders and submit to their authority, because they keep watch over you as those who must give an account. Do this so that their work will be a joy, not a burden, for that would be of no benefit to you."[213]

True shepherds want to encourage everyone onwards in the heavenly calling in Christ Jesus.[214] True leaders work themselves out of a position continually trying to raise up others, they never try to be in demand or control but rather are subservient to the Lord's will. Servant leaders are genuine and real about their walk with the Lord, their faults and weaknesses. Paul exemplifies this when he says: "I came to you in weakness with great fear and trembling."[215]

There has never been a faultless perfect leader in the body of Christ but rather weak, broken vessels that God has raised up for His glory to build a testimony for His Name. Moses was being prepared by the Lord as a vessel for His purposes in the earth. When God was finished with Moses, he was inadequate and a nobody in the eyes of the world. When His man was ready, reduced to *nothing* weak and useless in his own flesh, God said, "he's ready!" Leaders in the body of Christ must be humble and broken from the Lord's hand to be truly useful in His kingdom.

---

[211] 2 Corinthians 11:20
[212] 2 Corinthians 10:1
[213] Hebrews 13:5
[214] Philippians 3:14
[215] 1 Corinthians 2:3

Believers will recognize the gift and calling of leadership on a brother and as an early Church document states: "Appoint, therefore, for yourselves, bishops and deacons worthy of the Lord, men meek, and not lovers of money, and truthful and proved; for they also render to you the service of prophets and teachers. Therefore do not despise them, for they are your honored ones, together with the prophets and teachers."[216] May we honor those the Lord puts in the body to mature and help us along the narrow way to conformity to the image of God's Son.[217]

True shepherds realize they are accountable to the Chief Shepherd, Jesus Christ[218] and will be judged more harshly for what they have taught and done.[219] Therefore they serve in the fear of the Lord, in meekness, grace and love, considering others better than themselves.[220] Servant leaders lastly have a main purpose, which is to bring all the body to unity[221] in Jesus Christ and to protect them from division and doctrines of demons.[222] God has given servant leaders the ministry of protecting His precious Bride on the earth. To keep her as a chaste virgin to Christ till His coming.[223] Such is a great responsibility and honor as servant leaders shepherd and love the body of Christ as Christ loves Her deeply.

---

[216] Didache (A.D. 80-140)
[217] Romans 8:28
[218] 1 Peter 5:4
[219] James 3:1
[220] Philippians 2:3
[221] John 17:20-23
[222] 1 Timothy 4:1
[223] Revelation 21:9, Ephesians 5:27

Principle 12

Jesus Christ: The Head of the Church

THE HEADSHIP of Jesus Christ was not just a doctrine or an idea to the early Apostles but rather a present reality to them. The Lord was the active Head of the Church. They realized it was His Church and everything was done in His Name for Him and through Him.[224] This apostolic dependency on the person of Jesus Christ allowed the Lord to be in control of each Assembly. "God placed all things under His feet and appointed Him to be Head over everything for the Church, which is His body, the fullness of Him who fills everything in every way."[225]

In the life of the Church and in the function of the members of the body it is important to keep our Lord as Head. He should be the center of our thoughts, actions, reactions and endeavors so that all the body looks to the Head for direction and thus unity ensues. He should be spoken of much for all things are from Him and relate to Him.[226] He is the Head of the Church.[227] Paul the apostle stated:

---

[224] Colossians 1:16-18
[225] Ephesians 1:22-23
[226] Romans 11:36
[227] Colossians 1:18

"For I resolved to know nothing while I was with you except Jesus Christ and him crucified."[228]

The truth of Jesus Christ being the Head of each Assembly (*gathering of believers*) is not just important; it is everything. We find in the Book of Revelation statements of great significance towards this. For instance, our Lord says that He will remove the *lampstand*[229] from an Assembly if they lose their first love and their first works—the following closely of the Lord's commands and ways. A lampstand has the light at the top of the stand which represents the presence and testimony of Christ as Head of that Church or Assembly. The light at the top of the lampstand is vital to the life of the Church or Assembly. If the light is severed from the lampstand then Christ is separated from the body being the Church, and the Assembly is dead. Such is the danger when a gathering of believers is not under the Headship of Jesus Christ but under some specific prominent teacher, ism, practice, or even doctrine.[230]

We have a great rest and happiness when as a Church we simply are the body and allow Jesus to be the glorious Head. The Head is able to direct the body as it wishes and so it should be with our Assemblies. The Lord should be able to direct us easily through His Holy Spirit without complaints and contention. Opposition and disobedience grieve the Holy Spirit.[231] We have the example of the Apostle Paul and others in Antioch who were waiting before God with prayer and fasting, and then the Holy Spirit spoke to give them orders.[232] This should serve as our example that God wants to continually give orders to the Church by the Spirit of Christ so that we can fulfill His good pleasure and will.[233]

So therefore, to look to Jesus Christ as the active present Head of the Church will bring much fruit to God.[234] If we accept God's heart and direction, to look to Christ and not men,[235] then division,

---

[228] 1 Corinthians 2:2
[229] The letters to the seven Churches in the Book of Revelation (*see Revelation 2-3*).
[230] 1 Corinthians 1:12-13
[231] Ephesians 4:30
[232] Acts 13:2-3
[233] Ephesians 1:9
[234] John 15:5
[235] 1 Corinthians 3:3-4

competition, debating and strivings would surely cease as Jesus Christ Himself is put in His rightful place.

When we are gathering in meetings we are gathering together to commune and meet with the Godhead. Meetings of believers are not merely for knowledge and good fellowship. Rather the most important aspect of meeting is to meet with the living God. Do we come to our gatherings with this focus and prayer? It is very helpful to prepare one's heart with the Lord in prayer and confession before coming to a gathering of believers. So when at the gathering there will be a purity of spirit and a hunger in the hearts of the saints [236] to meet with God. Such, *hungering after God* is necessary and important to obtain the full blessings in Christ Jesus. There is such great blessing He wants to pour out on His Church if we would allow Him to.[237]

We must also not just treat the Lord Jesus Christ as a truth or principle but a very person of God. A personal vital relationship with Him[238] will result in a healthy believer who will have a bright burning first love[239] relationship with Jesus Christ. Thus the desire of such believers will be to exalt the Lord as the Head of the Church in every gathering of believers.

[236] Psalm 27:8, Psalm 42:1-2, Psalm 108:1
[237] Ephesians 1:3
[238] John 15:15
[239] Revelation 2:4-5

Principle 13

A Growing Vibrant Movement

THE EARLY Church was a growing movement of multiplying house Churches.[240] God was adding to the number daily such as would be saved[241] and there were many being saved through the preaching of the Gospel. Radical evangelism was not an option in the early Church but the only logical response to the great offer of the Gospel of Jesus Christ. Not just a few but all the disciples[242] were gripped with the burden to reach the whole known world with this message of eternal life. Though all efforts were made, the early disciples' true reliance was on the Spirit of God in their evangelism. There was a sovereign working of God's Spirit drawing men to Himself.[243] Such a working can happen when men allow God to build His Church so that great grace can be upon them. "With great power the Apostles continued to testify to the resurrection of the Lord Jesus. And God's grace was so powerfully at work in them all."[244]

---

[240] Acts 12:24
[241] Acts 2:47
[242] Acts 8:4
[243] Acts 16:14
[244] Acts 4:33

Once God is given His rightful place in the Church and is fully reckoned and trusted, a move of His Holy Spirit is something that should be expected. The early Church did not try to work God down from heaven but simply waited before Him for active instructions.[245]

As we look to the Book of Acts as our model we see great growth of the Church in just a few days. Through the first 10 chapters of the Book of Acts we see continual references to the growth of the Church, adding of disciples, and spreading of the Word of God. God had the Church focused on making new disciples from all nations. He had just sacrificed His Son Jesus for all mankind.

Together with direct instructions to share the way of salvation through His Son Jesus, He also put into the hearts of the Apostles the burden to go out preaching. Immediately, they felt led to share the Good News in the market place, in the temple and abroad. The passion for souls brings opposition especially where other religions and practices exist. It is not strange therefore that in the end all the Apostles died martyrs' deaths—except John—while spreading the Gospel not only in and near their homeland but also to remote countries. God desires all men to come to repentance[246] and not just a holy few. As we share the burden of the Lord we will feel the call to share the Gospel with many who have never even heard the Name of Jesus.

Any true apostolic movement of the Church always multiplies and grows. This is the economy and will of God that men would come to salvation in Jesus Christ[247] and part of that fruit of conversion is that they would speak of Christ[248] to others. In the Book of Acts we see the Gospel verbally being proclaimed,[249] calling men to repentance and belief in Jesus Christ,[250] in His death and resurrection. It is no different in our day, the same verbal call must be made through written literature and preaching.

The call of the Chinese underground Church is: "Hurry up, share the Gospel!" In so doing they risk their lives to bring others new life

---

[245] Acts 13:2-3
[246] 2 Peter 3:9, 1 Timothy 2:4
[247] Matthew 28:16-20
[248] Matthew 10:32
[249] Acts 8:5, Acts 9:28, Acts 17:13, Acts 28:31
[250] Acts 2:38

and to fulfill the great commission from God.[251] Before the night comes in other countries, will we fulfill the task that God has given us? We need to pray as the disciples did when threatened with beatings and jail: *"Now, Lord, consider their threats and enable Your servants to speak Your Word with great boldness. Stretch out Your hand to heal and perform signs and wonders through the Name of Your holy servant Jesus."*[252]

God answered that prayer in the Book of Acts, He is answering this prayer in the underground Church with signs and wonders today, and God will do so again: "After they prayed, the place where they were meeting was shaken. And they were all filled with the Holy Spirit and spoke the Word of God boldly."[253]

The Lord is raising up networks of underground gatherings of believers all over the world. Will you consider being a part of such a move of God's Spirit? He is pouring out new wine in new wineskins.[254] Though the Lord still works through more rigid denominational groups, there will be a greater openness to the Spirit's working in these new gatherings where the Lord will be able to accomplish His end time purposes.[255] Gatherings of believers that hear the Chief Shepherd's voice clearly.[256] Such a movement will not just be a meeting you go to but a body of believers you commit to. A Church and kingdom that you labor for everyday.

May the Lord open your heart to His will and plans.

---

[251] Matthew 28:18-20
[252] Acts 4:29-30
[253] Acts 4:31
[254] Mark 2:22
[255] Ephesians 3:11, Isaiah 14:26-27
[256] John 10:14-16

Principle 14

Making Disciples Not Just Converts

MANY EVANGELICALS in our day simply believe that to have someone confess Christ with their lips is fulfilling the great commission.[257] There are great campaigns to simply have people say a quick prayer and make confession. Though salvation begins with this confession that Jesus Christ is Lord[258] yet it is not enough for someone to only be converted, for each convert should be a disciple who follows the Lord daily. "Then He said to them all: 'Whoever wants to be My disciple must deny themselves and take up their cross daily and follow Me.'"[259]

Jesus said in the Gospel of Matthew: "Not everyone who says to Me, 'Lord, Lord,' will enter the kingdom of heaven, but only the one who does the will of My Father who is in heaven."[260] Therefore, true conversion results in Christians who live for Jesus Christ every hour of the day. These are the true Christians who are love-slaves[261] of Jesus

---

257 Matthew 28:16-20
258 Romans 10:9-10
259 Luke 9:23
260 Matthew 7:21
261 Romans 1:1

Christ and who know they have been bought with a great price.[262] Therefore, serving and pleasing God[263] is their aim everyday.

It is a strange thing when one can embrace and understand the Gospel and it does not result in giving up everything to God because of this Good News. When we truly see the great sacrifice and love in God's Son dying for us, this will change everything about our lives and we will freely give all. A famous missionary to Africa[264] said in response to the Gospel: "In light of the sacrifice of Jesus Christ there is nothing too big I can give up, no sacrifice too big."

God knows who are true disciples. There were many disciples that fell away from following Christ.[265] Judas was considered a disciple but was actually a traitor.[266] "God knows who is a citizen of His kingdom and who is an impostor. We must accept His Word and live by it, aligning our lifestyle and choices to match the commands of the King. This is repentance."[267]

Disciples are those who have seen the cross. They have met with the living Christ. They have died to this present world. So now they live fully for the will of God. Disciples are those that shape their entire lives around the truths of the Bible. A disciple is called to obey all the commands of Jesus Christ[268] to follow in all of His ways by the Spirit of grace.[269] Discipleship is not an option, it is the call for every believer in Jesus Christ. Disciples making more disciples is a principle of the Scripture.[270] To have one brother who preaches the Gospel is not the Biblical model but rather all of God's people should be preaching the Gospel through their words and lives as obedient disciples. All the calls for discipleship[271] in the four Gospels are 100% applicable to us as modern day Christians.

Whoever has ears, let him hear.

---

[262] 1 Corinthians 6:20
[263] Colossians 1:10
[264] David Livingstone (1813-1873)
[265] John 6:66
[266] Luke 6:16
[267] Brother Yun
[268] John 14:15
[269] Colossians 1:29
[270] 2 Timothy 2:2
[271] Matthew 8:18-22

Principle 15

Not Pleasing Men but God Alone

WE MUST always in our walks with Jesus Christ keep our eyes on the Lord and seek to please Him alone. The fact is that we belong to Jesus Christ. He has redeemed us with His precious blood and therefore we are not our own.[272] This is a liberating truth if we can realize that all we do is in the clear view of God and therefore seek His approval alone. The early Church walked in the fear of the Lord[273] and did not seek the accolades and esteem of men. "Then the Church throughout Judea, Galilee and Samaria enjoyed a time of peace and was strengthened. Living in the fear of the Lord and encouraged by the Holy Spirit, it increased in numbers."[274]

The early Church sought to please God rather than men,[275] for as our Lord had said: "Do not be afraid of those who kill the body but cannot kill the soul. Rather, be afraid of the One who can destroy

---

[272] Romans 14:7-8
[273] Acts 2:43
[274] Acts 9:31
[275] Acts 5:29

both soul and body in hell."[276] The fear of man is a snare[277] but the fear of God is freedom to do His will.[278]

The religious men of our day exercise control and apply rules of men thereby bringing to naught anything born of the Spirit of God. Such men must be resisted in the fear of God.[279] The early Apostles learned through the example of our Lord not to fear men even if it would get them killed. We must realize that when we fear men it hinders the work of God;[280] may God keep us clear from this hindrance and allow us to have the fruitfulness of the early Church. May God keep us low always before Him as we seek to do His will,[281] not caring about the opinions of men.

Another important aspect to this truth is that we will all stand before the judgment alone. In 2 Corinthians it says: "For we must all appear before the judgment seat of Christ, so that each of us may receive what is due us for the things done while in the body, whether good or bad."[282] So this should put a holy fear of God in our hearts that the decisions we make matter more before God than men. Each day as we follow the Lord we should seek to please Him knowing that one day soon we will stand before Him to give account. Sadly so few of God's workers in our day clearly want to please God alone, for many struggle to get approval from men at the same time. We cannot please men and God always, there will be a dividing line that will come. In John 6 after the miracle of the loaves of bread, our Lord uttered some hard sayings and many were offended and left Him.[283] We have to remember that Jesus said nothing except what was given to Him from the Father.[284] May we follow in His example to speak the Words of God even if it brings great offense before men.

---

[276] Matthew 10:28
[277] Proverbs 29:25
[278] Ephesians 6:5
[279] Acts 8:20-21
[280] Galatians 1:10
[281] John 5:30
[282] 2 Corinthians 5:10
[283] John 6:53-66
[284] John 8:28

Principle 16

The Church Was Birthed in Prayer

PRAYER IS not just one of the functions added to an Assembly meeting, it needs to be the life and atmosphere of a New Covenant gathering under the Headship of Christ. The Church was birthed in prayer. It was sustained in prayer. When they were persecuted they called a prayer meeting.[285] Prayer was the beginning of the great commission. The disciples prayed for a successor after Judas died.[286] Peter prayed for the lame man at the temple gate.[287] Stephen prayed for his persecutors when he was being martyred.[288] Prayer was the main activity of the Church. Ananias was praying when God directed him to anoint one of the early key leaders of the Church.[289] Peter the Apostle was praying when God directed him to preach the Gospel to the Gentiles.[290] Paul prayed for direction many times in his missionary journeys. The Apostle Peter prayed for the resurrection of Tabitha from the dead.[291] Prayer was the engine of the early Church

---

[285] Acts 4:24-30
[286] Acts 1:24-25
[287] Acts 3:6
[288] Acts 7:59-60
[289] Acts 9:10
[290] Acts 10:9
[291] Acts 9:40

that helped it grow and reach the world with the Good News. "The Lord Jesus Christ did not begin his ministry without prayer. We see this in *Luke 3:21*. This is the first thing we must learn as Gospel vessels."[292]

There are thousands of references to prayer in the Bible. One of the greatest privileges of the child of God is to speak to His Holy Father in heaven by prayer. Prayer is the litmus test of the health of the Church and the child of God. Prayer is our reliance on God and the lack of prayer shows our independence from God. "If weak in prayer, we are weak everywhere. A sinning man stops praying, a praying man stops sinning."[293]

Corporate prayer is needful for any Assembly. When spending time together in prayer it is always a good use of time, even if waiting on God and with very little said. Yet believers all across the world—in the busyness of modern society—have decided not to spend time in prayer meetings, for the work of the local Church. This sad choice has kept many Church meetings prayerless and ineffective. Many pastors spend less than 5 minutes a day in prayer: "And it will be: Like people, like priests."[294] So the private prayer walks of many is lacking. Few are praying. Few are spending time in intimacy with the Lord Jesus. Few are prevailing with God.

Prayer meetings are a tremendous place where God births life in a local area. To gather with 2-3 other believers and spend time seeking the Lord in prayer allows for a testimony to be established for the Lord's Name. A simple practical encouragement is for believers to spend a few minutes quieting themselves before praying.[295] They should then enter into a time of thanksgiving towards the Lord[296] for His character, goodness and for the mighty works done in His Name. Then they should lead into a time of intercession—with thanksgiving[297]—guided by a servant leader who will highlight various prayer requests to the body. He should present such requests individually allowing brothers and sisters to pray into one request

[292] Bakht Singh (1903-2000)
[293] Leonard Ravenhill (1907-1994)
[294] Hosea 4:9
[295] Ecclesiastes 5:2, Psalm 37:7, Habakkuk 2:20
[296] Matthew 6:9
[297] Philippians 4:6

until there is a sense of breakthrough and fulfillment of the burden from the Lord for that topic. This prevailing prayer is necessary and what a blessing it is to sense the prayer already answered from the Lord. There can be a sense of cry and burden[298] that can be expressed in prayer with fervency.[299] At other times prayers might be more intimate and soft spoken before the Lord. This is all according to the leading of the Spirit of God and there is no system or pattern for praying except as given by way of examples in the Holy Scriptures.

In the underground house Church in China when new converts come to the Lord they literally are locked away with others—out of their own free will—for 2-3 days to learn the basics of Christian life and to learn how to pray. Such praying is done on their knees for many hours before the Lord and God listens! "When desperate prayer outweighs stale religious observance, God listens."[300]

"Samuel Chadwick, one of God's great men of past years, taught that Satan's greatest aim is to destroy our prayer lives. Satan is not afraid of prayerless study, prayerless work or prayerless religion—but he will tremble when we pray. Remember we are in a spiritual warfare. Prayer is one of our main weapons and faith is closely linked with it. We must not expect it to be easy. Satan will counterattack any efforts made towards effective prayer. We must refuse any form of discouragement and press forward whatever the cost."[301]

Through the history of the Church there have been many true saints who have been great examples to the body of Christ through their prayer lives. One such brother was *George Mueller* of Germany. He prayed up to 6 times per day. He only asked God to supply the needs—not people—as he endeavored to take care of orphan children. He proved that it is sufficient to only ask God without relying on people. When he died, there were 2100 orphans and staff solely provided for by faith. Money just came in. All was done by faith and God supplied all needs solely based on prayer for over 64 years. Mr. Mueller taught on *five conditions* for prevailing prayer:

1.) Our entire dependence must be on the Lord Jesus Christ, as the only ground to claim any blessings.

---

[298] Hebrews 4:16
[299] James 5:16
[300] Ron Pearce
[301] George Verwer

"Whatever you ask in My Name, that I will do, that the Father may be glorified in the Son. If you ask anything in My Name, I will do it."[302]

2.) We must separate from any known sin.

"If I regard iniquity in my heart, The Lord will not hear."[303]

3.) We must have faith in God's Word of promise as confirmed by God's oath. Not to believe Him is to make Him a liar.

"But without faith it is impossible to please Him, for he who comes to God must believe that He is, and that He is a rewarder of those who diligently seek Him."[304]

4.) We need to ask according to God's will. Our motives must be godly. We must not ask to fulfill our lusts.

"Now this is the confidence that we have in Him, that if we ask anything according to His will, He hears us."[305]

5.) There must be waiting upon God and waiting for God. (*Persistence with patience*).

"Be patient, then, brothers and sisters, until the Lord's coming. See how the farmer waits for the land to yield its valuable crop, patiently waiting for the autumn and spring rains."[306]

May God stir us again as the body of Christ to fervent,[307] prevailing, private and corporate prayer. May we share the burden of the Lord Jesus Christ as He continues to intercede for us[308] according to God's will.

---

[302] John 14:13-14
[303] Psalm 66:18
[304] Hebrews 11:6
[305] 1 John 5:14
[306] James 5:7
[307] James 5:16
[308] Romans 8:34

Principle 17

The Spirit is Essential

CHRISTIANITY WAS birthed in the Baptism of the Holy Spirit[309] and will only continue as we have this empowering from above. When we look at Church history the only truly significant stories of men that influenced and built the kingdom of God were men who were filled with the Holy Spirit. This anointing is something that not only signifies leadership in the Church but also usability before God for His work.

Christianity in this way is quite simple, it is a work of the Spirit of God. This simplicity can offend men but God clearly states in 1 Corinthians 1 that He uses the weak, the unwise, the unlearned and the despised of this world.[310] It happened when God chose 12 disciples. Two wanted to send fire from heaven down on towns,[311] three could not stay awake during a prayer meeting,[312] one was a traitor and thief,[313] and one betrayed Christ denying that he even knew the Lord.[314] They argued over who would be the greatest and all of them fled away when hard times came.[315] Yet with this group of

---

[309] Acts 1:8
[310] 1 Corinthians 1:27-28
[311] Luke 9:53-56
[312] Luke 22:45-46
[313] Luke 6:16
[314] Matthew 26:75
[315] Matthew 26:56

weak, unlearned simple men God was building His Church against which the gates of hell will not prevail.[316] This can give us great consolation and hope to be usable in the work of the Lord for He is looking for those who are not self-seeking but rather are humble, weak and needy. They are the ones that are calling out to God for His Spirit because they literally need Him in every situation.

Sadly, even the weak soon learn how to be strong, how to rely on their own experiences, successes and victories. It becomes a dangerous practice of taking glory away from God for accomplishments we believe we have achieved. We then deny the proper recognition and glory which belongs to God alone because it is His work. God will only entrust His work with those He knows will give Him 100% of the glory for what is done and take no glory to themselves.[317]

In the same way many denominations, churches and ministries start off as a vibrant move of the Spirit of God but then turn into methods, traditions and formulas. Such groups then depend on their history, on the last move of God, on structures, buildings and all other things rather than a fresh dependence on God daily for their purpose and growth. A famous evangelical pastor said of the church in his day: "The average church has so established itself organizationally and financially that God is simply not necessary to it. So entrenched is its authority and so stable are the religious habits of its members that God could withdraw Himself completely from it and it could run on for years on its own momentum."[318]

God is always looking for the willing vessels that will trust Him afresh for the impossible,[319] for in such cases He gets the glory and the individual being used simply gives the glory to this God of the impossible.[320] Every true move of the Holy Spirit primarily elevates and glorifies[321] the person of the Lord Jesus Christ. Furthermore, He gives a fresh expression and expansion[322] to the kingdom of God according to the model of the early Church when His Son is exalted.

---

[316] Matthew 16:18
[317] 1 Corinthians 1:29
[318] A.W. Tozer (1897-1963)
[319] Ephesians 3:20
[320] 1 Corinthians 1:31
[321] John 15:26
[322] Acts 4:31

Principle 18

The Satanic Counterfeit

THOUGH GOD is always working in different ways and with different means, it is still only by the Spirit of God that the Church will grow. Over the past 50 years particularly originating in Western countries there have been such excesses and abuses of what is considered *Spirit-filled* Christianity that many true believers have been repulsed completely from even seeking the Lord for the true filling of the Spirit. This is not only a tragedy but one of Satan's tactics[323] to hinder the growth of the true Church of Jesus Christ. The genuine believer should never feel scared to call out to God for fresh infusions of the Spirit of God for service[324] and to foster a dependence on the Holy Spirit of God daily in his life.

We have to remember that Satan is the father of lies. He is a murderer from the beginning and dwells in falsehood.[325] He never wants the glory to go to Jesus Christ but rather twists the truth and deceives those in the Lord's work to take glory to themselves.[326]

He is also the master counterfeiter who has been deceiving God's people since the beginning. He spoke to Eve and deceived her by

---

[323] 2 Corinthians 2:11
[324] Ephesians 5:18
[325] John 8:44
[326] 3 John 1:9

twisting the truth of God saying: "Has God indeed said?"[327] Such twisting of the truth is his normal activity.

Since the earliest days of the Apostles, even with our Lord Himself there were deceivers and false brethren present. Those who secretly come into God's flock for personal gain and to infiltrate the liberty[328] of the believers. Betrayers,[329] deceivers,[330] false brethren,[331] false prophets,[332] and those desiring preeminence among the saints. We must have a strong trust in the Lord to see these individuals purged away from the flock of God as believers meet in gatherings under the Headship of Jesus Christ.

One key to understand is that if the Spirit of God is working in a meeting then Jesus Christ will be glorified.[333] If men, manifestations and even the Holy Spirit Himself is glorified then you can start to know that this is not a pure work of the Lord. A brother said this same truth in this way: "Any spirit that focuses on the Holy Spirit and glorifies the Holy Spirit is not the Holy Spirit. It is contrary to His whole nature and purpose. Once you've grasped that [truth] it will open your eyes to many things which are going on in the church that are otherwise difficult to understand."[334] The Scripture states: "He will not glorify Himself."[335] Those that worship, honor, and glorify the Holy Spirit more then Jesus Christ are not led by the Holy Spirit to do that. The Holy Spirit will always honor Jesus Christ, thus the true working of the Spirit can be distinguished in measure.

"With the spread of truth and liberty have come a million false lights—men who like 'clouds without water'[336] speak 'great swelling words'[337] without substance; those 'perilous times'[338] prophesied by the apostle Paul have long set in. As people give way to 'itching ears' and as their fleshly appetites grow, opportunities multiply to new

---

[327] Genesis 3:1
[328] Galatians 2:4
[329] Mark 14:43-45
[330] 2 John 1:7
[331] 2 Corinthians 11:26
[332] Matthew 7:15
[333] John 5:22-23, John 13:31-32, John 15:26
[334] Derek Prince (1915-2003)
[335] John 16:13-14
[336] Jude 1:12
[337] 2 Peter 2:18
[338] 2 Timothy 3:1

heights for skilled deception from the enemy. Today, Satan takes advantage of centuries of experience in creating his cunning devices, even disguising his wolves as 'angels of light.'[339] The airwaves are filled with those who 'call themselves by His Name,'[340] but who do not know Him. Multitudes follow them because they have not been willing to fully surrender to the absolute Lordship of Christ. They continue to secretly embrace some sins, and in doing so they run the unthinkable risk of God sending a strong delusion[341] so that they should believe a lie."[342]

God brings judgment and expresses His displeasure over those who disobey even while deceived by Satan. As a Church we must be on guard from this deception so that we will not be deceived by the evil one, but rather follow the simplicity of truth and obedience found in Jesus Christ and His glorious Gospel.[343]

As we are in the end times there will be an influx of those in the Church teaching doctrines of demons to deceive even the elect of God. There will be many false teachers who claim to be of the truth but are not. Perhaps one of the most dangerous weapons against the Church is not persecution, but apathy and deception.[344]

At times the deception in teaching is not obvious but in character it becomes more obvious. Does the minister live like Christ or is he full of greed, selfishness, self-exaltation, soulish and carnal? "The opposite of Christ is called the *antichrist* in the New Testament. If Christians do not see this clearly, then when the antichrist turns up on the world's stage, with his false signs and wonders, they too will blindly accept him."[345]

A brother from the past century said of this demonic counterfeit: "When Satan gets into the pulpit, or the theological chair, and pretends to teach Christianity, when in reality he is corrupting it; pretends to be teaching Christian evidences when in reality he is

---

339 2 Corinthians 11:14
340 Matthew 7:23
341 2 Thessalonians 2:11
342 Mark Case
343 2 Corinthians 11:3
344 Amos 6:1
345 Zac Poonen

undermining the very foundations of faith—then look out for him; he is at his most dangerous work."[346]

"Where the Spirit of the Lord is, there is liberty.[347] But where religious flesh is, we can almost always find evil spirits parading as *anointed* vessels. Without keen discernment we will be taken in by one with a false anointing. The devil's servants know how to act and talk like the Lord's servants—but they are counterfeit, and we must learn to recognize them by their fruit. They are all around us and will continue to increase in number as the coming of the Lord draws near."[348]

We must be on guard against Satan's coworkers[349] who appear to have a form of godliness,[350] who seem impressive with a show of power but are devoid of the truth. We must be on guard against Satan as he can transform himself into an angel of light to deceive us. This calls for a need of discernment in the body of Christ especially as it relates to the end times. As we near the end of the age there will be many false prophets and teachers using supernatural miracles[351] and healing to deceive even God's elect.[352] Our prayer must always be for discernment[353] and a love of the truth as we near the coming of our Lord[354] and as we gather under the Headship of Jesus Christ.

---

[346] R.A. Torrey (1856-1928)
[347] 2 Corinthians 3:17
[348] Stella Paterson
[349] 2 Corinthians 11:13-15
[350] 2 Timothy 3:5
[351] 2 Thessalonians 2:9
[352] Matthew 24:24
[353] Mark 13:6
[354] 2 Thessalonians 2:10

Principle 19

Dependence on the Spirit of Jesus

A GODLY writer over 200 years ago lamented the lack of the actual presence of God[355] in Christian Assemblies with these words: "By this process the Church steadily ceased to be a testimony to the existence, presence, and working of the living and true God. Less and less often did unbelievers coming into the Assembly, and beholding in the spirit and unity and conscience-searching power of the worship, the evidences of His presence and control, exclaim: 'God is among you indeed.'[356] God was worshipped, but as absent; and presently the beauteous divine simplicity of the first days had been materialized into the lifeless magnificence of Roman ritual."[357]

Those *first days* referred to are the simple and glorious days of the Acts of the Apostles which can be better titled the *Acts of the Holy Spirit.* The Spirit of Christ in the meeting of believers together[358] is to be deferred to and depended upon. For any believer to share or speak

---

[355] It is important to note that some churches in our day focus solely on creating an atmosphere where there is a feeling of a presence. This is not what the writer is stating but rather the convicting holy awe-inspiring presence of God. Such a presence (*the Holy Spirit*) comes to lead into truth and true worship of God.

[356] 1 Corinthians 14:24-25

[357] G.H. Lang (1874-1958)

[358] 1 Corinthians 5:4

anything of spiritual worth requires the anointing[359] and present working of the Spirit.[360]

Such should be our attitude when gathering together that we would come "poor in spirit"[361] begging for spiritual nourishment of the Lord. It is a true spiritual principle that those who come to the Lord full and not needing anything will never receive anything of the Lord.[362] The wonderful picture is given by our Lord Jesus Christ of a small child asking a father for bread. The response of the father surely always will be to feed the child and not give him a stone to eat! "If you then, though you are evil, know how to give good gifts to your children, how much more will your Father in heaven give the Holy Spirit to those who ask Him!"[363] The conditions for being filled with the Holy Spirit are surrender, emptiness of self, no pride, no known sins and asking the Father to fill us.

In the local Church in 1 Corinthians 12 we are encouraged to esteem the weakest amongst us and elevate them to learn from them. Such is always the spirit of a true New Testament Assembly where there is a dependence on others in the body of Christ, even the weakest, who we should esteem as indispensable![364] More than that we should consider the very Spirit of the living God to be greatly needed, so much so that if He is not present it is vain to meet together as the Church.

"The Holy Spirit does not come to entertain, to provide signs and wonders and miracles just to thrill us or make us feel good. No, every one of His workings has this divine purpose: *I'm preparing a Bride.* The work, ministry and mission of the Holy Spirit is singular: It is to wean us from this world, to create a longing in us for Jesus' soon appearance, to convict us of everything that would blemish us, to turn our eyes away from everything but Jesus, to adorn us with the ornaments of a passionate desire to be with Him as His Bride!"[365]

---

[359] 1 Corinthians 12:7
[360] 1 Peter 4:11
[361] Matthew 5:3
[362] Luke 1:53
[363] Luke 11:13
[364] 1 Corinthians 12:23-25
[365] David Wilkerson (1931-2011)

This dependency on the Holy Spirit and crying out for fresh infusions of His grace needs to be a core principle for the gathering of believers who are meeting under the Headship of Jesus Christ.

We are following a crucified King who died on a Roman cross. This Savior of the world died after only 33 years of earth-life. His life was constantly dependent on the work and power of the Holy Spirit of God. From the baptism, to the wilderness and every Word He spoke our Lord relied on the Spirit. Thus should not our lives be spent in the same way with the same dependency?

"While we are looking for better methods and stronger men and women, God is looking for weak vessels with no confidence in their own abilities. He does this so that His work will be done His way and so that all the glory will go to Jesus Christ."[366]

"God will confound the strong and wise by anointing as His instruments those who are considered weak and foolish. The Lord will bypass those who lean on the arm of flesh, who trust in their talents, their knowledge, their background, their family reputation. Instead, He will raise up the brokenhearted, the weak and the weary. He will pour on them a spirit of praise and a baptism of love. He will show them His greatness, His faithfulness, His covenants, and they will become strong in the Lord and in the power of His might."[367]

May this be our desire to simply be weak vessels that the Lord uses. We will then depend on the Lord Himself and seek things above and not things of the earth.[368] May there be a renewed testimony of the Spirit of the Lord in our meetings as we come together with great dependency on Him with hearts of full-surrender to God's ways. This way all the glory can go to Jesus Christ, God's Son.

---

[366] Brother Yun
[367] David Wilkerson (1931-2011)
[368] Colossians 3:2

Principle 20

Holy Spirit Normal Christianity[369]

AS ONE reads through the Book of Acts, the work of the Holy Spirit in the early Church is evident on every page. If you remove the work of the Holy Spirit from the Book of Acts you have virtually nothing left. Truly, He empowered the first disciples to "turn the world upside down."[370]

The places in the world today where the Church is expanding the fastest are those places where Jesus' followers are yielded to and empowered by the Holy Spirit. This should not surprise us. The Holy Spirit can accomplish more in ten seconds than we can accomplish in ten thousand years of our own efforts.[371] Thus it is of vital importance that the disciple-making minister understands what Scripture teaches about the work of the Holy Spirit in the lives and ministries of believers.

---

[369] This principle is all attributed to *David Servant* excluding the Scripture portion at the end of the section.

[370] Acts 17:6

[371] Though we do the work of the Church daily and labor, we must always remember a great harvest will come in the Lord's timing as we faint not. "*And let us not grow weary while doing good, for in due season we shall reap if we do not lose heart.*" (Galatians 6:9).

In the Book of Acts, we frequently find examples of believers being baptized in the Holy Spirit and empowered for ministry.[372] We would be wise to study the subject so that we can, if possible, experience what they experienced and enjoy the miraculous help from the Holy Spirit that they enjoyed. Although some claim that such miraculous works of the Holy Spirit were confined to the age of the original Apostles, we find no Scriptural, historical or logical support for such an opinion. It is a theory born from unbelief.[373] Those who believe what God's Word promises will experience the promised blessings.[374] Like the unbelieving Israelites who failed to enter the Promised Land, those who don't believe God's promises today will fail to enter into all that God has prepared for them.[375] Which category are you in?

"There are different kinds of gifts, but the same Spirit distributes them. There are different kinds of service, but the same Lord. There are different kinds of working, but in all of them and in everyone it is the same God at work.

"Now to each one the manifestation of the Spirit is given for the common good. To one there is given through the Spirit a message of wisdom, to another a message of knowledge by means of the same Spirit, to another faith by the same Spirit, to another gifts of healing by that one Spirit, to another miraculous powers, to another prophecy, to another distinguishing between spirits, to another speaking in different kinds of tongues, and to still another the interpretation of tongues. All these are the work of one and the same Spirit, and he distributes them to each one, just as he determines.

"Just as a body, though one, has many parts, but all its many parts form one body, so it is with Christ. For we were all baptized by one Spirit so as to form one body—whether Jews or Gentiles, slave or free—and we were all given the one Spirit to drink. Even so the body is not made up of one part but of many.

"Now if the foot should say, 'Because I am not a hand, I do not belong to the body,' it would not for that reason stop being part of the body. And if the ear should say, 'Because I am not an eye, I do not

---

[372] Acts 2:4, Acts 10:44-46, Acts 19:6
[373] Hebrews 3:12, Psalms 78:19-20
[374] John 11:40
[375] Hebrews 4:6

belong to the body,' it would not for that reason stop being part of the body. If the whole body were an eye, where would the sense of hearing be? If the whole body were an ear, where would the sense of smell be? But in fact God has placed the parts in the body, every one of them, just as He wanted them to be. If they were all one part, where would the body be? As it is, there are many parts, but one body.

"The eye cannot say to the hand, 'I don't need you!' And the head cannot say to the feet, 'I don't need you!' On the contrary, those parts of the body that seem to be weaker are indispensable, and the parts that we think are less honorable we treat with special honor. And the parts that are unpresentable are treated with special modesty, while our presentable parts need no special treatment. But God has put the body together, giving greater honor to the parts that lacked it, so that there should be no division in the body, but that its parts should have equal concern for each other. If one part suffers, every part suffers with it; if one part is honored, every part rejoices with it.

"Now you are the body of Christ, and each one of you is a part of it. And God has placed in the Church first of all Apostles, second prophets, third teachers, then miracles, then gifts of healing, of helping, of guidance, and of different kinds of tongues. Are all Apostles? Are all prophets? Are all teachers? Do all work miracles? Do all have gifts of healing? Do all speak in tongues? Do all interpret? Now eagerly desire the greater gifts. And yet I will show you the most excellent way."[376]

[Editor's note: It is important to understand that this passage from 1 Corinthians fully applies to modern day believers just as it did 2000 years ago and that these gifts are still in operation in the body of Christ today.]

---

[376] 1 Corinthians 12:4-31

Principle 21

Hungering After the True Holy Spirit Baptism

IT WAS asked of one brother that travels amongst the house Churches in the Chinese Church and speaks with the underground leaders, "How do the Chinese choose the leaders?" The answer was simple; the brother responded: "Whoever is the hungriest after God, they are the leaders." Such a need is present in our time for more leaders who are hungry for the Lord and baptized in His Holy Spirit. There is a vast difference between one that seeks the Baptism of the Spirit simply for power[377] and one that seeks to know the Lord intimately and desires to be His vessel, fully surrendered.[378] One seeks God for what he can get, the other seeks Him for what he can give. There is a crying need to see believers seeking God for God Himself and nothing else. Jesus Christ spoke of these whom God the Father seeks[379] who will worship Him in Spirit and truth. One who worships God only out of obligation and reward is not a true worshipper. God is making a separation in the end times of those who are serving Him for their own selfish desires from those that have the true bridal love for Jesus Christ. This Bride will be endued with

---

[377] Acts 8:18-19
[378] 2 Timothy 2:21
[379] John 4:23

power from on high having her vessels full of oil when the Bridegroom comes.[380]

One of the greatest reasons that God hesitates to pour out His Spirit on His Church is that we will not cherish the blessing. When someone has gone without food for many days a simple piece of bread is enjoyed immensely and cherished. In the same way God requires us to have a hunger for the things of God, and to pray and wait on Him. Such waiting and hungering after God produces in us a respect and value for the gift He is giving. The Holy Spirit is given by the grace of God, it is not earned by righteous deeds. Yet, God does require an obedient heart[381] which desires God's will and not its own. Some are just looking to get the power of the Spirit for their own purposes, their own kingdoms, their own ministries.

So may we be renewed in our hunger and desire to wait before the Lord for this precious infilling of the Spirit of Christ. The true Baptism of the Spirit is given through personal abiding relationship with God. It is not something apart from this. We need to be like a child before a Father and have that simple dependence and faith. God is always more willing to bless us than we can imagine. The qualifying evidence of the Baptism of the Holy Spirit is a life of unselfish love and exaltation of the person of Jesus Christ.

"Many millions of Christians around the world, after being baptized in the Holy Spirit, have experienced a new dimension of power, particularly when witnessing to the unsaved. They found that their words were more convicting, and that they sometimes quoted Scriptures they didn't realize they knew. Some found themselves called and specifically gifted for a certain ministry, such as evangelism. Others discovered that God used them as He willed in various supernatural gifts of the Spirit. Their experience is thoroughly Biblical. Those who oppose their experience have no Biblical basis for their opposition. They are, in fact, fighting against God."[382]

---

[380] Matthew 25:4
[381] Acts 5:32
[382] David Servant

Principle 22

God Uses the Weak by His Spirit

GOD DOES not look to find those who are the elites and those who are the most skilled. Rather He looks for the weak[383] and foolish who trust in Him. God uses broken pots and vessels,[384] He uses imperfect people who trust in a perfect God. Thus all men will know that it is God who has manifested His power and glory through a brother or sister. It is realized then that it was not the work of men[385] but the work of God. To bring maximum glory to His Name the Lord is assembling an end times movement of weak, poor, helpless, and despised people who the religious system of our day have written off as unusable for their purposes.[386] These believers God is going to anoint to carry the message of the Gospel in power to a lost and dying world. We see evidence of this in the underground Churches of the world where unknown itinerant evangelists go from town to town sharing the Good News.

For the Scripture declares: "But God chose the foolish things of the world to shame the wise; God chose the weak things of the world

---

[383] Isaiah 40:29
[384] Jeremiah 18:6
[385] 2 Corinthians 4:7
[386] Acts 4:13

to shame the strong. God chose the lowly things of this world and the despised things—and the things that are not—to nullify the things that are, so that no one may boast before Him."[387] The question is, are we weak enough for God to call and use us? Are we empty of all the traditions of religious men[388] so that we can learn from the Lord Himself? This is the way of the Lord. God is looking for a Gideon's army[389] of those that are willing to trust fully in His power and not in any might or power of their own. God uses nobodies that will trust Him implicitly and fully. Are you going to be part of this Gideon's army today?

Imagine the odds of 1000 to 1, or perhaps 100,000 to 1, yet this is God's economy, for one with God is a majority. It could be 1 million to 1 and if God was with that one person, he would be the victor. In these end times God is looking to magnify His Name greatly and therefore is using the weak and the lowly so it will be clearly evident that it was a work of God and not men. My strength is made perfect in weak people![390]

The Lord is sovereign and will raise up those He wills especially to shame the wise and capable. God desires a Remnant of saints who will do His bidding and work no matter the cost. The overlooked and weak will be raised up so that God will get the glory. This glory that is soon to cover the earth as the waters cover the sea[391] will be all to promote and exalt the testimony of God in the earth.

"The Lord Jesus calls people who realize they cannot function at all apart from His grace and empowerment. God chooses to use those individuals who know Him intimately! This is the primary qualification for service in the kingdom of God."[392] Such a group of weak people who know God will be those who accomplish God's end time purposes in the earth. We must not be angry with the Lord when He starts to raise up workers in the last hour that have not been laboring all day. Such God will raise up and even give them a greater inheritance in the work of spreading the Gospel to the Nations. We

---

[387] 1 Corinthians 1:27-29
[388] Mark 7:13
[389] Judges 7:7
[390] 2 Corinthians 12:9
[391] Habakkuk 2:14
[392] Brother Yun

must never be jealous of another worker or person's anointing but rather desire to accomplish God's will for our own life.

Another well-known yet vital Biblical picture is that of the thousands of Israel's army shaking in their armor as the mighty Philistine giant Goliath comes forward to challenge them. Yet God calls a simple shepherd boy David who had faith towards God. Holding a simple sling and a few stones, God fought for him. What proceeded was a great victory wrought for God's glory and Name. Davids, Samuels, Samsons, Abrahams, Gideons, God is calling us today—weak as we may be—to follow in their ways and trust God for the impossible. With God all things are possible.

May we be stirred with faith to believe God today.

Principle 23

Cults, False Gospels and Division

RELIGIOUS FREEDOM has its benefits for unhindered preaching of the Gospel. These freedoms have allowed some vibrant godly forms of Christianity to grow and prosper and yet *these freedoms* have sadly also allowed many of the vilest perversions of Christianity to prosper. One cannot begin to calculate the effects of cults, heretical groups and false gospels that have been allowed to prosper under the banner of religious freedom and expression.

In the past hundred years more cults then ever in Church history have sprung up and many with end time focus and deception. Such groups start as a guise and deception of the true working of the Holy Spirit in that day. We must "test the spirits to see whether they are from God, because many false prophets have gone out into the world."[393] We must not shun away from focusing on God's end time purposes and the second coming of Jesus Christ, though many cult groups[394] are perverting this great hope of the Church.

However, a far worse epidemic of division in the body of Christ has also been fostered in this environment. There are groups of people meeting in homes, churches, and in public meeting areas all divided

---

[393] 1 John 4:1
[394] Mormons, Jehovah Witnesses, etc.

from each other under the premise that a specific doctrine they hold is right. Therefore the rest of believers are not *with them* in their truth.[395] Such thinking has resulted in the splitting and splintering of denominations to the place where there are easily over 40,000 registered denominations[396] worldwide in Christendom.

Not all division is wrong and there are times for groups to be formed for a recovery of lost truth.[397] Therefore, some of these groups are started for good reasons, namely, the preserving of the testimony of Jesus Christ in their local area. Many groups splintered from a larger group because of the defection from truth (*apostasy*) that was beginning to happen.[398] Even some church bodies that claim themselves to be the only true church started from a sincere desire to preserve the truth when so many around them were deviating from God's Word.

Yet this calls for the maturity of the saints of God in our day who are gathering together under the Headship of Jesus Christ to also have a heart for the larger body of Christ.[399] In some areas a specific group will exist for the purpose of calling the body of Christ to further purity, holiness and life. Yet these groups also need to have a realization and acceptance for others in the body of Christ who are even in churches they do not agree with.[400] God has a Remnant in many fellowships all over the world who have not bowed the knee to baal.[401]

One way we can start to pray is for God to unify the elect people of God in local areas who are of the true body of Christ. God will hear such a prayer for His desire is to see victorious overcomers in local Assemblies gathering together.[402] Devoting ourselves to such prayers will begin to build in us a spiritual vision of how the Lord sees His end times Bride.[403]

---

[395] Matthew 12:25

[396] This is a conservative number.

[397] 1 Corinthians 11:19

[398] Revelation 3:4

[399] Romans 14:1-12, John 13:35

[400] 1 Corinthians 1:10, Ephesians 4:3, Philippians 2:2

[401] Romans 11:4

[402] Revelation 2:11

[403] Ephesians 2:15, Ephesians 5:27

Principle 24

Christ the Unity of the Body

DENOMINATIONS, BEING splintered by slight shades of truth, are not pleasing to God, but rather grieve Him, though like a precious diamond we can see something good in every denomination.[404] There is always some truth that one specific denomination knows, believes and preaches that is noteworthy and admirable for us to learn from. Yet overall it is not God's perfect will for His body to be divided.

In the Book of Corinthians we find that God calls division in the Church, "carnality."[405] Carnality has its root in pride which is in opposition to God and His ways.[406] One brother said on this topic: "We must never forget that we are Christians, believers, brethren, disciples and saints—and so are all who have been redeemed by the precious blood of Christ. To deny this by any form of sectarianism, denominationalism or exclusivism is to deny the truth of the Bible and to be guilty of carnality and pride."[407]

If we are honest with this situation we can see that there is truly only one Church—the body of Christ, believers who are in-dwelt by

---

[404] Count Nicolaus Zinzendorf (1700-1760)
[405] 1 Corinthians 3
[406] James 4:6
[407] William MacDonald (1917-2007)

the Holy Spirit of God and declare Jesus Christ to be the risen Son of God. If we were to strip away most of these extra doctrines, ideas and explanations of how one is to be identified as a Christian we would find in the most basic principle that either men *have* Christ or they *do not have* Christ.[408] If we were to gather all the leaders of Christianity in one room and put away all of these in many cases extra-biblical doctrines, we would find many to be in unity and agreement.

"No assembly, no church, no movement, no testimony, no fellowship, is justified in its existence from God's standpoint except insofar as Christ is expressed by it."[409]

The house Church movement in China has some separations into different networks. Yet this underground Church is unified. They all agree with each other and declare there are no denominations or sects in China but one faith, one Baptism and one Lord.[410] Of course there is the activity of some cults and even some denominations yet surprisingly there is a great unity in the body of Christ there, just like we find in the Book of Acts. At times we feel the prayer of Jesus for the unity of the body of Christ[411] rarely sees fulfillment, but not so in China!

Yet as persecution—even worldwide persecution—ensues against the Church there will be unity that will come, which will only be explainable as a miracle. There are such carnal strong walls that men have built up against each other in the body of Christ that for all those walls to crumble requires the power of God Himself.[412] This will happen as God unifies and gathers the body of Christ in local areas for a last days testimony[413] of His grace and love to a lost world. May those who are gathering under the Headship of Jesus Christ seek to find unity with any true believer no matter what sect they are involved in or church they still attend.

---

[408] 2 Corinthians 13:5
[409] T. Austin Sparks (1888-1971)
[410] Ephesians 4:5
[411] John 17
[412] Matthew 19:26
[413] Matthew 24:22, Mark 13:27

Principle 25

Not Judging Others

MANY IN our day will judge and consider a believer not saved or born-again if they do not meet a specific man-made standard. If a believer is not overcoming 100% in a specific area, or is partaking in some worldly activity, one may judge and claim that believer is not saved. Such merely outward judging is not spiritual but an immature and dangerous thing to do. Of course, if a believer is blatantly continuing in outward sin he must be dealt with in gentleness and love. As God taught us through the Book of Acts and Epistles of Paul, corrective measures as determined by the Holy Spirit might be necessary. This may include asking a believer to leave the Assembly for a period of time.

In the early Church the Holy Spirit was doing such a work of purifying that all who joined their ranks were quickly corrected by the Lord if they were wrong in an area.[414] Those that grieved the Lord to the point of great compromise ended up in some cases dead![415] The result of this Holy Spirit purification was even greater unity amongst the brethren: "All the believers were one in heart and mind."[416]

---

[414] Acts 8:21
[415] Acts 4
[416] Acts 4:32

We must have a high standard for the Church, the Gospel, the Scriptures and ourselves, for God says: "Be holy, because I am holy."[417] We must likewise have the highest standard for exercising the love of Christ and His great mercy. Without love we are nothing. Jesus exemplified His love and mercy for us when He died for us while we were yet sinners.[418] He taught us through living examples when dealing with the woman caught in adultery, the woman at the well, the tax collector and many more, how to walk in love and mercy. Jesus calls us *hypocrites* if we make ourselves better than the sinners who ask for God's mercy.[419]

Scripture teaches us to gently help a struggling brother or sister pointing them in the right direction but to watch for the beam in our own eyes.[420] We give such help through the guidance of the Holy Spirit, with love, mercy, long-suffering, gentleness and grace without interfering with the Lord Himself who is correcting, changing and growing believers. Likewise, we are all under construction and will not be perfect until we see Him face to face. The Lord reminds all of us: Learn to love your neighbor[421] and learn mercy.[422]

We need to look at every brother and sister in Christ as being *in Christ* which gives us a foundation and basis for fellowship. If someone is not in Christ then there will be no fellowship of the Spirit and no common love for the things of God. Christ is the unity of the Church and as each member of the body looks to the Head to whom they are connected they also find their unity with others in the body to whom they are also connected.

It is a dangerous thing to judge others, for God will measure that judgment upon us with the same severity.[423] Judging others reflects in our speech, emotions, thoughts, our hearts, and our actions and makes us a hypocrite before God. It is maturity in Christ to pray for those we are concerned about and not talk about their problems with others.

---

[417] 1 Peter 1:16
[418] Romans 5:8
[419] Luke 18:10-14
[420] Matthew 7:3
[421] Matthew 5:43-44
[422] Matthew 12:7, Matthew 23:23
[423] Matthew 7:2

A mature godly brother in the Lord once said:
"I have found that I can fellowship with any person who will
meet with me around the person of Christ. If he won't insist that I
accept his mode of Baptism, we can enjoy some wonderful fellowship.
I have marvelous fellowship with some people who believe that you
ought to be put under the water three times, and I can fellowship
with those who sprinkle. I got out of the Presbyterian church, but I
can fellowship with them, provided we meet around the person of
Christ. Separation is unto, not just from, something."[424]

Love never wishes a brother harm and seeks at all cost to do good
to others in the household of faith no matter how much they have
seemed to fail. Love covers a multitude of sins.[425] True love seeks to
put others before themselves and even die for others.[426] Such love has
opportunity to be exhibited as we gather together with others under
the Headship of our Lord in small groups.

Neither do we wish the judgment of God on men in this
dispensation of grace. We can warn lost people that the wrath of God
is over them, but we should act like our Lord who sought to seek and
save souls. For our Lord said that He came not to condemn the world
but to save the world.[427] When the disciples asked the Lord to send
fire down from heaven to destroy a village He responded with mercy
and rebuked the disciples for such thinking.[428] Our heart should be
for the good of all men[429] especially brothers and sisters in the Lord.

Paul the Apostle wisely says: "Therefore judge nothing before the
appointed time; wait until the Lord comes. He will bring to light
what is hidden in darkness and will expose the motives of the heart.
At that time each will receive their praise from God."[430]

---

[424] J. Vernon McGee (1904-1988)
[425] 1 Peter 4:8
[426] Romans 5:7, John 10:11
[427] John 3:17
[428] Luke 5:54-55
[429] 1 Thessalonians 5:15
[430] 1 Corinthians 4:5

Principle 26

Having a Right Doctrine but Wrong Spirit

THERE IS a saying: "You can be so right that you become wrong." Sadly some in Church history were 100% right in their doctrines but in their practice they were wrong. The goal of the Christian life is to know and love God the Father, God the Son and God the Holy Spirit, receiving eternal life through the Son, and resulting in a glorious and personal relationship with the Triune God. Where we love Him, worship Him serve Him, obey Him and where we experience His love and His care for us.[431]

Scholars and theologians can write about God but at the same time not experientially know Him.[432] Doctrines coming from such men in many cases will lead believers into scholastic studies about God but not the very experience of Him. Good doctrines can provide us with foundational principles based on a correct interpretation of the Word of God. But, only the most basic doctrines are necessary to help unify the body of Christ—which is the Church. Too many

---

[431] Zephaniah 3:17
[432] John 17:3, 1 John 3:6

doctrines divide without being essential to the faith.[433] Doctrines rooted in man-made terms, ideas and explanations can even lead a believer away from the Lord Himself. Good doctrines are helpful, but growing in discipleship with the Lord Jesus Christ is more important.[434] Though there is Scriptural warrant and benefit to study the character of God and His ways. God does not call us to be theologians merely but disciples who practice what Jesus taught. "Christians now choose churches based upon particular doctrines, and having the right theology has become the most important thing rather than having the right lifestyle, all because a Biblical model has been abandoned."[435]

A rereading of the New Testament with this as our mindset helps us to see clearly that the early thinking and lifestyle of Christians has changed in many countries of the world. The effects of humanism, secularism, materialism, and entertainment have brought doctrines of Satan to the Church,[436] resulting in counterfeit churches accepting such doctrines as ordaining profane ministers who are living in sin and practicing sin, and other new doctrines such as the prosperity doctrines.[437] Some churches and denominations are misusing the miracles of God for their purposes to obtain money. Other churches, denominations and many bible colleges in the world today deny that the miracles of God took place and they deny the power and miracles of God being applicable to our lives today. In some countries, witnessing for Christ has become an exercise of not offending the freedom of other faiths and keeping our mouths closed. If this is true of us then we truly have become the lukewarm Church that Jesus spoke about. He will spit us out of His mouth unless we repent.[438] We must return to the principles and doctrines of the early Church as a way of life[439] and as a living response to knowing the very person of God through the blood of Christ and indwelling Holy Spirit.

---

[433] There was a danger in the early Church of those who looked into many obscure doctrinal teachings but were not living in obedience to the simplicity of the faith in Jesus Christ and being led of His Spirit. (*see 1 Timothy 1:3-4, 1 Timothy 6:3-4*).

[434] James 1:22

[435] David Servant

[436] 1 Timothy 4:1

[437] 1 Timothy 6:5

[438] Revelation 3:15-16

[439] 1 Timothy 6:3

"The Pharisees sat in the chair of Moses, which meant that they had gone to Bible colleges and got their doctorate degrees and had a lot of accurate knowledge. Jesus even told His disciples to do all that the Pharisees taught. So what the Pharisees taught must have been right. But they did not obey what they knew to be right."[440] If we do not combine our knowledge with obedience it will bring spiritual death and disaster to all around us. Salvation is not knowing a doctrine or understanding all the nuances of salvation. Salvation is experiencing the very person, the Lord Jesus Christ.[441] When Paul the Apostle preached the Gospel he did not have a specific list of doctrines but rather preached the person of Christ, presenting Him to the people.[442] "Not a doctrine, or a religion, or a catechism, but a Person, an exceedingly great and precious Person, this Preeminent Christ."[443]

"If 'Christ is all' to you, you are Christians; and I, for one, am ready to give you the right hand of brotherhood. I do not mind what place of worship you attend, or by what distinctive name you may call yourselves, we are brethren; and I think, therefore, that we should love one another. If, my friends, you cannot embrace all who love the Lord Jesus Christ, no matter to what denomination they may belong, and cannot regard them as your brethren in the Lord, and as belonging to the universal Church, you have not hearts large enough to go to heaven."[444] May this be the experience of all those who claim to have the right doctrines that they themselves will represent God's love, unity and all aspects of His character according to the Word of God. The proof will be by the way we love one another.[445] The world needs to know that we are His disciples.[446]

---

[440] Zac Poonen
[441] John 5:40
[442] Colossians 1:28, Acts 8:5
[443] Chip Brogden
[444] C.H. Spurgeon (1834-1892)
[445] Galatians 5:6
[446] John 17:23

Principle 27

The Priority of Love

THE LORD is crystal clear in the priority and importance He puts on our love one for another. This is not an option but a reality that will manifest when true believers are together.[447] If love is lacking there should be a sense of alarm that something is wrong in the body life.[448] The law of love says: "Do nothing out of selfish ambition or vain conceit, but in humility consider others better than yourselves."[449] Our Lord not only commanded the early disciples to love one another but said that it would be a fruit that would show the world that God has assembled a Church on the earth. Every believer should consider reading through 1 Corinthians chapter 13 on a regular basis to keep the right priority in Christian discipleship.

The phrase *one another* occurs over 25 times in the New Testament. Here are some of the phrases: Wash one another's feet,[450] love one another,[451] honor one another,[452] live in harmony with one another,[453] stop passing judgment on one another,[454] accept one

---

[447] Colossians 1:4
[448] Galatians 5:15
[449] Philippians 2:3-4
[450] John 13:14
[451] John 13:34
[452] Romans 12:10
[453] Romans 12:16
[454] Romans 14:13

another,[455] instruct one another,[456] greet one another,[457] agree with one another,[458] serve one another,[459] bear with one another,[460] be compassionate to one another,[461] submit to one another,[462] forgive one another,[463] encourage one another,[464] do not slander one another,[465] act in humility towards one another,[466] fellowship with one another.[467] These statements are not just a rule sheet to keep but rather truths that the Holy Spirit of God wants to work into our lives, for us to become more like Jesus Christ. To walk in this New Covenant way of love requires a resting and dependence on the grace of our Lord. In an individualistic society we need to be watchful what we think of others, especially those of the household of faith.[468]

"Beware of schism, of making a rent in the Church of Christ. That inward disunion, the members ceasing to have a reciprocal love 'one for another,' is the very root of all contention, and every outward separation."[469]

The two greatest commandments in the Bible given us by our Lord are based on love: "Jesus replied: 'Love the Lord your God with all your heart and with all your soul and with all your mind.' This is the first and greatest commandment. And the second is like it: 'Love your neighbor as yourself.'"[470]

The Scriptures says that if we do not love, we are nothing: "If I speak in the tongues of men or of angels, but do not have love, I am only a resounding gong or a clanging cymbal. If I have the gift of prophecy and can fathom all mysteries and all knowledge, and if I

---

[455] Romans 15:7
[456] Romans 15:14
[457] Romans 16:16
[458] 1 Corinthians 1:10
[459] Galatians 5:13
[460] Ephesians 4:2
[461] Ephesians 4:32
[462] Ephesians 5:21
[463] Colossians 3:13
[464] 1 Thessalonians 5:11
[465] James 4:11
[466] 1 Peter 5:5
[467] 1 John 1:7
[468] Galatians 6:10
[469] John Wesley (1703-1791)
[470] Matthew 22:37-39

have a faith that can move mountains, but do not have love, I am nothing."[471]

Our Lord taught on the principle of loving the least brethren by saying: "Then the righteous will answer him, 'Lord, when did we see You hungry and feed You, or thirsty and give You something to drink? When did we see You a stranger and invite You in, or needing clothes and clothe You? When did we see You sick or in prison and go to visit You?' The King will reply, 'Truly I tell you, whatever you did for one of the least of these brothers and sisters of Mine, you did for Me.'"[472]

"A sober revelation indeed: In the day of judgment, the Lord is not going to separate the sheep from the goats based upon how many sermons we preached, or how many souls we were able to convert to Christ, or how many things we accurately prophesied, or how many demons we cast out. Nay, here in this passage it is shown people being accepted or condemned based upon how they treated (*and in the most practical ways*) the 'least' of Christians—for how people treat the least of Christians is how they treat Christ Himself!"[473]

May we gain this priority of love as essential in our Assemblies and towards the weakest of believers as we meet together under the Headship of Jesus Christ.

---

[471] 1 Corinthians 13:1-2
[472] Matthew 25:37-40
[473] Adam Kautz

Principle 28

Examine Yourself and Correction in Love

IN THIS age of technology when we get hurt it is easy to go to Facebook, or other social media to voice our feelings. For many of us having mercy or asking: *Am I correct in feeling this way?* can become an afterthought. Scripture reminds us to examine oursèlves first. Judging, criticizing, maligning character, slandering and speaking to tear down another is probably one of the easiest things to do. Sadly, in the Christianity of our day such unedifying practices are applauded as righteous and discerning. Tearing down has become a ministry preoccupation with many in the blogosphere and Internet in general.

It is so easy for one to just spend a few minutes typing at the computer and the result can be devastating. The defiling of the testimony of a brother who has loved the Lord for many years can happen in minutes when the tongue is uncontrolled.[474] Such correction and criticism usually comes with little or no prayer, and without speaking to the individual himself, while appearing to be very holy on the outside. Yet the fruit produced from many of these types of rebukes, is usually the increase of a critical spirit in others.

---

[474] James 3:6

Of course, there are some brothers who have fasted and prayed, sought the Lord and had a burden from His heart. There are those who have pleaded with the individual involved and even worked through other brothers and sisters in the local area where that person is located.[475] They have only, as a last resort and plea to this precious brother or sister in the Lord, chosen to post a public warning.[476] Such warnings in love are needed for those who are continuing in sins.[477] It is also Biblical at times to warn the Church of God of others that are clearly false teachers.[478]

No public warnings must be posted on the Internet or on other social media until the intent and love of Scriptural correction is fulfilled. Disputes in the body of Christ must be resolved first in the household of God according to principles set out in the Bible. According to Matthew 18:

"If your brother or sister sins, go and point out their fault, just between the two of you. If they listen to you, you have won them over. But if they will not listen, take one or two others along, so that 'every matter may be established by the testimony of two or three witnesses.' If they still refuse to listen, tell it to the Church; and if they refuse to listen even to the Church, treat them as you would a pagan or a tax collector."[479]

Also in Luke 17 it says: "So watch yourselves. 'If your brother or sister sins against you, rebuke them; and if they repent, forgive them.'"[480]

In Galatians 6 it says: "Brothers and sisters, if someone is caught in a sin, you who live by the Spirit should restore that person gently. But watch yourselves, or you also may be tempted."[481]

Here is a simple outline on how to proceed:

1.) Examine yourself. What evidence is there of this sin in my own heart and life. Do I do the same things in my hidden life?

---

[475] Matthew 18:15-17
[476] Proverbs 27:5
[477] 1 Timothy 5:20, Ephesians 5:11
[478] Acts 20:29-31, Philippians 4:14-15
[479] Matthew 18:15-17
[480] Luke 17:3
[481] Galatians 6:1

2.) If the person has propagated doctrines different from yours, are you certain you are in the faith and correct? Have you sought advice from a good spectrum of servant leaders? Is the *beam* in your eyes greater than the little speck you are complaining about?

3.) Have you attempted to solve the problem based on Biblical principles?

4.) Christ's exhortation to watch over one another and to bear one another's burdens in the spirit of meekness and love should be foremost in our mind.[482]

5.) The primary aim must be the restoration of the offender and not to destroy him or her.

6.) Loving the sinner or enemy but not their sin, is the guiding principle. We attempt to restore the person in gentleness and love. This then gives a worthy witness of our faith during correction for a testimony to the sinner, the Church and the world.

7.) It is also true that we cannot overlook sin, as many do in churches today. We do not want to create problems, nor dissension or offense. We say, "We leave it to the Lord." This is wrong. Scripture tells us we have the duty to oppose sin against us in our Churches or Assemblies. One rotten apple can destroy the whole barrel. Satan and his demons are active in the Church to plant dissension, opposition, division and anger. He seeks to sow evil so that we might devour each other. Satan goes where he can find people of faith to destroy them.

8.) We must forgive 70 times 7 but we should not have fellowship with such a person unless he or she repents and turns around. God tells us that if we forgive, He will forgive us. If we don't forgive, He will not forgive us.[483]

9.) The offender must be readmitted to fellowship when he or she has repented, asked for forgiveness and made restitution where possible. Warnings in love and correction in love, including expulsion from fellowship for a time are necessary for those continuing in sin.

In any correction in the body of Christ, may we follow the example of Moses who flung himself in the dust before rebellious Korah.[484] This humble servant leadership that does not seek evil for anyone but rather forgiveness and mercy that is approved by God.

---

[482] Galatians 6:1-3
[483] Matthew 6:14-15
[484] Numbers 16:4

God still judged Korah in the end for his disobedience[485] but Moses gave every opportunity for Korah to repent as he humbled himself in a great way before him. Moses was not trying to build his reputation but rather was simply following the Lord in humility. We must be ready for such situations to occur in gatherings of believers who are meeting under the Headship of Jesus Christ. Where the light is shining greatly the enemy will be active to disrupt.

May God grant us such great humility and Christ's love in correcting any brother or sister in the Lord.

---

[485] Numbers 16:27-33

Principle 29

Being Rich in Mercy

IN MANY of the Epistles, the Apostles began with the wonderful phrase: "Grace and mercy."[486] If God began writing many of His holy Letters to us in this manner, then we should do also in our own correspondence with others in the body of Christ. In the beginning of the Book of Jude we read, "Mercy, peace and love be yours in abundance."[487]   Do we find it easy to wish mercy on others in abundance or are we quick to condemn? One that finds it easy to judge others has lost the perspective that he was shown much mercy from God. For it is by grace and mercy we have been saved by the blood of God's Son. In the Book of Titus it says: "Not because of righteous things we had done, but because of His mercy."[488]

When we start to look at another's problems more than our own, we are in a dangerous place in our walk with the Lord. Our Lord Jesus taught a wonderful parable on mercy in *Matthew 18*. Sadly, it ends with the judging of the *wicked servant* who did not show mercy but rather had a ministry of choking others: "Shouldn't you have had mercy on your fellow servant just as I had on you?"[489] Do we demand of others what we do not accomplish ourselves?

---

[486] 1 Timothy 1:2
[487] Jude 1:2
[488] Titus 3:5
[489] Matthew 18:33

As Jesus told the Pharisees, God considered justice, mercy and faithfulness much more important than tithing, sacrificing and being *right* before others. We need to get a revelation from the Lord on how important and crucial mercy is to Him. Thus, we will see it as a precious gift to share with others: "You have neglected the more important matters of the law—justice, mercy and faithfulness. You should have practiced the latter, without neglecting the former."[490] When we are seeking to be closer to God we must covet His wisdom and the fruit of His Spirit. Yet even these very attributes are full of mercy, bathed in mercy. Jesus taught us to love our enemies.[491] We should seek to ensure there is no division with others by first showing great mercy to that believer. May our testimony be that we are as full of mercy as is our God.[492]

We should constantly remind ourselves that we were forgiven much and therefore should show mercy to all other believers. If we do not and begin to judge and accuse others the Lord will allow us to be in a prison on this earth in our hearts:

"Then the master called the servant in. 'You wicked servant,' he said, 'I canceled all that debt of yours because you begged me to. Shouldn't you have had mercy on your fellow servant just as I had on you?' In anger his master handed him over to the jailers to be tortured, until he should pay back all he owed."[493]

"Speak and act as those who are going to be judged by the law that gives freedom, because judgment without mercy will be shown to anyone who has not been merciful. Mercy triumphs over judgement."[494]

May God fill His body with a powerful unity as we look to Christ our chief Shepherd and emulate His love, care and mercy toward others. Though we can be radical, fervent and know the Bible better than anyone near us, let us not deceive ourselves but prove our Christianity in action by exhibiting great love and mercy for all sinners and the body of Christ, our sisters and brothers.

---

[490] Matthew 23:23
[491] Matthew 5:44
[492] James 3:17
[493] Matthew 18:32-34
[494] James 2:12-13

Principle 30

Reading the Entirety of Scriptures

FOR MANY Christians in countries with no persecution, having a Bible—the full Scriptures[495]—is often not appreciated. We do not realize that the Bible is our greatest physical treasure in this world. In persecuted nations our sisters and brothers weep over the Word of God and often only have parts of the New Testament or literally scraps of paper with copied Scripture verses on them. Yet for some in the body of Christ there is great abundant access to full Bibles in literally hundreds of translations.[496] Amazingly, access to God's holy Word, in many languages and many countries in the world, has increased immeasurably via computers, whether on digital devices or in audio form, or in book form. Yet sadly, compared to the Christians in other persecuted countries we have the least desire and love to read

---

[495] Old And New Testaments.

[496] Some Christians will divide over Bible translations preferring the KJV or a specific translation. Though there are some better literal translations of the Bible we still can benefit from many different versions and even paraphrases to help contextualize the Scriptures in modern vernacular. We must take this to the Lord and not make it a point of division to separate over translations and if we hold one preferably above others we must do this first to the Lord and not cause other brothers to stumble by causing division and confusion. It is better to be in obedience to what the translation is saying rather than simply saying it is better. In this case we can deceive ourselves by reading and not obeying. (*see James 1:22*).

the Scriptures. As blood bought followers of Jesus Christ our life is not our own[497] and therefore we should have the desire to be in the Word of God daily. Even beyond that of our appetite to eat, the Scriptures should take precedent over anything else in our daily lives.[498] One reason for the lack of intense Bible study is the fact that we really do not believe what is written in the Book. If we truly believed the Scriptures and that the life to come matters much more than this life[499] then we would be more diligent to be steeped in what God desires of us now and for eternity.

Scriptures say we cannot live by bread alone but by every Word that proceeds from the mouth of God.[500] We need physical food and spiritual food. If we count the time it takes to eat physical food three times a day, and if we were to spend the same time every day to take in spiritual food—by reading the Word of God—we would have personal revival.

Of all the ways to read the Bible one of the most beneficial can be a survey reading of the entire Scriptures, verse by verse, chapter by chapter, and book by book. Beyond this even a chronological reading of the Scriptures can be of great benefit to know exactly when events took place. If all believers in many areas would commit[501] to being those who read the Word of God constantly and consistently in context, there would be a great strengthening of the body of Christ. Before reading the Word of God pray briefly asking the Holy Spirit to illuminate and explain to you what you will be reading. Then read the Scriptures slowly, taking time to let each word sink in. This slow reading and asking the Holy Spirit what you should learn will bring much truth and understanding to you, helping you every day in your daily activities. We must therefore read our Bibles carefully and slowly.

We must not be as those who take out a favorite few verses or even many verses to support individual viewpoints or doctrines. We

---

[497] 1 Corinthians 6:20
[498] Matthew 4:4
[499] Colossians 3:1-3
[500] Matthew 4:4
[501] We are suggesting to believers to be Bereans of the Word of God and commit to a systematic Bible reading method daily. This will also tend toward wonderful questions each time a fellowship meets, for all will be reading the same portions throughout each day. This must not take precedence over slow Bible reading devotionally for each person.

must follow the entirety of the Word of God as our standard and rule. We must not try to only delve into deep mysteries and secret things in the Word of God but rather read and believe simply[502] what is written and allow it be become real in our practical daily lives.[503]

The Holy Scriptures are to be read constantly, memorized, treated as more important than gold and silver. We should esteem the Scriptures more than our daily food. God's Words should be our delight and hope. May we follow the example of our dear underground Church brethren in different countries where they read the Scriptures for many hours daily.

To help with our practical response to this we have listed a reading schedule that goes through the entire Bible chronologically (*Arranged in order of time of occurrence*) in *Appendix III* of this book. Believers can commit to read a portion daily so that in 365 days the entire Scriptures can be read in context and in their fullness. We believe this will dispel many doctrinal errors[504] that have been held by some and allow us all to be more versed in the Holy Scriptures that are a light to our path[505] in this earthly pilgrimage.[506]

---

[502] 2 Corinthians 11:3

[503] Acts 1:1

[504] Many doctrinal errors are formed by simply taking a truth and putting it out of balance. Therefore a more balanced Bible reading can help put truths in their right order and place in the economy of God.

[505] Psalm 119:105

[506] 1 Peter 1:17

Principle 31

Godly Disciplines for Assemblies

ONE OF the hidden jewels of the Church is godly discipline. There has been a great lack of teaching and encouragement in modern evangelicalism towards the godly disciplines of: Fasting, waiting on God, early rising, head coverings, prevailing prayer, systematic Bible reading, Bible memorization, kneeling in prayer, and many other godly traditions in Church history.

Many have been taught that such things are legalistic and should be avoided if possible. Yet in the New Testament all these disciplines were taught and practiced by the early Apostles. Our Lord Himself taught and practiced fasting.[507] The early Apostles would wait on God in His presence ministering to Him.[508] Our Lord would rise early before all others to pray and seek His Father.[509] The Scriptures encourage women to cover their heads in prayer.[510] Some in the early

---

[507] Matthew 6:16-18, Matthew 4:1-11
[508] Acts 13:2, Isaiah 40:30-31
[509] Mark 1:35, Mark 16:9
[510] This truth should not be considered a bondage but rather a freedom and way to obey the Lord as a sister in Christ. Virtually all denominations, movements and Christian groups except for very few kept this practice in the life of the Church until largely in the last generation. (*see 1 Corinthians 11:2-16*).

Church had a ministry of intercession.[511]   The Apostles gave themselves to the careful study of Scripture.[512] Memorizing Scripture has been a principle of the people of God through both covenants.[513] The Apostle James prayed on his knees[514] till they were worn like a camel.[515] There are countless other examples of those whose works followed their faith.

Godly disciplines not only help us grow spiritually but are a great means of how the Lord ministers to our inner man and encourages our dependence on the Spirit of Christ. It is much more important for us to be disciplined in our spiritual life than in our physical life. Many suffer the loss of sleep, time, and money to succeed in a job, hobby or some game. But many will not suffer any discipline to be able to grow in their spiritual walk with the Lord.

The busyness of our lives[516] and the modern church culture can rob us from being attentive to simple devotion and discipline with the Lord, as one brother said: "When our service for the Lord becomes so busy that we forget the Lord Himself, it is time to stop everything and seek Him."[517]

There are some disciplines that are for our private walk with the Lord and some disciplines are for the assembling of the body of Christ. There are clear Scriptural directives on traditions and practices that the early Church practiced so we can emulate them. It is with such confidence we can meet together as the Church, over 2000 years later, and still practice many of the simple disciplines that those early Assemblies practiced.

With the same joy, we can walk in and practice the same godly disciplines—in our own private spiritual life—that the Apostles practiced. May God give us fresh vision and encouragement to seek to do what is written in Scripture and follow the ways of the Apostles traditions; not the modern ideas of men.

---

[511] 1 Thessalonians 3:10
[512] Acts 6:4, 2 Timothy 2:15
[513] Deuteronomy 11:18, Colossians 3:16, Psalm 119:11
[514] Ephesians 3:14, Psalm 95:6
[515] Early Church tradition claims that James was called *camel knees* because of the calluses on his knees from praying so often.
[516] Luke 9:41-42
[517] K.P. Yohannan

Principle 32

Godliness Through the Act of Submission

ONE OF the most important areas of godliness in the life of a believer is the area of submission. If one is not submissive but rebellious in spirit, there is a great danger of pride and sin. Many warnings are given in Scripture towards that state of rebellion and un-submissiveness in a believer's life. We must recognize God's sovereignty and rule over all creation, our lives and the Church. We must submit our minds to the authority of Scripture as we submit to God in our spirits; He owns us now. We must submit to those whom He has equipped with callings and giftings in the Church to lead the body of Christ.[518] God always has and always will place shepherds in the body of Christ to help oversee and protect the flock of God under the chief Shepherd, Jesus Christ our Lord.[519]

When we follow the way of un-submissiveness and elevate our own selves we fall into the place of being ruled by the spirit of lucifer or Satan,[520] who was the first to rebel against God. Thus he will influence us to rebel against God and all of His delegated authorities that have been set up.

---

[518] Ephesians 4:11-12
[519] 1 Peter 5:1-4
[520] Isaiah 14:12-15

"As we examine what it means to have this spirit of submission, we need to let go of our human reasoning and our cultural trappings so we can fully accept what the Word of God teaches. Unfortunately, we have inherited this rebellious nature from Adam. So don't be surprised to discover it fighting to stay alive. We'll be helped if we allow the light of God's Word to reveal this rebellion and then deliberately choose to believe what the Scriptures say instead of what our flesh says.

"Biblical submission to authority is recognizing that God, my Creator, is the ultimate authority and has all power. As clay in the potter's hand, I, His creation, should yield full control of my life to His will. This includes submitting to and obeying all delegated human authority over me, realizing that when I do so, I am actually submitting to God's authority. Likewise, when I rebel against delegated authority,[521] in essence I rebel against God Himself.

"This definition identifies who God truly is and our place in His creation, which includes absolute obedience to Him and to His delegated authorities."[522]

Jesus Himself was submitted to God the Father.[523] Therefore, He was submitted to every other authority as led of God's Spirit. Such is an example for us to follow for when we are mistreated for the sake of the kingdom of God we are blessed.[524]

True submission can only happen as led by the Spirit of God. Many submit, but in their hearts they are too bitter and angry to submit to an authority. Godly submission is where the individual is able—by God's grace—in good and bad circumstances, to submit and obey God. One example of this in the Old Covenant is when David submitted to Saul's leadership even though the Lord had departed from King Saul's life. Even at times Saul tried to kill David

---

[521] In some cases, we must resist the authority God has ordained in order to obey what God has commanded. We must obey the authorities until they command us to disobey God, the ultimate authority. There are some other examples of civil disobedience in the Bible (*see Exodus 1:17, Daniel 3:12*). This calls for the wisdom of the saints and leading of the Spirit to know when to resist or fully submit even to injustice and mistreatment.

[522] K.P. Yohannan

[523] Luke 22:42, 1 Corinthians 15:27-28, Hebrews 5:7-8

[524] Matthew 5:11

y throwing a spear at him, yet under these circumstances he still submitted.[525]

In the Epistle to the Ephesians, we are clearly shown the Biblical precedent for submission: "Wives, submit yourselves to your own husbands as you do to the Lord. For the husband is the head of the wife as Christ is the Head of the Church, His body, of which He is the Savior. Now as the Church submits to Christ, so also wives should submit to their husbands in everything."[526]

While husbands seek a submissive wife, they must submit to God themselves and act towards their wives in the same way as Jesus did towards the Church. Jesus loved the Church so much that He laid down His life for the Church and likewise a husband needs to lay down his life for his wife. Ephesians says: "Husbands, love your wives, just as Christ loved the Church and gave Himself up for her."[527] This leads to a beautiful union where the wife has no problems to submit as she sees the love and sacrifice of her husband.

Submission exists in our everyday life and moreover applies to political leaders and the police. Submit to the government: "Let everyone be subject to the governing authorities, for there is no authority except that which God has established. The authorities that exist have been established by God."[528] Where we are forbidden to believe and share the Good News of the Gospel we must answer as Peter and John did: "But Peter and John replied, 'Which is right in God's eyes: to listen to you, or to Him? You be the judges! As for us, we cannot help speaking about what we have seen and heard.'"[529]

The Bible also teaches submission to each other. We don't have to be right all the time. We can humble ourselves to preserve peace: "Submit to one another out of reverence for Christ."[530]

We must submit to the leaders that Christ appoints in the Church. Here is an example of this exhortation for submission by an early Church Father: "For, if the prayer of one and another has so great force, how much more that of the bishop and of the whole

---

[525] 1 Samuel 18:11
[526] Ephesians 5:22-24
[527] Ephesians 5:25
[528] Romans 13:1
[529] Acts 4:19-20
[530] Ephesians 5:21

Church. Whosoever therefore comes not to the congregation, he does thereby show his pride and has separated himself; for it is written, '*God resists the proud.*' Let us therefore be careful not to resist the bishop, that by our submission we may give ourselves to God."[531]

1 Corinthians says: "To submit to such people and to everyone who joins in the work and labors at it."[532] Also Peter the Apostle said: "In the same way, you who are younger, submit yourselves to your elders. All of you, clothe yourselves with humility toward one another, because, 'God opposes the proud but shows favor to the humble.'"[533]

In the epistle to Hebrews we are exhorted to: "Have confidence in your leaders and submit to their authority, because they keep watch over you as those who must give an account. Do this so that their work will be a joy, not a burden, for that would be of no benefit to you."[534]

The most important submission is to God: "But He gives us more grace. That is why Scripture says: 'God opposes the proud but shows favor to the humble.' Submit yourselves, then, to God. Resist the devil, and he will flee from you."[535] If we do not submit and surrender fully to God there can be no victorious Christian life for us. By submitting to the Heavenly Father and asking Him to bring the victory, the conflict is won. For Christ is the victor. "But thanks be to God! He gives us the victory through our Lord Jesus Christ."[536] Jesus not only has freed us from the penalty of sin but He has also freed us from the power of sin.[537]

May we learn afresh the godly discipline of submission as we gather under the Headship of Jesus Christ.

[531] Ignatius (A.D. 35-105)

[532] 1 Corinthians 16:16

[533] 1 Peter 5:5

[534] "*Be obedient to those leading you, and be subject, for these do watch for your souls, as about to give account, that with joy they may do this, and not sighing, for this is unprofitable to you.*" *Young's Literal Translation.* (Hebrews 13:17).

[535] James 4:6-7

[536] 1 Corinthians 15:57

[537] Matthew 1:21, Romans 6:14

Principle 33

The Obedience of Believers Baptism

IN CHRISTENDOM there have been huge divisions over the doctrine of Baptism. Yet this practice is not something to be ignored for it is Biblical and needs to be exhibited in the life of the Church. Baptism is something that is reserved only for believers who have come "out of darkness into his wonderful light."[538] Many true believers became martyrs to defend and stand upon the truth of believer's Baptism. They stood up against the false ideology of infant Baptism perpetrated by the Catholic church system for many years. Those who were known in the 1500s as Anabaptists were those who *re-baptized* therefore named *Ana (re-)* Baptists. Many paid a dear price as the persecutors in that day made them martyrs through a *third Baptism* by drowning.

Repeated testimonies throughout Church history confirm the fact that when a believer confesses faith in the Lord Jesus Christ they will have a desire to obey the Lord in water Baptism. Whether this is by full immersion, sprinkling or any other method must not be a dividing point amongst believers. Some call Baptism the *first obedience* which is right because it is one of the first commands to a

---

[538] 1 Peter 2:9

new believer. Some will try to make Baptism of no importance because it is just one small command. But we must have the mindset that even the smallest commands from God in the Day of Judgment will be very important.

The Lord Jesus Christ Himself exemplified water Baptism—as an adult—being baptized by John the Baptist in the River Jordan. God the Father was pleased and opened up heaven and spoke by way of a voice: "You are My Son, whom I love; with You I am well pleased."[539] We are commanded to baptize in the Gospel of Matthew: "Baptizing them in the Name of the Father and of the Son and of the Holy Spirit."[540] Also in the Gospel of Mark: "Whoever believes and is baptized will be saved, but whoever does not believe will be condemned."[541] Throughout the Book of Acts believers followed Christ in Baptism, including the 3000 saved at Pentecost.[542]

When we are baptized we declare to the world our faith in Jesus Christ, that we are baptized with Him into His death—that sin has died with us—and that we rise into Jesus' resurrection, having put on Christ. We are baptized into one body, and by one Spirit, the Spirit of the Father, Son and Holy Spirit.

After accepting Christ no Baptism classes are necessary. "As they traveled along the road, they came to some water and the eunuch said, 'Look, here is water. What can stand in the way of my being baptized?' Philip said, 'If you believe with all your heart, you may.' The eunuch answered, 'I believe that Jesus Christ is the Son of God.' And he gave orders to stop the chariot. Then both Philip and the eunuch went down into the water and Philip baptized him."[543]

May we take heed to these things and treat every command of Scripture as important, more-important than anything else in this earth-life.

---

[539] Mark 1:11
[540] Matthew 28:19
[541] Mark 16:16
[542] Acts 2:41
[543] Acts 8:36-38

Principle 34

The Body of Christ: An Army of Evangelists

ACCORDING TO the Chinese rural underground Church witnessing, evangelizing and making new disciples is the number one task of the Church. Their cry to go and make new disciples is backed up with their very lives. In many cases if they speak to the wrong person about Jesus, they face prison, torture and even death. The task of sharing the Gospel is for every Christian, even if they give their life as a martyr. Chinese Christians teach us that when their seed (*their life*) has gone into the ground and died it will multiply and produce much more fruit.[544] With their blood new growth is coming. The seed, their body that died now produces 100 fold, 1000 fold or even more.

When we consider that the angels in heaven rejoice when one sinner repents[545] we know that God's heart is touched and He rejoices also. Modern Christians say: No, the number one task is to worship and love God. The answer: Then show how much you love and worship Him by *doing*. Witness and give joy to the Father. There are many excuses: I don't have the gift to witness, witnessing is for the pastor and missionaries, I don't want to upset people, I want to respect other religions, I don't know the Bible enough, what will the

---

[544] John 12:24
[545] Luke 15:7

people think of me, and I am not an extremist. All are lies from Satan, the world and our own sinful flesh. We don't trust God that He will help us and empower us. Please read the promise in Acts chapter 1 verse 8: "But you will receive power when the Holy Spirit comes on you; and you will be My witnesses in Jerusalem, and in all Judea and Samaria, and to the ends of the earth." If you feel you cannot speak out, would you be willing to give out a tract?[546]

Imagine gatherings of believers meeting regularly that are equipped with tract booklets so that during the week they can hand them out as the Spirit of God leads them. These tracts can be of great help for seekers to find the truth. You can add your contact information to the tract for them to contact you. As you invite them to your fellowship they will learn of Christ and become a disciple through the witness in your fellowship and the work of the Holy Spirit. We believe there is a need for a radical movement of believers who are fully engaged in evangelism during their work week no matter what vocation or work they are in. Imagine an army of believers who are constantly engaging in Gospel witness to the lost world around them! The evangelization and discipleship of the world is not an option but it is a command[547] from the Lord Jesus Christ. Men are ignorant of the Gospel message, they do not know the Scripture nor Christ. We must proclaim to them the Gospel and the messages of Scripture through our lives and through our mouths, so the Holy Spirit can bring men and women to repentance.[548]

A time is coming when we will not be able to do the work of spreading the Gospel to our neighbor as easily. We must be active now! Only those believers who are awake to God will have this burden. Many do not have any tears for lost souls around them because they have grieved the Holy Spirit in their lives. When our Christianity has little self-denial we will be lead by the lusts of the flesh and not share the spiritual burdens from the Lord. One reason for the exceptional growth of the Church in China is this one fact: All believers in the house Church movement are considered evangelists!

---

[546] There are many good Biblical tracts that can be obtained freely or printed from home. Be in prayer for what strategy and tract that the Lord would lead you to use in your local area. We must be led of the Holy Spirit in every way we reach out with the Good News.

[547] Matthew 28:16-20

[548] Romans 2:4

"How, then, can they call on the One they have not believed in? And how can they believe in the One of whom they have not heard? And how can they hear without someone preaching to them? And how can anyone preach unless they are sent? As it is written: 'How beautiful are the feet of those who bring Good News!'"[549] May God raise up an army of the bearers of this Good News today!

We want to encourage gatherings of believers to have printed tracts available for the Lord's people as you assemble so they can distribute them in your local area.

In Scriptures we see Antioch as a larger gathering of believers where many prophets and teachers were.[550] Also this place was a missions sending base where the Apostle Paul and others were sent out[551] and came back to rest, be edified and encouraged. In the same way we can look and see each home gathering as a missions sending base to send the Gospel out to the entire neighborhood and local area. May the Lord grant a broken heart for the lost[552] and a passion to reach out with the Gospel of our Lord. May we realize that every Christian is a Missionary!

The Church has never expanded without sacrifice, to have a harvest means hard work to sow, plow and reap. We must be willing to be a follower of the Lord and deny our selfish ways[553] in this matter so that the Gospel can go forward. Therefore we will be able to say as in the days of the Apostles: "The Word of God continued to spread and flourish."[554]

---

[549] Romans 10:14-15
[550] Acts 15:35
[551] Acts 13:4-12
[552] Jeremiah 8:20, Matthew 9:36-38
[553] Luke 9:23
[554] Acts 12:24

Principle 35

The Lord's Supper: The Death of Christ

THE LORD'S Supper is clearly a New Testament practice that the early disciples kept, as its significance is tied into the end of the age. The Scripture says that as we *remember the Lord* we are proclaiming His death until He comes back.[555] This death is important because by the death of Christ, He took upon Himself our sins and absolved the wrath of God on our behalf.[556] What a glorious Good News to celebrate that this is a finished work[557] and we do not have to suffer the wrath of God for our sins if we are in Jesus Christ and walking in a life of true discipleship with Him.[558]

The Lord's Supper is not just a symbol but a very important reminder of the holy act of God shedding His blood for the sins of men. If we partake of this supper in an unworthy way and are not having a reverential fear of the Lord in our daily lives then we can incur God's discipline on the Church and ourselves.[559] Thus taking

---

[555] 1 Corinthians 11:26
[556] Ephesians 2:3, 2 Corinthians 5:21
[557] 2 Corinthians 5:18
[558] 1 Thessalonians 5:5-10, 1 Peter 4:4
[559] 1 Corinthians 11:27

the Lord's Supper is part of realizing that Jesus Christ is Head of His Church and that He corrects and shepherds His own. All true believers are invited to participate in the Lord's Supper. "But let no one eat or drink of your Eucharist [Lord's Supper], unless they have been baptized into the Name of the Lord; for concerning this also the Lord has said, 'Give not that which is holy to the dogs.'"[560] In 1 Corinthians we are reminded to examine ourselves: "So then, whoever eats the bread or drinks the cup of the Lord in an unworthy manner will be guilty of sinning against the Body and Blood of the Lord. Everyone ought to examine themselves before they eat of the bread and drink from the cup. For those who eat and drink without discerning the Body of Christ eat and drink judgment on themselves. That is why many among you are weak and sick, and a number of you have fallen asleep. But if we were more discerning with regard to ourselves, we would not come under such judgment."[561] The Lord wants us to examine ourselves and confess any sins in our lives before participating in the Lord's Supper. "If we confess our sins, He is faithful and just and will forgive us our sins and purify us from all unrighteousness."[562] Confession also includes repentance and turning away from such sins in the future. If you are weeping over your sins you may want to abstain from participating in the Lord's Supper. However, the Lord loves you and wants you to partake of the Lord's Supper provided you have confessed and have asked for cleansing.

The Lord's Supper reminds us to visualize and remember the great sacrifice of our Lord. An old Apostolic prayer states: "To us you have graciously given spiritual food and drink, and eternal life through Your servant."[563] Thus we should be thankful and humbled in the breaking of the bread.

The Holy Spirit is jealous to magnify and elevate the person of Christ[564] and this occurs through the practice of the Lord's Supper: "At the beginning it was Christ who was preached: the Person who was kept in full view, and the One through whom the Gospel came.

---

[560] Didache (A.D. 80-140)
[561] 1 Corinthians 11:27-31
[562] 1 John 1:9
[563] Didache (A.D. 80-140)
[564] John 15:26

It was 'the Gospel of God concerning His Son.' The emphasis was not upon what men could have, but upon God's rights and Christ's glory. This may seem to be straining things, but let it be understood that the Holy Spirit—the Custodian of Christ's honor—is most jealous on this matter, and will only commit Himself to this keeping of Christ in view."[565]

The Lord's Supper also always keeps us humble showing that we are great sinners in need of salvation. This truth was shared by one of the early Church Fathers in this way: "The Word of God becomes the Eucharist [Lord's Supper], which is the body and blood of Christ; so also our bodies, being nourished by it, and deposited in the earth, and suffering decomposition there, shall rise at their appointed time, the Word of God granting them resurrection to the glory of God, even the Father, who freely gives to this mortal immortality, and to this corruptible incorruption, because the strength of God is made perfect in weakness, in order that we may never become puffed up, as if we had life from ourselves, and exalted against God, our minds becoming ungrateful."[566]

During a powerful time of revival and restoration the Lord was working through believers called *Anabaptists*. Here is a quote from the year 1527: "The Lord's Supper shall be held, as often as the brothers are together, thereby proclaiming the death of the Lord, and thereby warning each one to commemorate, how Christ gave His life for us, and shed His blood for us, that we might also be willing to give our body and life for Christ's sake, which means for the sake of all the brothers."[567]

In closing, here is a beautiful hymn by the founder of the Moravians, whose movement sent missionaries to the farthest reaches of the globe declaring the bloodied Lamb of God who died:

"Jesus, Your blood and righteousness. My beauty are, my glorious dress; Lord, I believe were sinners more Than sands upon the ocean shore, You have for all a ransom paid, For all a full atonement made."[568]

May God see fit to raise up such a movement again to bring the Gospel of God to lost perishing souls.

---

[565] William MacDonald (1917-2007)
[566] Irenaeus (A.D. 130-202)
[567] Schleitheim Brotherly Union (1527)
[568] Count Nicolaus Zinzendorf (1700-1760)

Principles 36 to 42

Principles from the Underground Church in China

Principle 36

Dependence on the
Moving of the Holy Spirit

IN THE Book of Acts the Church was birthed, led, sustained and grew in the power of the Holy Spirit. For many there is a hesitancy to speak much of depending radically on the moving of the Holy Spirit. Today for many sincere Bible believing Christians this terminology brings to mind many excesses of the worst kind—whether it's the selfish seeking after the Spirit of God for a feeling,[569] an anointing to enjoy for ourselves,[570] some sort of extravagant healing such as gold in the teeth or other blatant extra-biblical manifestations that grieve the heart of God. The Devil our enemy always makes a pseudo[571] of the genuine in attempts to deceive[572] some and deter others. Some in these charismatic circles claim the Chinese Church is experiencing the same manifestations, but this is not true.

"The gifts of the Holy Spirit are widely accepted and practiced, *in the underground House Churches in China,* but certain activities like speaking in tongues and prophesying are not emphasized. What

---

[569] 2 Timothy 3:4
[570] Acts 8:18-19
[571] 2 Corinthians 11:15
[572] Matthew 24:24

makes the charismatic element unique in China is that it is not disorderly."[573]

The rural underground Church in China relies upon and even expects that when the Gospel of the Lord Jesus Christ is declared there will be verification at times with great signs and wonders.[574] This dependence on the Holy Spirit to move, direct, guide and verify the Gospel is Biblical and needed in the Church. It was not unusual for healings to occur in every village that the pioneers of the house Church movement went into when they were driven all across China because of persecution. It must be asked in our lives, how much do we rely and truly depend on the Holy Spirit on a daily basis?

"They are *on fire* Christians with a real vital walk with the Lord Jesus Christ. There are no denominations in the rural underground Church. There are no Methodists, Presbyterians or Baptists, or any other. They are just simply *followers of Christ*. In the underground Church no one has seminary training. Their dependence is upon the Holy Spirit to teach them."[575]

Without a strong institutional and hierarchic structure some of the house Churches rely on the Holy Spirit for 100% guidance. Just like the Holy Spirit gave directions to the early Christians, the house Churches also receive direct instructions from the Holy Spirit.

During the Communist Cultural Revolution Bibles were scarce and difficult to obtain. A house Church prayed and asked the Lord Jesus Christ to give them His Word. There was an elderly deaconess who was over eighty years old. She had totally fasted (*abstention from food and water*) and prayed for nineteen days. She became filled with the Holy Spirit and would sit in the middle of the house Church. Everyone would sit around her. Through the unction of the Holy Spirit this sister would recite Bible verses loudly and clearly, and every one would write down the words in their books. Every word was the Word of God at the time when there were few Bibles in China. God had anointed a sister with a special charismatic gift of reciting Bible verses.

God has given us the Holy Spirit not only as a comforter and guide but also as a life-changing power. Any work done in peoples'

---

[573] Brother Zhu
[574] Romans 15:19
[575] E.A. Johnston

lives, without the Holy Spirit is void of any life-changes. In Zechariah this truth is shown where it says: "So he said to me, 'This is the word of the Lord to Zerubbabel: Not by might nor by power, but by My Spirit, says the Lord Almighty.'"[576] Yet many are denying the life-changing power of God and His Spirit: "Having a form of godliness but denying its power."[577] The Holy Spirit gives us the power to witness, as in *Acts 1:8*, but we must ask Him and we must surrender to Him.

Brother Enguan from the *Lixin* underground house Church network gives this testimony: "We were one of the most heavily-persecuted Churches in all of China. The police regularly swept through our area and conducted sting operations. Every year more than one hundred leaders would be arrested. Christians in our area were not Christians for long before they were rounded up by the police. You would have one believer who had been a believer for six years and had served five and a half of those years in prison. It was not uncommon to have believers that were baby Christians only being saved for a month or more before being martyred for their faith. This was life in those days. Those were hard days."[578]

Let us suppose we were being threatened with jail and beatings for proclaiming the Gospel. Would we do it? Many of us hardly witness now. The early Christians after being threatened did not pray for protection, or for safety, or for God to punish those that were threatening to hurt them. Here is what they prayed: "'*Now, Lord, consider their threats and enable Your servants to speak Your Word with great boldness. Stretch out Your hand to heal and perform signs and wonders through the Name of Your holy servant Jesus.*' After they prayed, the place where they were meeting was shaken. And they were all filled with the Holy Spirit and spoke the Word of God boldly."[579] God the Father was pleased with their prayer and shook the house and gave them boldness. God and His Holy Spirit's power was with them. Beloved sisters and brothers, do you want that? Ask the Father, He wants to give you His Holy Spirit, but it requires your full surrender. Pray as our sisters and brothers did in the Book of Acts.

---

[576] Zechariah 4:6
[577] 2 Timothy 3:5
[578] Brother Zhu
[579] Acts 4:29-31

Pray as our persecuted sisters and brothers do in China and wherever they are persecuted. God wants to send, through you and me, the Gospel and signs and wonders through the holy Name of His Son Jesus.[580]

---

[580] Luke 18:8

Principle 37

Jesus Christ as Lord and Head

THE CHINESE believers see the Gospel of Jesus' death and resurrection in all their activities. Out of a great love for this Savior they speak to Him and of Him often to everyone they meet. The simplicity of the message of the cross of Christ[581] has gripped them and persecution has allowed the Church as a whole to keep this as their main message. In every meeting of the underground Church, Jesus Christ is given the rightful place as Head[582] of the meeting and He is recognized in the midst.[583]

Many people in China carry the cross of Jesus. They see the verse as literal: "And whoever does not carry their cross and follow Me cannot be My disciple."[584] And the verse: "Then Jesus said to His disciples, 'Whoever wants to be My disciple must deny themselves and take up their cross and follow Me.'"[585]

Brothers and sisters carry the cross in China where many are imprisoned, beaten, tortured and even put to death. They say: The

---

[581] 1 Corinthians 2:2
[582] Colossians 1:18
[583] 1 Corinthians 5:4
[584] Luke 14:27
[585] Matthew 16:24

cross helps us to confess our sins and be right with Jesus. To carry our cross we have to walk side by side with Jesus to give a testimony of His love for salvation. We understand the persecution in *Hebrews chapter 11* and we walk with the Lord. For this reason He gives us His power and the presence of Jesus is with us. Our faith is only in Him and He gives us strength to endure.[586] We are the salt and the light of this world.[587] How will people know if we don't tell them?[588] We must be obedient to Jesus commands' so that He can return to us. The whole world must hear about Jesus' salvation and then Jesus will come back to us.[589] Many of us have been imprisoned many times. We don't know what the next day will bring. When we experience jail, beatings, electric shock, and other torture we feel that Jesus is with us. He won't let us suffer more than we can bear.[590] We experience how Jesus was crucified on the cross to carry our sins and we understand the cost of sin. That is why we love Him so much. We understand what He did for us to forgive us our sins. We feel sorry for our torturers. We say like Jesus said from the cross: "Father, forgive them, for they do not know what they are doing."[591] We also want them to know about Jesus and we try to tell them. We are ready every day to die. So we must be ready every day to face God in heaven.

We want to bring Jesus to the world because He won't return until all the world has heard the Gospel. Every Christian knows it is their responsibility to tell others the Gospel. We want to bring the Gospel to all of China, and then from there to Jerusalem. The Lord will reign forever when He comes back. In the meantime if we must suffer a little, He will give us strength and dry our tears. The suffering is only for a short while.[592] Please be obedient and take up your cross and walk next to Jesus.

"One night I was in Western China and the Spirit of the Lord filled the room. Everyone fell to their faces and started crying and

[586] 2 Thessalonians 1:4
[587] Matthew 5:13-16
[588] Romans 10:14
[589] Matthew 24:14
[590] 1 Corinthians 10:13
[591] Luke 23:34
[592] Romans 8:18

calling out to the Lord. During these meetings I couldn't sleep for two days and two nights. I couldn't stop praying. The Holy Spirit was so strong. Young people began to call out, '*Yes, Lord, I am willing to die in that country for you.*"[593] Such is the sovereign calling of Jesus as Head of His Church for believers in the end times to go to specific countries for His Gospel witness.

Instead of fancy Bible schools and seminary buildings these precious Chinese believers at times meet in caves: "On a recent visit to China, they were introduced to our underground seminary school and witnessed firsthand the high cost of following the Lord in China. They visited the secret seminary school one evening. Dressed in dark clothing, they ran silently across a field and crawled through the small cave opening undetected. While there they learned the real sacrifice these students make on a daily basis. For six months of the year, these students live in the cave, leaving infrequently and only under the protective cover of darkness. Their day starts at 6 A.M., with prayer and devotion. Around 8 A.M. the students receive their first meal of the day, which is a bun with mincemeat. They usually don't eat again until dinner, which features the *same meal* as breakfast. Their intense education takes place between these two small meals. After a rigorous day of learning, they fall asleep on a bed of hay on the cave floor."[594]

The urgency to share Jesus Christ with the world is deeply engrained in these believers' hearts as well as believing and proclaiming the soon literal coming of the Lord. We can learn much from this example to keep the message simple[595] and to not be as much focused on our church programs, ministries and resources. When Jesus Christ becomes the centre and Head of the Church again the message is simple, the way made plain and the power is given[596] by the Holy Spirit to accomplish the task of spreading the Gospel.[597]

---

[593] Brother Ezekiel
[594] WorldServe Missionary Report
[595] 2 Corinthians 11:3
[596] Acts 1:8
[597] Matthew 28:16-20

Principle 38

The Spirit of Martyrdom

AS THE underground Church in China has been baptized in a fire of intensely severe persecution this has produced a theology of suffering with Christ.[598] They have realized that all suffering is because of Christ and for Christ.[599] It was clearly told to Paul the Apostle, that he was persecuting Jesus Christ directly when he was persecuting the early Church believers.[600] There is a willingness in the Church in China to suffer for Christ as the normal cost of being a believer. It is accepted as the will of God at times to suffer[601] and to even expect severe persecution. This type of suffering produces a joy[602] and sense of privilege that they are willing to identify with their precious Lord who has saved them.[603]

Suffering and persecution has not built a resentment against China or its government but rather a deeper love for all the Chinese who are simply sinners in need of God's great love.[604] In other countries we need to deeply learn and try to understand this lesson that we are to love our enemies as our Lord taught us.[605] As the spirit

---

[598] 1 Peter 4:1-2
[599] John 15:18-20
[600] Acts 9:5
[601] 1 Peter 4:19
[602] 1 Peter 4:13-16
[603] Acts 5:41
[604] John 3:16
[605] Matthew 5:44

of antichrist and persecution comes to us we need to learn the same theology of martyrdom[606] that this young underground Church has learned so well.

One beautiful example of this optimism in the face of severe persecution can be read in one of the hymns of the underground Church: "In the dark night, flowers are more fragrant. In the dark night, footsteps are more determined. A journey in the dark, is close to its end. Remember to remain faithful to God!"[607] Such a dark night of persecution is coming to many. May we be of good cheer and leap for joy[608] even as we reflect the character of God's Son to others.

"The Church thrives under pressure, that was the very birth of the Church. They were persecuted in Jerusalem and all over. In the Scripture, especially in Acts, they went out after being arrested and beaten and they went rejoicing because they were worthy to suffer for the Name of Jesus. I think it's a great privilege, but it's not something you seek, because then that is the wrong attitude."[609]

The pressures of persecution for the Name of Christ, and an unwarranted hatred will come against you in the end times simply because you adore and worship Jesus Christ. Will you be able to stand in that day?

It will be easy to follow the multitudes, the *many* who will be turning away from the faith.[610] Yet our Lord desires us to stay true to His calling and Name by His grace. He states to the Church at Philadelphia: "I know your deeds. See, I have placed before you an open door that no one can shut. I know that you have little strength, yet you have kept My Word and have not denied My Name."[611] Also in the city of Pergamum: "Yet you remain true to My Name. You did not renounce your faith in Me, not even in the days of Antipas, My faithful witness, who was put to death in your city—where Satan lives."[612]

---

[606] It would do us well to read accounts of martyrs and study the *New Testament Scriptures* in light of this theme.
[607] Canaan Hymn Book
[608] Luke 6:23
[609] Brother Andrew
[610] Matthew 24:10, 1 Timothy 4:1
[611] Revelation 3:8
[612] Revelation 2:13

May God find us with these faithful Churches that happily and with hope endured much for the kingdom of God and did not allow compromise and lukewarmness to cause them to drift away from being bold for the Lord.

This *falling away* is shown in 2 Thessalonians: "Don't let anyone deceive you in any way, for that day will not come until *the rebellion* occurs and the man of lawlessness is revealed, the man doomed to destruction."[613] May God preserve us in that day and allow us to faithfully cling to Jesus Christ as our hope and salvation to be willing to bear the loss of all things for His Name sake.[614] Our great security in Christ is never at jeopardy as long as we continue to abide in Him daily.

We can sit at His feet as He prepares a table in the presence of our enemies.[615] The Great Shepherd of the sheep will keep us. Let us stay close to our Master so that none of these things will overwhelm us. These words should bring strength to our souls for these coming days and a desire to do the will of the Father.

In the first century the Apostle John wrote: "Do not be surprised, My brothers and sisters, if the world hates you."[616]

Now, 2000 years later, let us not be surprised when the entire world system will hate us who call ourselves after the Name of Christ. Be valiant for His testimony, for very soon suffering and martyrdom will not be mere abstract theology but a practical reality. May we learn of the Lord how to endure now for that time that is coming upon us. His "grace is sufficient,"[617] He will bear us up in that day for His glory's sake.

Also, may God continue to build in us a profound respect for those martyrs that have gone on before us in the Church,[618] and to help us realize that the Christianity in our day needs more soberness in it—a martyr spirit that will proclaim the Gospel at all costs to the world around it.

---

[613] 2 Thessalonians 2:3
[614] Philippians 3:8
[615] Psalm 23:5
[616] 1 John 3:13
[617] 2 Corinthians 12:9
[618] Hebrews 13:3

Principle 39

God Actually Answers Prayer

WITH MANY in the Church prayer is treated as the last thing we do before God. We use prayer to ask Him to fulfill—in many cases—our own carnal plans. With thousands of books written on prayer many of us have still not placed prayer as the most important Christian activity we do, corporately[619] or privately.[620] We have special times for prayer once in a while, expecting that God should hear us and then go back to our normal lives without an intense reliance on God through prayer.

All the growth of the house Church movement in China stems from a base of intensely fervent prayer.[621] Whole congregations cry out to God with weeping and tears in intercession for the lost in their country and for their persecutors.[622] Such passionate praying will shock and disturb many of us, yet the Church there truly believes that God answers genuine prayer. As with the widow who cried out to the judge,[623] so this house Church movement cries out to God day

---

[619] Acts 4:23-24
[620] Matthew 6:6
[621] James 5:16
[622] Philippians 3:18
[623] Luke 18:7

and night and God hears them. If we realized that God would hear such praying, we would spend much more time as a Church in the blessed place of prayer and intercession. Persistent intercessory prayer may often go on in many underground meetings for up to three or four hours at a time in duration.

It is argued that over 80% of the believers in the underground house churches in China believed in the Lord Jesus Christ because they have either seen or experienced some miracles, signs and wonders. How else can you convince atheists there is a One True God? "God also testified to it by signs, wonders and various miracles, and by gifts of the Holy Spirit distributed according to His will."[624]

One underground Church pastor upon returning to China from America, stated to his movement: "Our brothers in the West know how to plan, but we know how to pray."

There is such a great commitment to pray that many in the underground Church wake up at 5 A.M. every morning to worship and pray before they start their day of manual labor. Prayer meetings gather at this early hour of the morning and there is even a hymn written with the title: *5 A.M. in China*. Some of the words are: "When dawn arrives in China you can hear people praying. They are rejoicing in the great love that unites all the peoples of the world. These prayers soar over the highest mountains and melt the ice off the coldest hearts."[625]

Should this not move us to spend much time with our Heavenly Father who is eager to hear the prayers of His children? "I love the Lord, for He heard my voice; He heard my cry for mercy. Because He turned His ear to me, I will call on Him as long as I live."[626]

The Lord will hear our cries as we seek His face daily and believe that what we ask in the Name of His Son He will answer.[627] Prayer must be the first thing a local Church does and not the last. Prayer declares our dependency on the Lord for everything. We end up being paupers by not accessing all the riches of Christ Jesus[628] through prayer.

---

[624] Hebrews 2:4
[625] Xiao Min
[626] Psalm 116:1-2
[627] John 14:13-14
[628] Ephesians 1:18

Principle 40

The Body of Christ is the Church

MANY TIMES we are preoccupied with the idea that the building where we worship is the Church. Yet in the early Church and Biblical record, God calls the people themselves the Church.[629]

One of the main desires in church planting in North America is the constructing of a church building after a group of believers is established. This is not always helpful. The true work of God is not dependent on money and resources to grow but rather on hearts that have been affected by the Gospel of our Lord. If we focus on building structures and churches, we can subtly deceive the people to depend on such structures[630] and not the living Lord.[631]

No structures, except the living structure of the body of Christ, are necessary in the rural underground Chinese Church. Almost the entire movement does not own buildings but rather they make use of fields, caves[632] and homes. What is most important to them is the people of God.[633] Such was the burden of Paul the Apostle who saw

---

[629] Ephesians 4:12, Ephesians 2:19-22
[630] Matthew 24:2
[631] Psalm 2:12
[632] Hebrews 11:38
[633] 1 Peter 5:2, Hebrews 13:17

the people as being the Church and the crown of his reward.[634] This was also the burden of the early Church which acknowledged the priesthood of all believers[635] where every part of the body had a job or function. They did not believe in leadership that *controls* the body of Christ but rather serves and equips it.[636]

This does not undermine the great usefulness of a building or structure where it can be used for a gathering of people, who are the Church. Some servant leaders of the rural underground house Church networks in China meet in a barn with animals walking around as they pray and receive instructions from the Lord for millions of believers. Meeting in a barn or even an old unoccupied church building is not wrong in itself. Though the underground Church in China is not as free as other nations to meet in various types of buildings, the Church is still growing and abounding in the work of the Lord. May we never see the building as *the Church* but only the people as God's true Church set apart unto Jesus Christ.

Bibles in the rural underground Church in China are scarce at times, and it is common that fellowships have handwritten copies of verses and Epistles similar to the early Church days. The Chinese love their Bibles greatly and treat them as the most cherished item that they own or have in the world. Some of the current servant leaders in the rural underground Church, early on, would gladly travel a full day, one way, to just be able to borrow and read a Bible. Most preaching, especially in the earlier days of the movement, was from verses they had memorized.[637]

"As the Holy Spirit teaches the Chinese Church, they are not *reservoirs* who selfishly keep what they learn; rather, they are clear and unobstructed *conduits* that flow to others. The believers have an unconditional and uncompromised love for each other.[638] They love each other according to Christ's command.[639] Our Chinese brethren are walking Bibles for they have memorized much of it. We must do

---

[634] 1 Thessalonians 2:19
[635] 1 Peter 2:5-9
[636] 1 Peter 5:2-4
[637] Psalm 119:11, Jeremiah 15:16
[638] Galatians 5:13
[639] John 13:34

likewise for if we in the West have our Bibles confiscated, how will we still minister to others if we cannot recall God's Word?"[640]

The underground Church in China has such a reverence for the Lord and His Words and they see themselves in the proper light of God's holiness. A short Chinese hymn[641] that reflects their humble hearts in realization that they were sinners in need of a Savior says: "Lord, how great You are! You didn't abandon us. We are dust. We are no better than worms and moth, but You took pity on us. You cared for us, and chose us." Such words show the humble attitude we should come to God's Word with to receive life, instruction and truth.[642]

The underground Church in China operates like a body and one part does not demand to be recognized above the rest. One Church leader who with 7 others oversees many million believers was asked if titles are used for them. He responded by saying, "No, we don't think like that. We're all just brothers and sisters." All believers in that house Church network know who the leaders are and respect them but they do not demand to be recognized by titles and other various elevated positions.

"The underground Church in China is basically a pure New Testament Church. No one is called *doctor* or *pastor*, they call each other *brother and sister*. What they do is defined by function or gifts, not title. One may be gifted as a teacher so he teaches. Another may be gifted in hospitality so they serve in that capacity. Their gift makes room for them to serve. They feel that titles divide. To them the Church is a familial entity; every member is essential. The Chinese see the Church as a family functioning as the body of Christ."[643]

They truly have a faith in the body of Christ and that Jesus Christ is the Head above the rest and He alone is the glorified One.

---

[640] E.A. Johnston
[641] Canaan Hymn Book
[642] 2 Timothy 3:16
[643] E.A. Johnston

Principle 41

The Back To Jerusalem
Movement

"'YOU MAY go Westward from Gansu, preaching the Gospel all the way back to Jerusalem, causing the light of the Gospel to complete the circle around this dark world.' I said, 'O Lord who are we that we can carry such a great responsibility?' The Lord answered, 'I want to manifest My power through those who of themselves have no power.'"[644]

And such was the call given to a dear underground Church worker in China in the 1920s. This vision to see the Gospel go across to the "ends of the earth"[645] has been kept alive by the Lord in the underground house Churches for many years and now it has begun to be fulfilled with hundreds of workers going out. What the Lord showed many of the house Church leaders was that the Gospel went out west, north, south and east from Jerusalem. This progression occurred so that all of Europe, Southern Africa and eventually the Americas were saturated with the Gospel. Now that the Gospel has reached over to China it will continue to go West until it finishes its course around the globe back in Jerusalem.

---

[644] Mark Ma
[645] Acts 1:8

The burden these dear brethren have is for over 100,000 missionaries to be sent out from the underground house Churches. This is not even the direct number they are aiming for because their goal is the total evangelization of many closed countries between China and Jerusalem until the Lord Jesus Christ comes back. So the burden they have is to not stop this mission until the second coming of the Lord!

"Many of our missionaries will be captured, tortured, and martyred for the sake of the Gospel, but that will not stop us. The Chinese Church is willing to pay the price."[646] These precious believers believe the Bible truth that our Lord taught us: "Very truly I tell you, unless a kernel of wheat falls to the ground and dies, it remains only a single seed. But if it dies, it produces many seeds. Anyone who loves their life will lose it, while anyone who hates their life in this world will keep it for eternal life."[647] They believe that imprisonment and death will not mean failure but success as the Gospel will go forward inch by inch through the testimony of Jesus Christ in these precious end times martyrs.

They are not building church buildings as they do this work or large ministry headquarters but are accomplishing this work in an underground fashion just as the Lord is working through them in China. This allows gatherings of believers to spread rapidly, to be flexible and thus give all resources to the spreading of the Gospel.

May this powerful example rouse the Church in America and other Nations to be burdened for the lost and unreached peoples of the world. May we realize that all Christians are Missionaries! And may we walk in the power of the Spirit as sent-out ones. Let us join in prayer and support for this last days work of the Lord by our Chinese brethren. May God protect this movement from men, methods and humanistic methodology and allow it to be a pure work of the Holy Spirit to reach those trapped in the spiritual darkness of Mohammedanism, Hinduism and Buddhism.

---

[646] Brother Yun
[647] John 12:24-25

Principle 42

The True Mission of the Church

THE CLOSING Words of Jesus Christ to His early disciples for their mission of making disciples of the nations has also become the mission of the Church in China.[648] Even the newest converts in the underground Church get the immediate burden to tell everyone of the great Savior of China and the world. [Every Christian is encouraged to witness daily and do the work of an evangelist.[649]] Therefore they do not just rely on a special few as missionaries but the entire underground Church of China is a throbbing missionary movement spreading the glorious Gospel of our Lord.

In many countries, we have special times to promote the need for missions and the spreading the Gospel of Jesus Christ. Yet do we have the same burden for this mission as the early disciples did? May we learn that the entire Church, meaning every one of us, is a missionary called to spread this Good News to everyone in the nations of the world.[650]

The underground Church in China has flourished and grown under the continual guidance and dynamic leading of the Holy Spirit

---

[648] Matthew 28:16-20
[649] 2 Timothy 4:5
[650] Mark 16:15

of God. May God birth a similar movement all over the world apart from any specific denomination or church. May God raise up all in the body of Christ to be active,[651] unified[652] and growing[653] in the Good News of our risen Lord.

In China there is an urgency to share the Good News with others. The thinking is simply that they have received such a wonderful Gospel, so how could they keep silent and not share it with others. You can almost hear the believers saying: "Hurry Up! Hurry Up! Let's share this Good News with everyone!" It is not surprising therefore that God birthed in the hearts of these simple Chinese rural famers a strategy to share the Gospel to every closed country westward of China. Many young Chinese believers are going out 100% without provision or money but trusting in the Lord so that they could share the Good News with others.

We have much to learn from this example of the urgency to share this Good News given to us in God's Son.

The Holy Spirit is reminding us to learn from the Chinese Church and for each one of us to start witnessing. Here is an easy start:

Please examine in 1 Peter: "But in your hearts revere Christ as Lord. Always be prepared to give an answer to everyone who asks you to give the reason for the hope that you have. But do this with gentleness and respect."[654]

a.) *Revere* means to set yourself apart for the Lord so He can use you through His Holy Spirit. Simply pray and say, *"Lord I want to be obedient to You. I would like to give my testimony to anyone who asks me. I need You and Your Holy Spirit to do the work through me. I surrender to You. Please help me."*

b.) Writing out your *testimony*. Now we need to get ready. How do we get ready to run in a race for a mile, with a prize of a million dollars? Will we be fast right away? No. Will we give up right away? No. Will we practice? Yes. What do we do? Write out in not more than half a page what Jesus means to you and how He saved you.

---

[651] 1 Corinthians 10:31-33
[652] 1 Corinthians 12:12-14
[653] Ephesians 2:19-22
[654] 1 Peter 3:15

Then memorize your testimony. Please ask Christian friends to listen to your testimony to practice.

Here is a song that describes what Jesus did.

"O what a wonderful, wonderful day, day I will never forget; After I'd wandered in darkness away, Jesus my Savior I met. O what a tender, compassionate friend, He met the need of my heart; Shadows dispelling, with joy I am telling, He made all the darkness depart. Heaven came down and glory filled my soul, When at the cross the Savior made me whole; My sins were washed away and my night was turned to day, Heaven came down and glory filled my soul!"[655]

You could use similar thoughts to write out your testimony, or if you have a testimony where you remember the details of how the Lord Jesus saved you, then use those words. Since this is a personal experience no one can argue with you.

c.) The next step is to *memorize* one verse of Scripture such as: "Jesus answered, 'I am the way and the truth and the life. No one comes to the Father except through Me.'"[656] Try and use your memory verse if given an opportunity during a discussion.

d.) Now you are ready to give a *defense*,[657] meaning an answer to anyone who asks you about your hope, but please do not argue.

e.) Sharing in *love*. Please give your testimony with humbleness and respect of the person you are speaking with. It is essential that you love the person and that you do not make yourself to appear better than that person. We are all sinners saved by grace.[658]

What is your *prize?* First, you are vying for a living soul where the Word says: "What good is it for someone to gain the whole world, yet forfeit their soul?"[659] The soul has a greater value than all the gold, all the diamonds, all the oil, all the money in the world. Furthermore, all the angels in heaven rejoice when a sinner comes to God.[660] Moreover, there is a soul winner's crown laid up for you in heaven which is a great reward for eternity.[661] Now please pray again, after

---

[655] John W. Peterson (1921-2006)
[656] John 14:6
[657] 1 Peter 3:15
[658] Ephesians 2:8
[659] Mark 8:36
[660] Luke 15:7
[661] Daniel 12:3, Revelation 3:11

having prepared and think of five people that do not know Jesus. Ask the Holy Spirit to give you an opportunity to give your witness to one or more of the five people. The Holy Spirit will prepare the way.

After you give a witness Satan will immediately come and tell you, that you have failed. He wants to discourage you from ever trying again. We must understand that there might be good soil or bad soil.[662] Please also understand that maybe you will be planting a seed, or you are watering a seed or sometimes God will allow you to *harvest* a soul.[663] You will always have done the job provided you witness. Only the Holy Spirit can change a man's heart—not you. The Holy Spirit will bring the new birth—not you. We are God's servants as we witness in love, and with our lives and our voices. Won't you start now before the night is upon us?[664] It is Jesus' command and He says to you and me: "If you love Me, keep My commands."[665] And He said to them, "Go into all the world and preach the Gospel to all creation."[666]

[Editor's Note: The revival in China continues. Many underground Churches still have an abundance of converts and new Christians joining. The tremendous move *of God's Spirit* in the rural underground Church in China is evident despite men. As happened in great revivals past men took control and quenched the Holy Spirit. Some of this is starting to happen in the Chinese underground Church. We must understand that the Church in China is not perfect. Some leaders are now permitting disunity between house Church networks. So one must make it clear that this is a *movement of God* and thus we have much to learn from God working among these believers. It is also true that when men start to add to what *God is doing*, disunity follows. Let us pray that the Lord continues the great revival in China in all areas and that the Holy Spirit does not withdraw despite imperfect men.]

---

[662] Mark 4:3-9
[663] 1 Corinthians 3:6
[664] John 9:4
[665] John 14:15
[666] Mark 16:15

Principles 43 to 55

Principles from the Underground Church in North Korea

Principle 43

North Korea's Leader, an Image of Antichrist

A GROUP of Christians was discovered in North Korea. They had worshiped God and His Son Jesus. Their children were with them. The adults were told by those who had captured them: "If you do not acknowledge our *Dear leader* as god and if you do not renounce Christ, your children will be hanged." One of the children looked up at her mother. What would she do? Earlier that morning, twenty-eight other Christians had been bound and taken before a screaming crowd of North Koreans. The guards made it clear: "If you don't deny your Christ you will die." The mother thought of her child but she could not deny her Lord. The other Christians quietly made the same decision. Their God was real. The North Korean guards again shouted: "Deny your Christ, or we will hang your children." The children looked at their parents. The parents loved their children but they knew there was an eternal heaven for them.[667] They could not deny their Lord. One mother leaned down to her child and whispered with confidence and peace: "Today, my love, I will see you in heaven."

---

[667] Colossians 1:5

All the children were hanged. The adults who were still bound had to lie down on the pavement. A large steamroller was brought which was used to flatten the road. They were given one more chance. The guards told them if you give up your Christ you will live. If you don't give Him up you will die. The Christians thought of their children in heaven and started to sing softly. As the steamroller started to roll over them crushing them to death they were singing: "More love, O Christ, to Thee, more love to Thee."

Christians in North Korea live under unimaginable horrors and tyranny. Worshipping in public or if caught in private brings systematic torture, imprisonment and at times death. Carrying a Bible or speaking to others about Jesus Christ can bring a cruel death. If a North Korean Christian believes, he affects three generations of his family including the children. The parents, spouses, uncles, aunts and children must all suffer and will be incarcerated in death camps. It does not matter whether they believe or not.

North Korean Christians aren't simply killed for their faith in Christ. They are annihilated with construction equipment and other means. In the death camps some Christians are killed by being tested with biological weapons, or starved to death, or worked to death, or shot or electrocuted. Others are shot in front of children. Newborn babies have their brains crushed or a needle inserted into their spine in front of their mothers. These are crimes against humanity reminiscent of *Auschwitz* to which the world declared "Never Again!" Just a few years later such atrocities are being perpetrated against North Korean Christians—and the world stands by.

The dictatorial rulers of North Korea have been members of the Kim family since the 1950s. They are ruling over the nation as god kings. Their control is absolute, they are secretive and they rule with unimaginable brutality and tyranny. Kim Il-Sung, who was the original leader of this family, died in 1994. He was made *god* and was deified, embalmed and is worshipped as a permanent *god*. His reign was followed by the son of *god* namely Kim Jong Il who died in 2011. He was succeeded by Kim Jong Un the grandson of the *god*. Kim Jong Un is the current leader.

He oversees a nation of approximately 25 Million people with the fourth largest army in the world of 1.1 million soldiers. No outside news is allowed. TV and the newspapers are state controlled. There is no internet nor are there cell phones for the public.

The state religion called Juche declares Kim Il-Sung, the first leader, as god. The Government claims that the second leader also has divine attributes. Supposedly Kim Jong Il was born on Mount Paektu, a sacred mountain on the border with China. His birth was to have been announced by birds, a double rainbow and the birth of a new star. The facts are different.

According to the North Korean constitution Article 1, section 1, all North Koreans are required to worship Kim Il Sung with all their heart and might, even after his death. They have to worship the pictures and statutes of Kim Il Sung. A North Korean witness said: "We must hang Kim Il Sung's picture in our homes. Displaying the portraits of the Kim family is compulsory for every household. The portraits must be hung on the best wall of every home, and nothing else can be hung under the portraits. The pictures indicate that Kim Il Sung is god. We hang the pictures for the purpose of reminding ourselves that we depend on him." Only Kim Il Sung is god in North Korea.

All citizens of North Korea are required to worship their god and their current leader. Citizens are required to attend regular *self-criticism* meetings which include the singing of songs of praise of Kim Il Sung from a 600 song hymnal, readings from the writings of Kim Il Sung (including Sung's *Ten Principles*, reminiscent of the Ten Commandments), and emotional professions of faith to the Kim leadership.

Everyone is trained from birth to love and worship their *Dear Leader* as god. The indoctrination starts in Kindergarten and requires total submission and allegiance to a divine supreme being, that of the *Dear Leader*. A refugee commented: "We must worship him. Christians say grace to their God. We must say grace to our god Kim Jong Il."

Having faith in the Christian God is an act of espionage. Any open worship of the true God, including Bible reading, Christian literature distribution and witnessing is met with horrifying executions and death camps. Where one Christian is found, three generations of that family will be eliminated through death camps and executions. North Korean Christians endure the most suffering in the world.

Kim Il Sung and Kim Jong Il are examples of a future world leader who will also declare himself as god.[668] Scripture says about the coming antichrist:

"Don't let anyone deceive you in any way, for that day will not come until the rebellion occurs and the man of lawlessness is revealed, the man doomed to destruction. He will oppose and will exalt himself over everything that is called God or is worshiped, so that he sets himself up in God's temple, proclaiming himself to be god."[669]

Antichrist will declare himself god and persecute Christians:

"It opened its mouth to blaspheme God, and to slander His Name and His dwelling place and those who live in heaven. It was given power to wage war against God's holy people and to conquer them. And it was given authority over every tribe, people, language and nation."[670]

"I saw thrones on which were seated those who had been given authority to judge. And I saw the souls of those who had been beheaded because of their testimony about Jesus and because of the Word of God. They had not worshiped the beast or its image and had not received its mark on their foreheads or their hands. They came to life and reigned with Christ a thousand years."[671]

In Revelation chapter 20, verse 4, we are reminded that Christians will be beheaded for their witness and faith worldwide when they do not worship antichrist. This will affect Christians in the future who are in the world at that time. For our sisters and brothers in North Korea—because of their witness—persecution and death is reality today.

The question we must ask ourselves: "Would we stand up for Jesus when the time comes for us or would we deny our faith?"[672] If we say we will stand up for Jesus then the question is why are we not witnessing today in our countries where there is no persecution?

---

[668] Matthew 24:15
[669] 2 Thessalonians 2:3-4
[670] Revelation 13:6-7
[671] Revelation 20:4
[672] Matthew 10:33

Principle 44

A Cost to Be Part of the Church

A WITNESS of the North Korean army who later became a Christian reported the following: "The team had been sent to widen a highway. When they demolished a vacated house they found a Bible and a small notebook with 25 names, one identified as pastor, two as assistant pastors, two as elders, and 20 other names, apparently participants in a Christian group. The Military Police Unit investigated and picked up the 25 persons without formal arrest. The 25 were brought to the road construction site. Four rows of spectators were assembled. The five leaders were bound hand and foot and made to lie down in front of a steamroller which was used at the construction site to crush and level the roadway. The other twenty Christians were held at the side to watch. The condemned were told, 'If you abandon your faith and serve only Kim Il Sung and Kim Jong Il, you will not be killed.' None of the five said a word. The steamroller started to roll over the five leaders. Some of the fellow Christians assembled to watch the execution cried, screamed out, or fainted when the skulls made a popping sound as their brothers were crushed beneath the steamroller."

Why must this happen we ask? The martyrs' blood drenched the ground. The soldier who witnessed the execution could not understand. Later he found Jesus because of the testimony of the twenty-five who saved His life for eternity. Each person is made in the image of God. Each person's soul has a greater value than all the gold, silver, diamonds and oil in this world. For what shall it profit a man if he gains the whole world and loses his own soul? Jesus laid down His life for all sinners in this world. Are we not to lay down our lives so that others might receive eternal life?

The soldiers took the other twenty prisoners to North Korean prison camps better described as death camps. Because of the three generation rule it is certain that their parents, uncles, aunts and children were also investigated and incarcerated. Generally, these family members will be sent to death camps regardless of whether they are believers. The average sentence for a prison death camp is 15 years. The average time a person survives in a death camp is 5 years. One prisoner described her experience:

"I want the world to know about the cruelty we faced in the North Korean prison camps. I was forced to go to Yodok prison camp. I spent nine long years there. They treated us like animals. Even animals lived better than we did. The thing that made me feel so sad—yet furious—was the fact they also put my parents and children in Yodok prison camp. Because only I was a Christian, my father, mother and whole family were imprisoned. It hurt me so much that they treated my kids like animals. It made me so angry, what they did. I want the whole world to know what they did." She said that she and her family members were forced to engage in heavy labor both day and night. For her father, it was more than he could physically endure. "First, I lost my father in Yodok prison," she said. "I had to wrap his body in a straw mat since there was no coffin. Not long after, my mother also died of severe hunger. She had been starved to death. When I also lost my children, my heart was so broken and I felt very sad and miserable. It hurt me so much. I'll never forget seeing so many dead bodies from famine stacked all around the fields and mountains of Yodok. I want to tell the whole world."

Another witness said: "We were in constant fear. Even the least infraction brought a reduction in food allowance. Being hungry all the time was the worst tragedy. Here I ate my first mouse. Escape attempts are punished by death. Not doing your work meant execution by firing squad. Stealing or taking food meant to be executed by firing squad. Disobedience is punished by death. Running away is punished by death and not reporting others trying to escape, is punished by death."

A survivor reported: "A grandmother, uncle and little sister were taken to a death camp as part of the purge of three generations. Everyone was so weak, fragile, thin in rags, bones showing, all ribs showing, and shivering in the cold. With no food they started dying slowly."

"For it has been granted to you on behalf of Christ not only to believe in Him, but also to suffer for Him."[673] The granting to suffer is a privilege. God will give each a martyr's crown called a crown of life, which is a reward for eternity:

"Do not be afraid of what you are about to suffer. I tell you, the devil will put some of you in prison to test you, and you will suffer persecution for ten days. Be faithful, even to the point of death, and I will give you life as your victor's crown."[674]

"They triumphed over him by the blood of the Lamb and by the word of their testimony; they did not love their lives so much as to shrink from death."[675]

The Gospel call is free for all to accept and believe.[676] Jesus Christ said that we are to come freely to His message of salvation. Yet to associate ourselves with Jesus Christ and His followers has a cost.[677] This is not a message preached or understood in nations where there is not immediate persecution upon becoming a believer. The early Church in Acts had great success by the Holy Spirit to bring in many souls even 3000 people during the first day of the Church.[678] Later on in that passage it is stated: "The Lord added to their number daily those who were being saved."[679] Yet in the midst of this revival when they were meeting publicly in Solomon's Colonnade,[680] we see that: "No one else dared join them, even though they were highly regarded

[673] Philippians 1:29
[674] Revelation 2:10
[675] Revelation 12:11
[676] Ephesians 2:8
[677] 2 Timothy 3:12
[678] Acts 2:41
[679] Acts 2:47
[680] Acts 5:12

by the people."[681] Whether it was understood by all or not there was a sense that to join this group would mean persecution, misunderstanding and even death as those rebelling against the religious system of the day.

Jesus Christ Himself was more interested in disciples than converts.[682] When the largest crowds would gather He would speak the hardest sayings and most would leave from following Him.[683] Paul the Apostle stated to Timothy who was a young elder and Apostle of many Churches: "In fact, everyone who wants to live a godly life in Christ Jesus will be persecuted."[684] Thus, we should have as our aim to encourage strong discipleship that speaks of the cost of following Christ in our gatherings.[685] "Then Jesus said to His disciples, 'Whoever wants to be My disciple must deny themselves and take up their cross and follow Me.'"[686] Such a following will cost us greatly.

A testimony from a believer of the underground Church in North Korea should move and challenge us greatly. The cost to confess Christ openly is death: "Many in the West are not aware of the suffering endured by North Korean brothers and sisters. In North Korea, if people believe in God and are caught by the Kim Jong Un government, they are killed along with three generations of their family. Believers do not care if they die by themselves. However, because entire families could get killed, many believers secretly follow Jesus, but do not know who else is a believer."

It is estimated that there are currently 100,000 Christians in North Korea of which 40,000 are in prison death camps. An additional 300,000 Christians who were formerly in North Korea are missing. Many left North Korea and became refugees in China, South Korea, Mongolia and other nations. Many have given their lives during the terrible persecution that continues to this day.

---

[681] Acts 5:13
[682] Matthew 4:19
[683] John 6:66
[684] 2 Timothy 3:12
[685] 2 Timothy 2:2
[686] Matthew 16:24

Principle 45

Five Challenging Reminders

A YOUNG woman was washing clothes in a North Korean river. When gathering her clothes, a small Bible or Christian book fell to the ground. Another woman reported the girl to the police. The young woman and her father—about sixty years old—were arrested and held by the local police for about three months. During that time, the woman and her father were investigated and interrogated. They were taken to a market area in town and accused of trafficking. A brief public *show trial*, was held which consisted of the charges. They were found guilty of a capital offense. Then they were condemned as traitors to the nation and their god leader. Before the execution, people were assembled to witness the deaths. This included teachers and students from fourth grade and up, students from middle school and high school, and people who had come to the market. Seven police fired three shots each into the two victims, who had been tied to posts. The force of the rifle shots caused blood and brain matter to be blown out of their heads.

The Martyrs' blood drenched the ground.

The Bible tells us about persecution in the Book of Acts: "On that day a great persecution broke out against the Church in

Jerusalem, and all except the Apostles were scattered throughout Judea and Samaria."[687]

The word *scattered* here means that they had to leave their homes. They left their jobs, they left many of their belongings, they left their security and they left friends behind. In those days there were no telephones, cell phones or other means to keep in touch. Would you follow Jesus if this were to happen in your country? The extraordinary thing that followed in the Book of Acts is described in Acts 8: "Those who had been scattered preached the Word wherever they went."[688] Do we have to lose all of our possessions[689] before we are willing to witness?

Just as the early Church in Jerusalem came under great persecution so the Church in North Korea has come under the same pressures. As with many underground Church movements across the world the Church in North Korea has principles that ensure its growth and continued existence. When there is great pressure from many forces outside the Church the real success of the Church is built upon Biblical principles that are outlined in the Book of Acts. The Church truly has no other blueprint for its growth, structure and daily life. Believers in the end times need to relearn much from other expressions of Biblical Christianity in the world that are under great pressure but bearing great fruit in the Gospel.[690]

Some of the underground Churches in North Korea recite certain truths to keep them united and to remind them of their faith in Jesus Christ. They recite the *Lord's Prayer* and the following five phrases when they meet:

1) Our persecution and suffering are our joy and honor.

2) We want to accept ridicule, scorn and disadvantages with joy in Jesus' Name.

3) We want to wipe others' tears away and comfort the suffering.

4) We want to be ready to risk our lives because of our love for our neighbor, so that they also become Christians.

5) We want to live our lives according to the standards set in God's Word.

---

[687] Acts 8:1
[688] Acts 8:4
[689] Hebrews 10:34
[690] Colossians 1:6

Are we ready and willing to state before the Lord that we want to live like that? May God help us to do so.

Along with these five challenging reminders the underground Church in North Korea lives by Biblical principles that guarantee its continued growth and survival. It should be encouraging to us that the New Testament was written under times of great persecution. Therefore it is the perfect roadmap for us as believers entering into the end of the age where great persecution will be evident. Alongside the Scriptures we have these wonderful examples of saints that are enduring much as part of the body of Christ.

We have much to learn from those who are in the most brutal and Christ opposing nation in the world today.

Principle 46

Meeting in Home Churches

THE NUMBER of home Churches in North Korea is estimated at 10,000. Based on a number of testimonies the average underground home Church size may be 3 or 4.

Such home Churches have evolved from primarily three sources:

1.) Believers that predate the Korean war. Today these are the grandparents or great-grandparents who have held on to the faith under traumatic persecution while worshipping in great secrecy for up to and over 60 years. They are sharing the Word of God and Jesus with their family, and others based on long-term trust.

For example, a Christian woman had a Christian mother who attended church until 1947 and who kept her Bible. She had a friend who listened to *Far Eastern Broadcasting.*

2.) Others became Christians while hearing the Gospel in China or South Korea and then returned to North Korea. They share with their families. For example, a woman brought back a Bible from China. She and her mother secretly read the Bible at home under a blanket. She also listened to the Christian radio station from South Korea and told her older sister and her husband about the Gospel.

3.) Others became believers due to life-risking evangelism by their sisters and brothers.

For example, a woman in prison never saw organized Christian worship, but in prison there was a *crazy woman* in her sixties who kept praying to God to save her. God did a miracle and she was released. This got the witness thinking: "This God must be able and real."

Home dwellings and other secret places are sometimes the only best option for North Korean believers because of the secrecy requirements. They not only risk their own lives but also the lives of three generations of their family.

In many countries Christians have access to large church buildings to meet, yet it is strange how little these buildings are used —primarily only a few hours a week![691] The Church in North Korea, meets in any place possible that is private, mostly in their homes. If their group gets to be over one dozen people they split to form another house Church.

"During the Korean War in the early 1950s, most Christians either fled to the South or were imprisoned or martyred, and church buildings were bulldozed. There are 40,000 Christians in the kwan-li-so, [penal labor colony], among the estimated 200,000 political prisoners who are imprisoned without trial. These prisoners' lives consist of extremely hard labour and they live under brutal conditions in permanent semi-starvation."[692]

Here is another powerful testimony from a believer who left North Korea and now works with the underground Church:

"Christians in North Korea endure the most suffering in the world. Even in the face of such hardship God provides them with the faith, strength and courage to persevere. God is with them and gives them the hope of heaven. That's why whenever there is contact with North Korean Christians they ask for prayer and understand the value of standing together before God in prayer."

Like the North Korean believers, may we begin to learn to meet together in small groups of believers sharing the Word with each other and praying often and from house to house.[693] In the end we can say: *What do buildings matter?* for the Lord's people are the true

---

[691] Of course there are exceptions to this but it seems very few church buildings are used as efficiently as they could be used for God's work.

[692] AsiaNews

[693] Acts 20:20

temple where God dwells by His Spirit.[694] A dependence on church buildings to meet can be unhealthy and could prove problematic when persecution comes.

Here is an example of how this can be accomplished. Recently, we heard of a pastor of a church in America who felt led of the Lord to appoint 12 pastors in his Church who would oversee 12 separate home Churches on Wednesday nights. They all still meet together on Sunday mornings to hear the main pastor teach, but these small groups also act as functioning Churches. These *pastors* of the small groups are perhaps not as well-trained or capable from a human perspective but this servant leader saw the heart of God to raise up brothers and sisters, to encourage and lead the body of Christ.

We believe following the example of this pastor would not only help prepare a larger church gathering for persecution—when we cannot meet freely in a larger venue—but it also encourages more discipleship, evangelism and growth in the body of Christ. This does not require over-organization and planning but simply a step of faith to trust the leading of the Lord to supply the Word of God through more than one leader. All small group pastors and people would still submit to the spiritual leadership and oversight of the main pastor.

May God start to lead and guide the leadership in many larger churches to take the same steps of preparation for coming persecution.[695]

---

[694] 1 Corinthians 3:16
[695] Matthew 24:9, 1 Thessalonians 3:4

Principle 47

The Lord's Day Can Be Everyday!

A YOUNG woman from a pre-Korean War Christian family relates: "My mother and her friends continue to gather in worship secretly."

Another believer relates: "I also had a pre-Korean War Christian mother who continued to worship in secret with two relatives, using a Bible that her grandfather had brought back from Japan years ago."

Another Christian said: "I participated in an underground Church of 12 members, all relatives, who sometimes had missionaries visit from China."

Korean sisters and brothers meet under the most secret circumstances to avoid detection. They also meet any time that is available and not only on a Sunday as is the practice in countries not yet persecuted.

These Christians worship their Lord when their circumstances permit it. There is a great doctrinal split in many evangelical churches over what day is the Lord's day, meaning which day did the early Church meet to worship. This freedom to try to attempt to practice worship on a specific day is not possible in North Korea where if they are found worshipping Jesus Christ, they will be arrested and even killed for their testimony. Thus they meet at all different times and in different places. As we look at the Book of Acts we can imagine that the early Church especially under times of persecution would meet in different homes at different times to avoid detection.[696]

In an underground Church in China in one area the people wake up at 4:30 to come together for two hours to pray and worship, they do this every day. There are Churches that meet in the only place they are safe, a cave! There are Churches that meet on farms far away from prying eyes.

Another testimony on the underground Church in China: "One thing I quickly realized about the Chinese Church is that it is a lot different from the American one. For one thing they think a four hour sermon is short, but more than that is how different their services looked from ours, I mean, see for yourself what happens when a desperate people plug into a powerful God."

Dear believer, will you argue over what day to meet in your country when believers all over the world in underground Churches are surviving persecution, and are hungry for the Word of God, and are spending hours at the feet of Jesus Christ and His Word?

There are those denominations who feel very strongly about the sabbath or Sunday. During the time of the Book of Acts there were two Jerusalem councils where the Apostles discussed the applicability of the law under grace. The first council is described in the Book of Acts.[697] It was declared that the New Testament Gentile Church is under grace and not the law except to abstain from certain sinful practices. The second Jerusalem council is described fourteen years later in the Book of Galatians.[698] Again *grace* was confirmed and not the law. In the Book of Colossians the Apostle Paul made it very clear concerning the sabbath saying: "So let no one judge you in food or in drink, or regarding a festival or a new moon or sabbaths, which are a shadow of things to come, but the substance is of Christ."[699] The Old Testament practice of keeping the sabbath was a "shadow of things to come" where Jesus Christ became our *Sabbath*—our Rest. He "wiped out the handwriting of requirements that was against us, which was contrary to us. And He has taken it out of the way, having nailed it to

---

[696] Acts 2:46
[697] Acts 15:1-29
[698] Galatians 2:1-10
[699] Colossians 2:16-17

the cross."[700] Therefore, we are rejecting Him when we believe we must observe a day which was only intended as a *shadow* of Him. Such a trust in a day to be our salvation will only make us estranged from Christ Himself.

Even though in the early Church believers would try to assemble at the same times each week to celebrate the resurrection of Jesus Christ. It was their desire to meet on the first day of the week where possible[701] yet at times it was not possible. When the disciples were scattered from Jerusalem[702] their first thought was not to try and persevere the Lord's day meeting, but share the Good News of the Lord Jesus Christ.

We need to be open as believers in Jesus Christ, in the non-persecuted countries, to learn to meet often, regularly and not necessarily at a set time on Sunday or other days. When we meet with as few as 2-3 individuals at a home we can have a time of Bible reading, discussion, prayer and worship. This will prepare us for persecution, as we learn from our dear brothers and sisters in North Korea.

---

[700] Colossians 2:14
[701] Acts 20:7
[702] Acts 11:19

Principle 48

We Are a Body of Christ Together

A FORMER policeman described how he was involved in the arrests of 11 Church members. Two of them were tortured to death during interrogation, while the others were executed, he said.

God is no respecter of persons. Each person has a value more than the world's riches and Jesus died for each person. The lesson that we learn in North Korea is that Christians lay down their lives and become martyrs, be they an apostle, or pastor, or a believer. We are rewarded and judged each based on our own works in relation to the gifts God has given us. As believers in Jesus Christ we are all disciples, and all have the same standing, yet leaders have a greater accountability before God.

Jesus had reminded His disciples about leadership many times. If you want to be the greatest become *the least* and servant of all. Don't *lord* over people. Wash feet. In the end all of us are simple servants of the Lord.[703]

The North Korean Church cannot afford the luxury of having para-church ministries and organizations as we see in many other countries of the world. There are no head denominational men or

---

[703] 1 Corinthians 3:5

gifted leaders on specific Christian subjects. Each Church member in North Korea is a generalist who understands and walks in normal Christianity based on the Bible.

The abundance of Christian denominations simply speaks of division and the unhealthiness of the Church worldwide. The local Church, if healthy and Biblical does not need the existence of denominations. The body of Christ is one and is self-sufficient with its gifting and callings.

God has made the body of Christ in such a way that each member supports the other. As we learn from Scripture under the guidance of the Holy Spirit, and as we learn from each other we become more balanced and not extreme in one doctrine or another.

Believers in the North Korean Church take turns teaching the verses they have memorized by heart. Thus sermons are preached from the heart, in the power of the Holy Spirit, by these precious saints and remind us of the early days in the Book of Acts where unlearned men taught the Word of God as moved by the Holy Spirit.

In our modern Church age we need to relearn the lesson the Lord taught the Corinthian Church. There was over-dependence on personalities and gifted leaders which was creating divisions in the body of Christ:

"Brothers and sisters, I could not address you as people who live by the Spirit but as people who are still worldly—mere infants in Christ. I gave you milk, not solid food, for you were not yet ready for it. Indeed, you are still not ready. You are still worldly. For since there is jealousy and quarreling among you, are you not worldly? Are you not acting like mere humans? For when one says, 'I follow Paul,' and another, 'I follow Apollos,' are you not mere human beings?

"What, after all, is Apollos? And what is Paul? Only servants, through whom you came to believe—as the Lord has assigned to each his task. I planted the seed, Apollos watered it, but God has been making it grow. So neither the one who plants nor the one who waters is anything, but only God, who makes things grow. The one who plants and the one who waters have one purpose, and they will each be rewarded according to their own labor. For we are co-workers in God's service; you are God's field, God's building.

"By the grace God has given me, I laid a foundation as a wise builder, and someone else is building on it. But each one should build with care. For no one can lay any foundation other than the one already laid, which is Jesus Christ. If anyone builds on this foundation using gold, silver, costly stones, wood, hay or straw, their work will be shown for what it is, because the Day will bring it to light. It will be revealed with fire, and the fire will test the quality of each person's work. If what has been built survives, the builder will receive a reward. If it is burned up, the builder will suffer loss but yet will be saved—even though only as one escaping through the flames. Don't you know that you yourselves are God's temple and that God's Spirit dwells in your midst? If anyone destroys God's temple, God will destroy that person; for God's temple is sacred, and you together are that temple."[704]

As part of this principle we also want to remind readers that North Korean believers are part of the body of Christ worldwide where we need to care for other parts of the body. Scripture reminds us that if one part of our body in Christ is hurting then all parts are hurting. It is the responsibility of Christians in non-persecuted nations to pray for sisters and brothers in nations where persecution is rampant.

"If one part suffers, every part suffers with it; if one part is honored, every part rejoices with it."[705]

"Continue to remember those in prison as if you were together with them in prison, and those who are mistreated as if you yourselves were suffering."[706]

Pray for them, intercede for them, help them, write to the government for them:

Here are specific things to *pray* for:

i) "*Now, Lord, consider their threats and enable Your servants to speak Your Word.*"[707] (*through the filling and power of Your Holy Spirit.*)

ii) "*Stretch out Your hand to heal and perform signs and wonders through the Name of Your holy Servant Jesus.*"[708]

iii) That God would give them forgiveness and love.

iv) That God would provide Bibles for them.

---

[704] 1 Corinthians 3:1-17
[705] 1 Corinthians 12:26
[706] Hebrews 13:3
[707] Acts 4:29
[708] Acts 4:30

v) That they would be able to find someone to fellowship with.

vi) That their friends and neighbors would discover Jesus through their witness.

vii) That they would remain strong under torture and not deny Jesus.

viii) Pray for the leader Kim Jong Un to accept Jesus as his savior.

ix) Pray for North Korea to become a nation more open to Christianity.

x) Pray for faith, strength, and courage for them to endure.

xi) Pray for comfort in tribulation.

xii) Pray for the torturers that they may become Christians.

xiii) Pray that the North Korean Christians would bless their torturers, pray for them and do good to them.

xiv) Pray for North Korean Christians to remain strong in faith and to believe in a God of miracles, knowing that God knows best.

xv) That they might not be led into temptation.[709]

xvi) That God would deliver them from evil, according to His will.

---

[709] Matthew 6:13

Principle 49

Sharing and Memorization of Scripture

A CHRISTIAN woman related: "They found my handwritten Bible verses. Three generations of my family were taken to the prison death camp. This included my parents, my husband and my children. I have never heard of them again. Prison camp is hell."

A woman in her sixties knew of eight persons who were Christians who met secretly in groups of three and four to read handwritten Bible verses.

A refugee reported: "Many times the authorities came to our house without warning. They always do this to people. It's not because we're Christian, it's because they want to scare people and make sure they can't cause trouble. This is their way of making sure everybody worships the North Korean leader. One time, I copied Bible verses by hand. I always prayed these would not be found because it would put my family's lives in danger."

"In North Korea, Christians constantly fear being discovered. There is severe punishment if they are found guilty. That's huge because it means death! The North Korea government can't stand Christians worshipping God since they force people to worship Kim Il-Sung and Kim Jong-Il as their gods."

Another reported: "One day the police came to my house and searched it. They found pieces of the Bible verses I copied by hand. They shouted many times at me, and took away my husband and kids. We were all taken to a prison camp where they worked us to death. Now, I'm not sure whether my parents and kids are still enduring hard labor or are even alive in prison. I'm always praying for Christians left behind in North Korean prison camps because I know that living there is like being in hell."

Another witness: "I watched 3 Christians being executed publicly. It was one woman about 22 years old and two men about 23 years old. Their crime was having smuggled Bibles into North Korea."

Sharing of Scripture is necessary in the North Korean Church for there are very few Bibles. Members in the underground Church regularly share Scripture verses and lines of hymns written on pieces of paper. Most Christians in other countries can have up to 5-10 Bibles in their homes. In North Korea each believer has very little access to Scriptures. These fragments of Scriptures are passed around as precious items and most texts are shared by spoken communication. This is a Biblical practice where we are encouraged to speak to one another with psalms, and hymns[710] and practice the reading of Scripture.[711]

We can learn from this and actively share Scriptures from memory in our own gatherings. Why not use technology to share the Word of God and add it to our emails, letters, text messages and in person with each other? Such constant sharing of Scriptures with each other in the body of Christ builds us up in our most holy faith.[712]

Psalm 119 is the longest chapter in Scripture and it is devoted to exclaiming the wonders of God's Word and Law. It would be a worthy practice for us to read this chapter over and over to allow God to build in us an admiration and love for His Scriptures again. Would you forfeit all the riches you possess, to simply have in your possession a copy of God's holy Word? The Psalmist might have for he proclaimed: "The Law from Your mouth is more precious to me than thousands of pieces of silver and gold."[713]

---

[710] Ephesians 5:19
[711] 1 Timothy 4:13
[712] Jude 1:20
[713] Psalm 119:72

May we emulate our North Korean brothers and sisters by treating God's Word as the most precious possession we have.

As we face the future and persecution, the memorization of Scripture must become a priority for us. In underground Churches the need to memorize Scripture is not an option but a necessity. When Bibles are scarce and imprisonment likely, the believer desires to prepare for such trials by storing up the Word of God in his heart. Also it becomes a great blessing to share Scriptures with others in everyday life without needing a physical Bible present.

Such believers become *living Bibles* where the Word of God is always present. We can learn much from this discipline. To study and memorize the Word of God shows our true love for the Scriptures—which we have in abundance in non-persecuted countries. Do we really desire to read the Word above eating, entertainment and the many other things that occupy our time? While we have freedoms may God instill in His Church a greater love and desire for the Word.

The Scriptures declare that they are our weapon: "Take the helmet of salvation and the sword of the Spirit, which is the Word of God."[714] They are more important than our physical food: "I have not departed from the commands of His lips; I have treasured the Words of His mouth more than my daily bread."[715] Our delight is to be in the Scriptures: "But whose delight is in the Law of the Lord, and who meditates on His Law day and night."[716] God's Word keeps us from sin: "I have hidden Your Word in my heart that I might not sin against You."[717] It is also a light to our path,[718] a help in temptations,[719] and as we trust in the principles of the Word of God we have great help in this life.[720]

This testimony of Brother Yun shows a great love for the Scriptures. May it encourage us greatly to consume God's Word and store it in our hearts:

---

[714] Ephesians 6:17
[715] Job 23:12
[716] Psalm 1:2
[717] Psalm 119:11
[718] Psalm 119:105
[719] Matthew 4:1-11
[720] Joshua 1:8

"Yun decided to fast and pray for a Bible, and for the next 100 days ate only one bowl of steamed rice every day. He cried out to the Lord for a Bible. His parents thought he was losing his mind. One morning, there was a knock at the door. Two men had brought a Bible to Yun. Yun began to devour the Word of God. Even though he could hardly read, every day, he would painstakingly look up one character at a time as he advanced through the Bible. When he had finished reading in this way through the whole Bible, he started memorizing one chapter per day. In 28 days, he had memorized the Gospel of Matthew, and then started on the Book of Acts."[721]

How do you start practically? Memorize at least one verse that you can quote in evangelism or a small portion of Scriptures. So you can practice this daily as you ask the Lord to give you opportunity to share with at least one person the verse(s) you have started to commit to your memory. Memorize also verses that can be prayed to the Lord in your private prayer time with the Lord. To pray through the Scriptures this way can be a tremendous way to grow in the Lord. To memorize one Psalm in its entirety will also be very important to quote during times of pressure and tribulation. The Scriptures testify of the living presence of God. We must have faith when memorizing each verse that it speaks of true realities and the person of God Himself.

May God instill in us a desire to read and memorize His written Word like never before.

---

[721] Paul Hattaway

Principle 50

Not Merely Listening

IN 2009, The Associated Press reported that a 33-year-old Christian woman, Ri Hyon-ok, was accused of distributing Bibles and "spying" for foreign countries was publicly executed in North Korea. Despite such persecution and threat of death, the Church in North Korea hears the Word and obeys it. The call to preach the Good News is obeyed by these believers at great cost.

The Bible to North Koreans is a roadmap for living. It is a roadmap for their life and it should be for our life. It dictates to them what they do. We should let the Word dictate to us what we do. To just listen to a sermon and Scripture and then to say "That was a nice message" is foreign to these believers. They desire to obey everything they hear.

The problem for us in most non-persecuted countries is that we think "right" doctrine will be the solution to having "life" but that is not the case. Of course if we have the Holy Spirit we will be led into all truth.[722] To seek after perfect theological doctrine in every area is not what the New Testament commands of us. Rather it exhorts us to be in communion with Jesus Christ and to follow and obey His commands. Jesus Christ did not tell us to be theologians, He told us to be followers of Him who embodied His truths and life, and then prove our faith by doing.

---

[722] John 16:13

When we start reading the Bible based on our human wisdom we deny the faith and accuracy of Scripture. Without the guidance of the Holy Spirit men have been making up entire systems of beliefs with theological words that are used blasphemously and do not represent the truth nor the heart of God. We are then misled to believe that such humanistic doctrines carry "life." Life is not found in a theological system or interpretation; Life is found in Christ Jesus, surrendering to Him and allowing Him to live His Life through us. That's what it means to be "born again" or "born of the Spirit."

"Surrender to Jesus Christ!" is the crying need of the day so that sin can be dealt with in our lives. Our focus should not be to try to figure out every mystery in the Bible. Those who study the character of God but do not have the fear of Him in their heart which causes them to depart from private sin in their lives have erred greatly. The underground Church in North Korea is more occupied daily with communion with God, hearing His voice and wanting to follow His direction. For them it is the choice between life and death.

Many of us need to hear the exhortation of James again: "Do not merely listen to the Word and so deceive yourselves. Do what it says."[723] We need to come to the Lord daily, asking Him to help us put into practice all that we hear.

A Church that does this is a fruitful Church. Such a Church will bring the Gospel to the people through their lives of obedience, and through verbally proclaiming the message of salvation, even if it means death.

The prophet Jeremiah heard these clear words from the Lord to His people: "But I gave them this command: 'Obey Me, and I will be your God and you will be My people. Walk in obedience to all I command you, that it may go well with you.'"[724] God's people are an obeying people, a people that walk in His ways.

Our Lord Himself echoed this important truth: "He replied, 'Blessed rather are those who hear the Word of God and obey it.'"[725] May the Church be "blessed" in this way as we grow nearer to that last day.[726]

---

[723] James 1:22
[724] Jeremiah 7:23
[725] Luke 11:28
[726] 2 Peter 3:10

Principle 51

Measuring True Christian Growth

THE MERE possession of a Bible can bring a death sentence. Attending a secret underground Church service in North Korea can result in gruesome public executions. Christians in North Korea have grown to a level of love and commitment to Jesus such that is not known in countries where there is no persecution.

In North Korea the Church is intimate and each member knows and observes the walk of the other believers within a fellowship. There is not a one-hour Church service where everyone faces the front, where people do not know each other. Rather, it is a face-to-face meeting as often as is possible. Whenever they meet as a part of the body of Christ, they share truths from Scripture and encourage one another in their trust in Jesus. To them, that is all that matters. Such meetings build accountability to each one's progress in the faith.

Paul the Apostle shares with the young Timothy: "Be diligent in these matters; give yourself wholly to them, so that everyone may see your progress."[727] It is possible for others to see your growth in the Lord. Thus gathering in homes and in more intimate meetings—not just once a week—will allow us to encourage each other to grow

---

[727] 1 Timothy 4:15

authentically in our walks with the Lord and not remain hid in the back of a large public church meeting.

Paul the Apostle had a great desire for the Church in Ephesus to grow in the grace of Jesus Christ. In chapter 4 he pleads for the believers to walk worthy of the Gospel:

"As a prisoner for the Lord, then, I urge you to live a life worthy of the calling you have received. Be completely humble and gentle; be patient, bearing with one another in love. Make every effort to keep the unity of the Spirit through the bond of peace. There is one body and one Spirit, just as you were called to one hope when you were called; one Lord, one faith, one Baptism; one God and Father of all, who is over all and through all and in all.

"But to each one of us grace has been given as Christ apportioned it. This is why it says: 'When he ascended on high, He took many captives and gave gifts to His people.' (What does *He ascended* mean except that He also descended to the lower, earthly regions? He who descended is the very One who ascended higher than all the heavens, in order to fill the whole universe.)

"So Christ Himself gave the Apostles, the prophets, the evangelists, the pastors and teachers, to equip his people for works of service, so that the body of Christ may be built up until we all reach unity in the faith and in the knowledge of the Son of God and become mature, attaining to the whole measure of the fullness of Christ. Then we will no longer be infants, tossed back and forth by the waves, and blown here and there by every wind of teaching and by the cunning and craftiness of people in their deceitful scheming. Instead, speaking the truth in love, we will grow to become in every respect the mature body of Him who is the Head, that is, Christ. From Him the whole body, joined and held together by every supporting ligament, grows and builds itself up in love, as each part does its work.

"So I tell you this, and insist on it in the Lord, that you must no longer live as the Gentiles do, in the futility of their thinking. They are darkened in their understanding and separated from the life of God because of the ignorance that is in them due to the hardening of their hearts. Having lost all sensitivity, they have given themselves over to sensuality so as to indulge in every kind of impurity, and they are full of greed. That, however, is not the way of life you learned when you heard about Christ and were taught in Him in accordance with the truth that is in Jesus. You were taught, with regard to your former way of life, to put off your old self, which is being corrupted by its deceitful desires; to be made new in the attitude of your minds; and to put on the new self, created to be like God in true righteousness and holiness.

"Therefore each of you must put off falsehood and speak truthfully to your neighbor, for we are all members of one body. 'In your anger do not sin': Do not let the sun go down while you are still angry, and do not give the devil a foothold. Anyone who has been stealing must steal no longer, but must work, doing something useful with their own hands, that they may have something to share with those in need.

"Do not let any unwholesome talk come out of your mouths, but only what is helpful for building others up according to their needs, that it may benefit those who listen. And do not grieve the Holy Spirit of God, with whom you were sealed for the day of redemption. Get rid of all bitterness, rage and anger, brawling and slander, along with every form of malice. Be kind and compassionate to one another, forgiving each other, just as in Christ God forgave you."[728]

When comparing our lives with those of the persecuted Church, we realize we must grow in the Lord to be able to deal with the coming persecution. In Paul's wonderful exhortation above regarding the body of Christ, he emphasized that there is *one body and one Spirit*.[729] We must all, together, grow to become in every respect the mature body of Him who is the Head, that is, Christ.[730] Although each part of the body has its own specific calling, it is that *one Spirit* who works in all, and who transforms us into the image of Christ, or, as Paul put it, to the whole measure of the fullness of Christ.[731]

It takes unwavering faith to be able to face persecution such as the North Korean believers do. In being willing to endure that kind of torture without denying their faith in Christ, their lives exhibit more spiritual maturity than can be found in most of the Christian world.

---

[728] Ephesians 4
[729] Ephesians 4:4
[730] Ephesians 4:15
[731] Ephesians 4:13

If we are going to grow in the Lord, there is only one way: through entrusting our spiritual well-being to Christ. We cannot change ourselves, but the Holy Spirit knows what we need. He will teach us as we seek the Lord and study the written Word. We need only submit to His working in us so that we can be made fully complete in Christ.

The measure of true Christian growth is how much of Christ can be seen in us. Jesus said, "A new command I give you: 'Love one another. As I have loved you, so you must love one another. By this everyone will know that you are My disciples, if you love one another.'"[732]

---

[732] John 13:34-35

Principle 52

The Practice of Teaching Children

ALL CHURCHES have been bulldozed in North Korea except for a few *show churches* in the main capital of North Korea. Christians practice their faith in secrecy and constant danger. Religious prisoners are often subjected to harsher treatment and given the most dangerous tasks, all to force them to renounce their faith. When they refuse, they have often been tortured to death. Likewise their children are sentenced to hard labor and starved to death.

When a Christian is caught with a Bible in North Korea he or she can be executed. It affects the children. Those caught worshipping God will be imprisoned with their whole family, where they will be beaten, starved and worked to death. The children are affected equally with the adults.

A witness said: "It is not just our life we give as a Christian. It also is the life of our children. We must watch our children suffer and die or they must watch when we are executed."

As a Christian child, growing up in a North Korean home means getting ready for the ultimate test. Children learn in school to worship Kim Il Sung as god. They have been brainwashed since kindergarten to believe in a false god, but they learn about the true God as seen and heard through their parents. They learn from the gatherings in their home and from their parents that our holy Heavenly Father is the real God and Jesus is the Christ who gives them eternal life. Some Christian organizations report that most Christian families exclude their children because of the fear that they may innocently disclose the worship at home. However, we believe that the lives of the parents teach their children.

In non-persecuted countries we have elected not to teach our children because of time limitations. Even on Sundays we elect to separate them into a Sunday school. The concept of Sunday school is a term that is understood by many to be the separation of the children from the adults during part of a public church service. Such a practice can not only hinder the growth of the children in the Lord but does not allow them to see the vibrant faith of the adults.

The early Church in Acts did not have separate meetings for children but rather had them all in the service. To have a child share a Scripture verse or short prayer can be a greatly edifying practice for the children themselves and even for the adults. The Churches in countries where there is persecution do not have even the liberty to have separate meetings for children with coloring crayons and other activities to entertain them. May we allow the children to witness the moving of God's Spirit as the Church meets, teaches and worships.

In the Scriptures there are occasions where younger women were taught by older women[733] yet in no place do we find the practice of children being taught by older children. The primary teaching place for children is the home of the believers. This is in its smallest way a meeting of the Church as believers assemble towards Jesus Christ in their family altars to pray, worship and read the Word of God.

Here are some Scripture passages that speak of this responsibility for the family to train and discipline the children in the ways of the Lord:

"Start children off on the way they should go, and even when they are old they will not turn from it."[734]

"These commandments that I give you today are to be on your hearts. Impress them on your children. Talk about them when you sit

---

[733] Titus 2:4
[734] Proverbs 22:6

at home and when you walk along the road, when you lie down and when you get up."[735]

"My son, keep your father's command and do not forsake your mother's teaching. Bind them always on your heart; fasten them around your neck."[736]

"Moreover, we have all had human fathers who disciplined us and we respected them for it. How much more should we submit to the Father of spirits and live!"[737]

In countries with no persecution and especially in rich non-persecuted nations the family unit has broken down. In most homes both parents work to keep up their wealth status. This leaves no time for the parents to teach their children. God seeks godly offspring.[738] However, these children are now growing up as a godless generation. We are already reaping what we have sown. In the Book of Hosea it says: "My people are destroyed from lack of knowledge. 'Because you have rejected knowledge, I also reject you as My priests; because you have ignored the Law of your God, I also will ignore your children."[739]

May God have mercy on us. God always shows mercy where we genuinely repent and turn around. Parents, if you repent, God will help you.

"He will turn the hearts of the parents to their children, and the hearts of the children to their parents; or else I will come and strike the land with total destruction."[740]

---

[735] Deuteronomy 6:6-7
[736] Proverbs 6:20-21
[737] Hebrews 12:9
[738] Malachi 2:15
[739] Hosea 4:6
[740] Malachi 4:6, Jeremiah 10:25

Principle 53

Raising Up Many Leaders in the Body

A FORMER North Korea civil servant related the brutal mistreatment of Christians and their babies being killed. Prison guards regularly attempt to get Christian prisoners to recant their faith. Abortions are forced on female prisoners, some in the late stages of pregnancy. There is the idea of collective punishment, where people with bad ideology must be stopped from producing children. The women are forced to have their babies removed and killed.

One forced abortion was on a woman in her ninth month of pregnancy. The baby was still born alive. While the mother pleaded for her baby's life as it writhed on the floor, the guard came and stepped on the neck of the baby. The mother was publicly executed for pleading for her child's life.

The blood of the martyrs drenches and waters the soil of North Korea. The civil servant could not understand such faith and later became a Christian.

What kind of Christian leadership is required under such trauma? It must be the Head of the Church Jesus Christ who leads. It must be Holy Spirit filled believers who are able to utter the Words of

God with power. The practice of the priesthood of all believers[741] is something vital to the growth and expansion of the Church, especially in persecuted countries. Christians in North Korea are expected to be servant leaders and Spirit filled, to share the Word, pray, and preach the Gospel. One of the reasons for the continued existence and growth of the underground Church in North Korea is that they have not been dependent on a few highly esteemed leaders in the Church but have rather emphasized the raising up of all to be servant leaders who are able to edify and build the Church. At the same time the Church in North Korea recognizes whom God has specifically gifted as shepherds. Such servant leaders are esteemed but not idolized.

The Church in non-persecuted countries can learn much from this. Rather than having the majority of the body of Christ inactive, all members of the body of Christ should again become active as in days of old. Instead of just receiving the Word from leaders who teach them weekly from pulpits, podcasts or television programs, they should become involved themselves in teaching small groups.

There is great need for an equipping and raising up of the body of Christ because all are servants of the Lord. A good starting place is for many to step out in faith and lead a small house Church that meets a few times a week where everyone can share and grow in the Lord.[742]

While we advocate many servant leaders, we agree with and underline the teaching of *1 Timothy chapter 3* where God has given the qualifications of Church leaders. God continues to use leaders He recognizes, calls and has ordained to help His body grow. Saints under persecution also need to submit to those who exhibit the graces and calling of Christ to be a shepherd of God's flock. The Church should continue to seek elder brothers with experience in the Lord, to teach and lead them. Such brothers not only protect the home Church spiritually but can also give encouragement and the spiritual direction to start a house meeting under the Headship of Jesus Christ.

---

[741] 1 Peter 2:5

[742] Frank Bartleman (1871-1936) said, quoting the church historian Merle D'Aubigne: "*In the beginning the Church was a company of brethren led by a few of the brethren.*"

Principle 54

Remembering The Poor

DURING THE greatest part of the North Korean famine an estimated two million North Koreans starved to death. This happened during the years of   1995-1998. The famine has continued in reduced measure and North Koreans have still been unable to feed themselves. The World Food Program annually still needs to feed 6 to 8 million of North Korea's 24 million people.

All food subsidies are received by the Government and are distributed under their control. The former leader Kim Jong Il has classified the North Koreans into three segments: loyal, wavering, and hostile. This system continues to this day. Privileges, including the right to eat, are given to the population based on their perceived loyalty to the leader. In 1996, Kim declared that he is willing to let the other two-thirds starve to death and to rebuild the country with just the *loyal* third. Yet, even the army of 1.1 million has little food. They rob villagers of their last food.

A refugee testifies: "We were looking for a way to provide food for our family. The vast majority of people are extremely hungry. Some ate grass, tree bark and sand. To go to the toilet afterwards is very difficult. Christians are the last to receive any allowance for foods."

Instead of distributing the food aid, the leader Kim Jong Il built and owned 17 luxury palaces, 20,000 movies and 10,000 bottles of fine wine. The *wavering* and the *hostile segments* of the population include the Christians. They are starving much physically, but they cannot live without reading God's Word, praying and praising God.

The typical denominational church's financial giving in many countries first goes to the building and then the pastoral staff. After such an expenditure very little is left for giving to the poor, missions and other needs. The underground Church in North Korea does not have pastors with large salaries or buildings they need to pay for. They are desperately poor and yet they share what little resources they have with each other.

Giving to the poor was not an option in the New Testament but rather one of the chief ways Jesus Christ emphasized dealing with money.[743] Also the Apostles followed this pattern and emphasized this as one of the traditions and tenets of the Church.[744]

Having a remembrance and love for the poor always is a vital part of New Testament Christianity and of the Spirit of Jesus Christ. Jesus said: "The poor you will always have with you."[745] So this is a continual God-given responsibility and ministry of the Church.

We are encouraged especially by the Apostle James to show love and no partiality to the poor in our Assembly meetings as the Church:

"My brothers and sisters, believers in our glorious Lord Jesus Christ must not show favoritism. Suppose a man comes into your meeting wearing a gold ring and fine clothes, and a poor man in filthy old clothes also comes in. If you show special attention to the man wearing fine clothes and say, 'Here's a good seat for you,' but say to the poor man, 'You stand there' or 'Sit on the floor by my feet,' have you not discriminated among yourselves and become judges with evil thoughts?

"Listen, my dear brothers and sisters: Has not God chosen those who are poor in the eyes of the world to be rich in faith and to inherit the kingdom He promised those who love Him? But you have dishonored the poor. Is it not the rich who are exploiting you? Are they not the ones who are dragging you into court? Are they not the ones who are blaspheming the noble Name of Him to whom you belong? If you really keep the royal law found in Scripture, 'Love your

---

[743] Matthew 19:21
[744] Galatians 2:10
[745] Matthew 26:11

neighbor as yourself,' you are doing right. But if you show favoritism, you sin and are convicted by the law as lawbreakers."[746]

We must learn quickly what a powerful opportunity there is for us in this area of truly using our money rightly before the Lord. If house Churches started with the premise that instead of having a building and a full-time paid pastor they used their resources to reach out to the poor, there surely would be an abundant harvest of people reached for the Lord.[747]

---

[746] James 2:1-9
[747] Luke 4:18

Principle 55

Witnessing and Missions Work by Faith

A 22-YEAR-OLD woman returned from China to North Korea with the purpose of sharing the Gospel with friends and family. She was arrested after one and a half years when she was discovered to be distributing Bibles and hymnals.

She was cruelly punished as if she was *a terrorist*, being required in one instance to sit in one position for 24 hours without moving. However, by a miracle of God she was not executed. He still had more work for her. One day a prisoner was sent to her in the same prison. The new prisoner was a spy for North Korea in China, who was trapping North Korean defectors. The former undercover spy had tried to defect from China to South Korea, but was caught. The new prisoner asked the 22-year-old Christian if God existed and if He could forgive her because she regretted what she did to others. The Christian, who had only been trained for 4½ months in China, led the spy to Christ. Then to help her she wrote down some Bible verses on paper for the former spy.

Witnessing in North Korea is generally very secretive. Christians in North Korea do not pursue the open sharing of the Gospel as it leads to immediate incarceration, beatings, torture and possible martyrdom. There are two added factors that cause Christians to act in secrecy. They do not mind to lose their own lives but if they are discovered in their faith they will give a death sentence to three generations of their families—their fathers and mothers, their grandparents, their uncles and aunts and their children. Government spies are sent to trap them. Many of those professing Christ openly are government spies and agents who want to trap underground Church members. The mere mention of the Name of God is enough to prompt an investigation if not a conviction. For fear of electronic surveillance, all Christian speech is conducted in secret places, sometimes far away in fields or very quietly, so as under one's breath.

North Koreans take a long time to create trust with another person before they share their faith. Yet evangelism goes on, a word here and a word there. God's Word does not return void and has great conviction. The power of the Holy Spirit is with those who witness if they are true Christians.

Within the concentration and death camps the proclamation of the Gospel is more open. Death by execution or starvation is presumed to claim its victims. Prisoners feel if one is dead already one should share that there is eternal life giving others hope for eternity; there is nothing left to lose. Some North Korean Christians prefer to meet their fate in the death camps finally being able to speak freely of Jesus Christ their Lord, and the gift of God giving eternal life to those who believe.

"For it has been granted to you on behalf of Christ not only to believe in Him, but also to suffer for Him."[748]

"But even if I am being poured out like a drink offering on the sacrifice and service coming from your faith, I am glad and rejoice with all of you. So you too should be glad and rejoice with me."[749]

Then there are those who are especially called by the Lord. They will go out in secret, doing witnessing and missions work by faith, and trusting the Lord for their needs.[750] Some will give up their jobs and security, preaching the Gospel across their country. It is inconceivable to our minds that some young people or older people would give up their home, job and comforts of life to share the Good

---

[748] Philippians 1:29
[749] Philippians 2:17-18
[750] Luke 12:22

News in such a deadly, torturous, and brutal country. They trust the Lord and they do not love their own life unto death.

Thus we must learn from the underground Church in North Korea to trust God again and afresh. We must do the work while the night has not yet come in countries where persecution is not rampant. God is able to do abundantly above what we can ask or even imagine.[751] We trust so much in wealth and freedom instead of putting our full confidence in the Lord. We rely on fancy tools and not on the Holy Spirit of God absolutely! We deny the power of God in our lives.

May we choose to seek the filling of the Holy Spirit to receive the power of God to witness and preach with boldness. If God then requires it He will provide the power of the Holy Spirit for us to suffer for the Gospel.

We need to change our lives to meet more as the body of Christ, to gain a deeper understanding and reverence for the Word of God, to repent of worldliness, to repent of seeking pleasures and wealth and to repent of our idolization of Christian leaders. We must learn to *walk in the Spirit* so as not to fulfill the lusts of our flesh[752] and to trust God afresh to be a part of His growing Church.

An underground Church leader in North Korea explained how the Lord is preserving His movement. He said: "People ask me, 'How are Christians surviving in North Korea?' They have a secret. They survive through *God's intervention, protection and miracles.* They are starving much physically but they cannot live without reading God's Word, praying and praising God. That's the secret to their survival!" This is how the North Korean Church survives: They trust a God of the impossible!

How needful it is for us today to not trust in the arm of the flesh[753] or the plans of men[754] but in God who does what is not humanly possible. May we agree with the underground believers that say: "We truly believe in a God of miracles. *Amen!*"

---

[751] Ephesians 3:20
[752] Galatians 5:16
[753] 2 Chronicles 32:8
[754] Jeremiah 17:5

Principles 56 to 60

Principles from the Underground Church in Iran

Principle 56

Explosive Growth in an Antichrist State

FOR READERS to understand the environment Christians face in Iran it is necessary to give a brief summary of the Iranian and Islamic global agenda. Iran is a totalitarian government, a dictatorship, which exercises suppression, persecution and, at times, the death penalty for those of other faiths. The Islamic Republic and its leaders, operate under a great desire for Islamic world dominion with a religious fervor that does not permit faiths other than Islam.

Though in a great minority Christianity is a present reality in Iran a solely Islamic state. Christianity in Iran has a long history, dating back to Jerusalem and Pentecost. According to Acts 2:9 in the Acts of the Apostles there were Parthians and Medes (*Persians or today's Iranians*) in Jerusalem who were among the first new Christian converts at Pentecost. Since then there has been a continuous presence of Christians in Iran, formerly Persia. Christians are severely persecuted in Iran, put into prison, are tortured, and put to death.

Mahmoud Ahmadinejad—the current president—has been reported as being called by divine decree to usher in the return of the Twelfth Imam, a pseudo savior of the world. Ahmadinejad gave his eighth address to the opening fall session of the United Nations general assembly in 2012. Here are two excerpts from his 34 minute speech:

"The arrival of the ultimate savior will mark a new beginning, a rebirth and a resurrection. It will be the beginning of peace, lasting security and genuine life."

"His arrival will be the end of oppression, immorality, poverty, discrimination and the beginning of justice, love and empathy."

Islam and other religions have been created by men deceived by Satan. The true God cannot be allah because he declares muhammad to be his prophet. The one and only true and living God our Father in heaven declares His Son to be Jesus Christ. He told us in His Word:

"Dear children, this is the last hour; and as you have heard that the antichrist is coming, even now many antichrists have come. This is how we know it is the last hour."[755]

"Who is the liar? It is whoever denies that Jesus is the Christ. Such a person is the antichrist—denying the Father and the Son."[756]

"Every spirit that does not acknowledge Jesus is not from God. This is the spirit of the antichrist, which you have heard is coming and even now is already in the world."[757]

The Bible gives some specifics about a future world leader. However, we do not know the identity of such a person. We are given in the Bible in *Revelation Chapter 20* an indication of beheading as a major execution method used by the antichrist. "Beheaded because of their testimony about Jesus and because of the Word of God."[758]

The execution method of *beheading* has been practiced by Muslim extremists. Will God use Iran and other Muslim nations to usher in the great tribulation? We do not know. We must continue to declare the truth of the Gospel despite persecution. God our Heavenly Father declared by way of a voice from heaven that Jesus Christ is His Son. The true Savior of the world Jesus Christ rose from the dead and will return to earth in great power and glory and with the heavenly hosts.

---

[755] 1 John 2:18
[756] 1 John 2:22
[757] 1 John 4:3
[758] Revelation 20:4

As Christians we love Muslims as God commanded us to do. We love all Muslim persons but we must not and cannot accept satan's aberrations of presenting us with a false faith and false messiah. There is only one true and living God, our Heavenly Father, and His Son Jesus Christ who can save us and create a new heaven and a new earth, without sin, sorrow and death.

Estimates of the number of Christians in Iran vary. Some report an estimated 1 million Christians in Iran.[759] Another organization reports a wave of revival. While not all reporting ministries say the same, we believe overall wonderful growth is taking place despite great persecution.

Christian Pastor Nadarkhani says: "The Word of God tells us to expect to suffer hardship and dishonor for the sake of His Name. Our Christian confession is not acceptable if we ignore this statement, if we do not manifest the patience of the Lord in our sufferings."

Is our Christianity in non-persecuted nations cold, hot, or lukewarm? If you say you are *hot* are you witnessing every day and at every opportunity? Those in persecuted countries risk their lives to share the wonderful news of Jesus. Why are we not sharing the Good News every day, every opportunity?

The Gospel of Jesus Christ since its inception in AD 33 has never been anything but explosive in its growth when it has been proclaimed by Spirit-filled, Christ-centered and totally committed Christians. Such Christians were not hindered by the traditions and religious ideas of men. The simple message of the Son of God crucified and resurrected for the sins of mankind has impacted millions of lives to surrender all their rights and life to God and receive forgiveness of sins. We see in the Book of Acts several accounts of this explosive growth:

"But many who heard the Message believed; so the number of men who believed grew to about five thousand."[760]

"Nevertheless, more and more men and women believed in the Lord and were added to their number."[761]

---

[759] Christian News Today
[760] Acts 4:4
[761] Acts 5:14

"So the Word of God spread. The number of disciples in Jerusalem increased rapidly, and a large number of priests became obedient to the faith."[762]

Some estimate that between Acts chapter 2 and Acts chapter 6 the growth of the Church was from 120 to upwards of 25,000 believers in this short duration of time! Some will caution against seeking after such growth in the Church but we must not try to hinder what God wants to do by His Spirit. When there are times of pressure that come upon the Church this can result in great expansions of the Gospel into the world. Some estimate that over the last 30 years more Iranians have given their lives to Jesus Christ then over the last 1,300 years put together![763]

Such a moving of God's Spirit is normal when God is allowed to work. Sometimes this demands a time of persecution and pressure for the Church so that men are not in charge of the Church but God is again given His rightful place to lead and direct. Sadly it takes sometimes great pressures for the dependence on God to be sought again. The early Apostles, after being brought before the Sanhedrin, came back to the other believers and cried out to God about the situation. They prayed for boldness to proclaim the Gospel and not protection. They prayed for God to stretch out His hand and to do signs and wonders in the Name of Jesus. They were filled with the Holy Spirit and the place was shaken. It is in times like this that God begins to work sovereignly in powerful ways. The economy of God is such that He will let us wait sometimes many years in a state of Christianity that is rebellious and full of sin in order to let us come to an end of ourselves so that we would cry out to Him again.

God has a Remnant in Iran who are dependent, crying out to Him day and night and trusting in His working. In such a place God is doing the impossible to glorify His Name and great numbers are being added to the Church.

If you are in a country that is not persecuted, would you be willing to cry out to the Lord[764] asking Him for the Holy Spirit to help you share the Good News, as Christians do in persecuted countries? Would you be willing to weep for your neighbors who do

---

[762] Acts 6:7

[763] Estimation from *Elam Ministries* which works extensively with the Church in Iran.

[764] Luke 18:7

not know the Lord? Would you be willing to weep for your country to come to repentance[765] and the knowledge of the Gospel[766] through Jesus Christ our Lord?

May we believe for wonderful growth of the body of Christ as we step out in small gatherings under the Headship of Jesus Christ.

---

[765] 2 Peter 3:9
[766] 2 Corinthians 4:6

Principle 57.

Sharing the Faith Constantly in All Situations

A CHRISTIAN who was jailed in Iran was told that if Christians would simply agree to stop evangelizing, all the prisoners would be freed. Church leaders point to this as evidence that Christians in Iran follow the instructions of the Lord and share their faith.

"One imprisoned female Christian, though facing health challenges, says she has had the opportunity to lead three people to the Lord, including a criminal on death row, making her trial worthwhile."[767]

Pastor Irani, whose hair has turned white in an Iranian prison addresses the Christians in Iran with a letter:

"Despite the pressure and difficulties in prison, I am pleased to share, what is like a fountain, my Christian joy with you in the new special days to come. And I know that you, who are the saints and spiritual children of God, are acquainted with this joy. As a minister of God, I allow myself to announce you to be happy. Know that all the happiness that we have on earth is the first fruit of that great joy

---

[767] AG World Missions

provided for us in heaven. The Father provides. I understand your worries at a time of reported persecution, which forced some of you to flee abroad. However, please pay attention to what God says in Matthew in the Bible: 'Look at the birds of the air; they do not sow or reap or store away in barns, and yet your heavenly Father feeds them. Are you not much more valuable than they?'"[768]

Another Christian Pastor Farshid Fathi has been detained in prison since December 2010. He was charged with possessing religious propaganda. The evidence presented by the regime was that Pastor Fathi had Bibles printed in Farsi, that he had unlawfully distributed Bibles, and that he possessed Christian literature. The regime argued that his Christian activities were equivalent to *actions against national security*. Pastor Fathi is presently serving a 6-year sentence in Iran's notorious Evin prison. His crime is being a Christian and freely exercising his faith. Pastor Fathi has a wife Leila and two children, Rosana and Bardia. They suffer with him.

Under an oppressive regime—such as Iran's government— believers who share their faith can be reported for apostatizing from the Muslim faith. Yet there is a Holy Spirit boldness in many in the underground Church to share their faith publicly and daily with other Iranians. Believers share their faith with people in the buses, taxis, in the shops, and even when stopped at a red light. The openness in many hearts for the truth is such that some Iranians, when given the truth of the Gospel, want to accept it right away.

They do not hold any special crusades, rallies or any type of evangelism outreaches. All the Iranian believers go about their daily lives, sharing the Gospel with many they come across. Because none of them are foreign missionaries they blend right in with their country and culture and are therefore able to share their faith naturally in daily life.

An example of this boldness and obedience to the Holy Spirit is that of a Christian whose car was stopped at a red light in Tehran. The believer felt led of the Holy Spirit to get out of his car, knock on the window of another car and give the driver a New Testament. They also exchanged phone numbers and, shortly after that, the man who received the New Testament believed on Christ. When he met with

---

[768] Matthew 6:26

the man that gave him the Scriptures, the new convert testified that he had felt an overwhelming desire to follow the believer's car and for 20 minutes had driven behind the Christian throughout the streets of Tehran not knowing why. This is the way the Holy Spirit is working and drawing many to Christ by what we would call miracles and impossibilities. This is the normal working of God's Spirit to bring men to Himself through Jesus Christ.

A Christian taxi driver demonstrates another example of this boldness. He has a cross dangling from the front mirror in his taxi. He has a Bible on the seat next to him. He realizes and knows that his livelihood, his freedom and even his life are at stake. Yet, he says: "How can I not share the great salvation through Jesus Christ?"

In Acts 1:8 we are reminded that this is the work of the Holy Spirit. When we deny the power of God to witness through us, we become the salt that has lost its savor.[769] We can return to God in repentance and ask Him to endue us with His Holy Spirit. His power will become evident in our lives if we follow in obedience and in dependence on Jesus. In the Book of Acts God's power was revealed by His angel and by the Spirit to guide the deacon Philip:

"Now an angel of the Lord said to Philip, 'Go south to the road —the desert road—that goes down from Jerusalem to Gaza.' So he started out, and on his way he met an Ethiopian eunuch, an important official in charge of all the treasury of the Kandake (*which means 'queen of the Ethiopians'*). This man had gone to Jerusalem to worship, and on his way home was sitting in his chariot reading the Book of Isaiah the prophet. The Spirit told Philip, 'Go to that chariot and stay near it.'"[770]

May we seek such direction of the Lord daily in our circumstances to be a witness for Christ.

---

[769] Matthew 5:13
[770] Acts 8:26-29

Principle 58

New Converts Every Church Meeting

IT IS now a normal thing to see many new converts in Iranian House Churches. Iranian believers expect to see new people coming in repentance to Jesus every week. This is very much like the account of the Book of Acts where it says the Church was: "Praising God and enjoying the favor of all the people. And the Lord added to their number daily those who were being saved."[771] In some cases, when they have meetings where there are no stories of a conversion they examine what they have done wrong to hinder the Lord working. Such growth has happened in the last 30 years to where many say conservative estimates put the size of the Iranian house Churches at over one million people.

Iranians find the Lord Jesus Christ through evangelization by Iranians and personal one-to-one witnessing. The Lord commands us to make disciples. After the person makes a decision, they need discipleship. It involves walking and talking with those that have accepted Christ and teaching them what the Bible says. As Iranian Christians rely on the Holy Spirit they are Spirit-led to reach those that should be saved. They risk their lives to do so because they believe it is a sin not to share the Good News of the Gospel of the

---

[771] Acts 2:47

Lord Jesus Christ. Their commitment to Jesus Christ is reflected in many reports.

The cost to see this growth in the Church is at the price of great persecution and imprisonment. Rev. Mehdi Dibaj was in prison for 9 years for refusing to deny his faith in Christ and return to Islam. He said: "I am a Christian. As a sinner I believe Jesus has died for my sins on the cross and by His resurrection and victory over death, has made me righteous in the presence of the Holy God. The true God speaks about this fact in His Holy Word, the Gospel (*Injil*). Jesus means Savior 'because He will save His people from their sins.'[772] Jesus paid the penalty of our sins by His own blood and gave us a new life so that we can live for the glory of God by the help of the Holy Spirit and be like a dam against corruption, be a channel of blessing and healing, and be protected by the love of God.

"In response to this kindness, He has asked me to deny myself and be His fully surrendered follower, and not to fear people even if they kill my body, but rather rely on the creator of life who has crowned me with the crown of mercy and compassion. He is the great protector of His beloved ones as well as their Great Reward.

"They object to my evangelizing. But if one finds a blind person who is about to fall in a well and keeps silent then one has sinned.[773] It is our religious duty, as long as the door of God's mercy is open, to convince evil-doers to turn from their sinful ways and find refuge in Him in order to be saved from the wrath of the Righteous God and from the coming dreadful punishment."[774]

Three months after he was released from prison, Rev. Mehdi was abducted and later found hanging from a tree.

Such dedication in the life of Iranian Christians brings the results that God desires. Heaven rejoices when a sinner repents. God gives the eternal reward, that of a martyrs' crown, to His faithful servant. We in non-persecuted countries take the easy road. We say, *Let our life speak*. Yet we are drowned in the sea of the world. Our voices are not raised and therefore are not heard. We have lost the salt from our Christian lives. When Jesus prayed for us He talked to His Father about future Christians that would believe on Him because of their

---

[772] Matthew 1:21
[773] Matthew 12:11
[774] Mehdi Dibaj (1935-1994)

word: "My prayer is not for them alone. I pray also for those who will believe in Me through their message."[775] By saying *their message* Jesus is indicating that we Christians are to use the words of our mouths to testify about salvation. We are to share with others by word of mouth what Jesus has done for us. We are to speak with our voices about our faith, humbly, gently, and with much love. "For it is with your heart that you believe and are justified, and it is with your mouth that you profess your faith and are saved."[776]

In Iran, confession of the faith is also transmitted through technological means. A wonderful testimony is that of a family in Iran that watched a Gospel broadcast on an illegal satellite station. In response to hearing the Good News of the Son of God and eternal life in Him they prayed this prayer together as a family:

"Dear God, we confess that we are sinners. I confess that I cannot save myself through my own good works. I believe that You died on the cross for my sins. And they put You in the tomb and You rose from the dead after 3 days. I believe that You are alive and have the authority to forgive my sins. And to make me righteous in front of the Everlasting God. I ask that You accept me and as You promised, please give me new life. I thank You for hearing my prayers, Amen."

With this prayer they wrote in to the Gospel station and asked if the prayer was correct. Such simple faith and response to the Gospel is how God is working in a powerful way in this country to turn people from a harsh religion that demands many outward religious forms to the true and living God.

---

[775] John 17:20
[776] Romans 10:10

Principle 59

Networking Small Groups of Believers

JUST LIKE the Church in the Book of Acts began to meet in homes as a network of believers when it came under great pressures from the Jewish atrocities, the believers in Iran today have similar pressures that have encouraged them to meet in small home fellowships that are all networked together with other believers.

As persecution intensifies in certain areas, believers will move to different cities and start home fellowships there also, so that the spreading of these gatherings is something that is continually happening. The Iranians believe that Jesus Christ is with them in their small gatherings and therefore there is a confidence that they are meeting as a Church even if there are just a few believers present. They count it a necessity to network with others and consider themselves all part of one Church. There is no choice to try to find a different church for doctrinal preference or worship style; all believers are content to meet simply with each other.

In the Book of Acts, arguably over 25,000 new converts occurred within the first year of the history of the Church. Yet all of this growth was easily assimilated into small house Churches as they networked together seamlessly. The Gospel was preached in homes[777] and the older brothers and sisters taught the younger when there were no Apostles or elders present. This life of the Body, where everyone was able to teach each other, allowed for fast growth and for adjusting to how the Lord was adding to the Church daily those who were being saved.

For the next 250 years, before there was ever a church building constructed, this practice of meeting in homes and of loose networking was the pattern for the early Church. The home itself was a Church where the husband would teach his family. In Iran and other countries closed to the Gospel, this is a method used by the Holy Spirit to preserve His Church. It is noteworthy that Jesus Himself primarily ministered in homes[778] during His three years of public ministry. And not surprisingly the Lord taught His disciples to also use private homes in their ministries also.[779] The same was true of the early Church Apostles.[780]

There is a great vacuum in the lives of the people of Iran. Eighty percent of the younger generation is dissatisfied with the fundamentalism of Islam which cannot meet their deepest needs. They are searching for real answers for the problems in their lives. Most young Iranians do not adhere to the Islamic faith. When they choose Jesus Christ they know they have chosen eternity in heaven, but they realize they must *forsake all* in this earthly life.[781] The great Gospel of God given through His Son Jesus is recognized as worth leaving all behind and, if necessary, losing one's life. There is no in-between; it is a total commitment of taking up their cross and following Jesus, becoming a living sacrifice. The following accounts exemplify the danger:

A house Church was raided by security forces on Friday, October 12, 2012 in the city of Shiraz in Fars Province, Iran. Two members of the Church were arrested and summoned to the Intelligence Ministry's detention centre, Pelak, where seven other members of their house Church were being held.

---

[777] Acts 5:42, Acts 20:20
[778] Matthew 8:14, Matthew 9:9-10, Luke 22:7-12
[779] Matthew 10:11-14, Luke 10:5-7
[780] Acts 9:43, Acts 10:22, Acts 5:52
[781] Luke 14:26-27, Luke 14:33

A 27-year-old Iranian Christian was spending a quiet evening at home with his wife and young daughter when plainclothes security forces entered his house and arrested him. The security officers searched the home and seized personal belongings such as a computer, CDs containing films of Christian seminars and teachings, Christian books and Bibles, and family photo albums. The Christian was incarcerated. No information about his condition and whereabouts was given to the family for months.

In another case: Fifteen Christians were thrown in jail. They were put under severe pressure to recant their faith but refused to do so.

Nonetheless, "While it is safer to start a church in the West, it may actually be simpler to plant one in Iran. Go to a church planters' conference in North America, and you will hear about budgets, programs, marketing campaigns, and the need for a good worship set. Attend a conference for Iranians, and you get a very different picture. They'll talk about starting by sharing Christ with friends and family, gathering new believers for a weekly Bible teaching and fellowship, and then encouraging and praying with them to go and share with their friends and family."[782]

We can follow their example by starting small fellowships under the Headship of Jesus Christ in the same way as our Iranian brothers and sisters.

---

[782] Elam Ministries

Principle 60

Martyrs Esteemed in the Church

THE THOUGHT of any believer in Christ being martyred is something hard to bear. Yet from an eternal perspective the Iranian believers hold in high regard those who have laid down their lives for the cause of Christ. The stories of the martyrs in Iran are many. These are just a few:

On January 19, 1994, Haik disappeared from the streets of Tehran. The authorities reported his death to his family on January 30; he was stabbed 26 times in his chest: "Indeed, Haik gave his heart to Christ twice. Once when he invited Christ to his life as his Savior, and second, when his heart was torn apart for his faith in Christ."[783]

Martyr Mehdi Dibaj wrote:

"I have always envied those Christians who were martyred for Christ Jesus our Lord. What a privilege to live for our Lord and to die for Him as well. I am filled to overflowing with joy; I am not only satisfied to be in prison but am ready to give my life for the sake of Jesus Christ."[784]

Iranians Abbas Amiri and his wife Sakineh Rahnama, who hosted an underground house Church service died from injuries sustained

---

[783] Hovsepian Ministries Testimony
[784] Farsi Net

when secret police raided their house Church service and severely beat them to death. Abbas died right away. Before becoming a Christian Abbas had been a devout Muslim even making a pilgrimage to Mecca. His wife died less than a week later. At the house Church service were seven other men, six women and two children.

Martyr Mohammad Ali Jafarzadeh, was executed by hanging in Evin Prison in Iran.

Martyr Mohammad Jaberi was also executed by hanging in Evin Prison in Iran.

Martyr Pastor Ghorbandordi Tourani an Iranian house Church leader was murdered near his house.

Martyr Pastor Mohammed Bajher Yusefi, affectionately known by his flock as *Ravanbaksh*, or *soul giver*, was murdered. He had left his house to spend time in prayer, but he never returned. The Iranian authorities notified the family later that evening that his body had been found hanging from a tree in a nearby forest.

. Recently a brother was arrested and put on trial for his faith in Iran and he shared this exhortation in a letter: "One day there are intense pains after beatings in interrogations, the next day they are nice to you and offer you candy. These hot and colds only make you a man of steel for moving forward in expanding His Kingdom. When for 120 days you are asleep in a room with one big light that is constantly lit and does not separate day or night and when you can only see true sunlight for a few minutes a week, that's when you are becoming His workmanship and you can be a vessel in bringing His kingdom in a dark place and you are able to share the Gospel of peace and life to the dying world. And this is where you learn you can love your enemies with all of your heart."[785]

The sadness and hurt of any believer in Christ being martyred is hard to bear. Yet from an eternal mindset and perspective there is a glory and esteem the Iranian believers have for those who have laid down their lives for the cause of Christ. The stories of the martyrs in Iran are many. Above we have mentioned a few.

Such lives are not laid down in vain, but are paving the way for the furtherance of the glorious Gospel of Jesus Christ. As Tertullian[786]

---

[785] Saeed Abedini
[786] A recognized early Church father

said in his Apology in AD 200: "The oftener we are mown down by you, the more in number we grow. The blood of Christians is seed." This seed is being sown in Iran today and we should expect a vibrant harvest of souls in the coming days before the coming of our Lord.

Martyrdom is a sobering subject. Maybe it will sober us back to the place where the Church needs to be. The martyr spirit is the spirit of New Testament Christianity. We have to recapture a faith that is worth living for and worth dying for in our day. Christ demands our all in His call for discipleship. If we seek to save our lives we will lose them.[787]

The Bible is filled with the testimonies of martyrs; from the first Book of Genesis where Abel becomes the first martyr,[788] to the end of the Book of Revelation, where the last of the martyrs are killed for the testimony of Christ.[789] From the beginning to the end of the Bible, martyrdom is not only keenly present but overwhelmingly obvious to any reader of the Scriptures.

The Apostle John gives us this exhortation: "Do not be surprised, my brothers and sisters, if the world hates you."[790] It should not surprise or startle us in anyway when we are recipients of the fact that the world hates us. When we are on the receiving end of a slander, blasphemy, rejection or even a violent act we should not be surprised. This world and all of its inhabitants are offended by the Gospel and by Christ in us. Our light and righteousness speaks of their condemnation.[791] Daily, our lives make manifest the fact that they will be judged by God one day.

Hebrews chapter 11 is not only a *hall of faith*, as many call it but it is also a *hall of martyrs*. "Some faced jeers and flogging, and even chains and imprisonment. They were put to death by stoning; they were sawed in two; they were killed by the sword. They went about in sheepskins and goatskins, destitute, persecuted and mistreated—the world was not worthy of them. They wandered in deserts and mountains, living in caves and in holes in the ground."[792] This

[787] Mark 8:35
[788] Genesis 4
[789] Revelation 20
[790] 1 John 3:13
[791] John 3:20
[792] Hebrews 11:36-38

passage along with others should build in us a great sobriety on this subject as we consider those who went on ahead of us in the body of Christ.

Another passage largely misinterpreted and overlooked in its context is in Romans chapter 8: "Who shall separate us from the love of Christ? Shall trouble or hardship or persecution or famine or nakedness or danger or sword? As it is written: 'For Your sake we face death all day long; we are considered as sheep to be slaughtered.'"[793]

Evangelicals quote this passage to speak of the greatness of God's love; and surely God's love is great, but unfortunately we have misinterpreted its true meaning. Paul speaks of famines, danger and swords! Shall a sword separate us from the love of Christ? Or, using modern vernacular, shall a gun pointed at our head separate us from the love of Christ? The answer of course is, No. Nothing will separate us from the love of Christ, even when men torture and martyr us for that precious Name, they will not be able to touch our souls. We are safe in Christ's love. All that men can do to us is destroy this earthly tent, the body we are living in. This was the Apostle Paul's emphasis and point in this passage. Martyrdom is the secret weapon of the Church. No one can take away the victory of Christ's love on the cross and the redemption of men for Himself.

We can see clearly that the end of following Christ whole-heartily is to share in His very end: "Martyrdom is not some kind of rare experience for the very few because they were not wise enough to avoid the consequence; it is the normative, logical result of faith in Christ, if we pursue Him truly, because we live in a world that is hostile against Him."[794]

May we trust the Lord afresh for a vibrant work of His Spirit in our lives today to be His witnesses *(martyrs)* of the Gospel.

---

[793] Romans 8:35-36
[794] Art Katz (1929-2007)

Epilogue: The Call To Gather as Fellowships

THIS BOOK has been prepared to encourage believers to gather in small gatherings under the Headship of Jesus Christ.[795] Thus no man is head over the fellowships as a whole that gather in this way. Though servant leaders are submitted to, there is no one brother over all fellowships controlling them. True submission to authority in the Church should not be because of someone who was voted in or hired but because of their spiritual walk with the Lord. Thus people submit to them willingly seeing Christ formed in them and desiring to emulate their walk with the Lord.[796]

Each *Gospel Fellowship* meeting is autonomous and accountable to the Lord directly,[797] and as the Lord networks groups together they will mutually submit to each other for accountability as the Spirit leads them. Leaders will be raised up by the Lord as He brings out their giftings.[798] When gatherings multiply and expand some brothers will have responsibility over many groups to shepherd them.[799] We believe there is a movement of the Spirit to gather believers as the Bride of Christ. We believe this book is simply a response to what the

---

[795] Colossians 1:18
[796] 1 Peter 5:3
[797] Revelation 2:7
[798] Ephesians 4:11-13
[799] 1 Peter 5:2

Lord is already doing in these last days, to purify and grow His Church and His Kingdom.

Even though being called of God to start a gathering does not demand that you be accountable to another spiritual brother, there is great wisdom in seeking to be under an elder brother. It is helpful to be connected with other brothers in the local area that you can respect and unify with who are in already established house churches. Even if a brother is involved in a denominational church, it can be wise to be spiritually submitted to[800] that brother although the new gathering of believers will not be under that denomination. Yet, in a time of apostasy especially, there will be situations where you cannot submit to other pastors in your area and you are free by the leading of the Lord to start a new work though it can come with ridicule and misunderstanding.

You do not need permission to gather as the Church in groups of even just 2-3 believers.[801] You do not need permission to break the Lord's Supper or baptize someone who is clearly following Jesus Christ as a disciple.

"The first step to starting a house Church is to pray. House Church ministry must be birthed in prayer. Though it is a simple step, without prayer and God's leading, we invite trouble."[802] Prayer is the foundation of every true work of God that builds the Lord's kingdom. Thus to begin to pray and cry out to the Lord together in small gatherings will be a healthy atmosphere for the Lord to begin to *show favor to the humble.*[803] From there also allow the Lord to practically guide and be Head of the meetings.

The rest of the book is given as a resource for such groups gathering under the Headship of Jesus Christ: Preparing the body of Christ for persecution *(Appendix I)*, Select teachings for *Gospel Fellowships (Appendix II)*, *Gospel Fellowships* additional resources *(Appendix III).*

These *Appendix* sections are here for reference and study as needed. We encourage believers gathering in small groups to use them as a basis of unity. Believers might not fully agree with every

---

[800] Ephesians 5:21
[801] Matthew 18:20
[802] Larry Kreider
[803] 1 Peter 5:5

statement in this book but we do believe the majority of statements are an effective unifying tool for the body of Christ as they gather together under the Headship of Jesus Christ.

Gospel Fellowships is about Jesus Christ.[804] He is the purpose for everything.[805] He is the reason for us gathering.[806] His Name is the greatest Name.[807] He is the Head of the Church.[808] The Life of the believer.[809] The glory of God![810] Jesus and Him alone should be our attention. Many have not yet experienced and know[811] this glorious Name above every name.[812]

May God give us a firm faith in the work of the Holy Spirit to network and birth gatherings in local areas as we follow the Lord in obedience.

"At midnight the cry rang out: 'Here's the Bridegroom! Come out to meet Him!'"[813] "Blessed are those who wash their robes, that they may have the right to the tree of life and may go through the gates into the city."[814]

Lord, Your Church will never fail. We look to You as the end of the age approaches. May all glory be to the Lamb. May His Gospel be shared with all. Please do this Father for Your Name's sake and honor. We long to be with You in robes of white in endless eternity. Redeem Your Saints at the appointed time. Gather Your Elect to be a Bride for Your Son. Through Your Spirit work a work no man can put his name on so all glory will be given to You. Amen.

---

[804] Hebrews 12:2
[805] Colossians 1:16
[806] Ephesians 1:22-23
[807] Isaiah 45:23, Philippians 2:9-11
[808] Colossians 1:18
[809] Galatians 2:20
[810] John 1:14
[811] John 17:3
[812] Philippians 2:9
[813] Matthew 25:6
[814] Revelation 22:14

Appendix I

Preparing the Body of Christ for Persecution

Preparing for Persecution;
To Be a Christian

by brother Edgar

THE GREATEST failure of the Church in many nations is the lack of preparing Christians for persecution.

Persecution is certain. It is told to us by the Lord Jesus Christ, the Son of God, Himself. In the Gospel of John it says: "Remember what I told you: 'A servant is not greater than his Master.' If they persecuted Me, they will persecute you also."[815] We can believe what Jesus says and we can rely on it. Also in the United States of America and Canada, persecution is certain. In the second Epistle to Timothy it says: "In fact, everyone who wants to live a godly life in Christ Jesus will be persecuted."[816]

Chinese Pastors lamented that they had failed to prepare their Churches for persecution. During the Boxer rebellion in China, 236 foreign missionaries were killed and became Martyrs. Twenty-three thousand Chinese Christians were killed and became Martyrs. Later, missionaries were admitted again and the Chinese Church grew. Thousands of Christians were martyred in the following years and hundreds of thousands were imprisoned during the cultural revolution of Mao Zedong. Following Mao Zedong, there was further

---

[815] John 15:20
[816] 2 Timothy 3:12

persecution by Chinese Communism. Again thousands were martyred and hundreds of thousands were imprisoned and tortured for Christ. During each wave of persecution the seeds of the Gospel in China were planted anew in the blood of the martyrs. With persecution the Church in China is flourishing. Estimates of the number of Christians vary up to *100 Million Christians*. How is that possible with such persecution? They are endued with the power of God.[817] He is with them. He leads them and they follow.

If we follow Jesus and if we live godly lives we will be persecuted and hated.[818] If I am not persecuted I likely do not live a godly life. I am missing out somewhere on what it means to be a Christian. I need to remember that the meaning of the word martyr is *witness*.

THE CHANGE IS COMING

The world is changing quickly. Our faith is also beginning to be under attack also in the Western hemisphere. We see a rapid progression towards a one world government and a single world leader. The club of Rome, a secret group of political and financial leaders, has proposed 10 world regions. A one world religious system is in the plans that will be headed by a single leader. The Bible calls him the false prophet. This religious system will deny Jesus, the Son of the living God. We will have to stand for the Truth.

The Book of Revelation describes a great tribulation. In the Book of Revelation, the Apostle John had been taken into heaven and he saw in heaven a multitude which no one could number.[819] Since they were in heaven, they must have died and gone to heaven. So who are these people? How did they get there and how did they die? In Revelation chapter 7, John is told: "These are they who have come out of the great tribulation."[820] In other words, these are Christians who have lived on earth, endured persecution and then died. What did they die of? Scripture does not tell us in Revelation chapter 7, but there is another passage that gives us an indication. In Revelation 20 it says: "I saw thrones on which were seated those who had been

---

[817] Luke 24:49
[818] 1 John 3:13
[819] Revelation 7:9
[820] Revelation 7:14

given authority to judge. And I saw the souls of those who had been beheaded because of their testimony about Jesus and because of the Word of God. They had not worshiped the beast or its image and had not received its mark on their foreheads or their hands. They came to life and reigned with Christ a thousand years."[821] Please note the word *beheaded*. This indicates a martyr's death, where the head of a person is cut off from his body.

Many Christians, if they stand strong for the Lord Jesus will be beheaded for their witness. Some have been beheaded already in Middle Eastern countries and in past persecutions. If we think of nations where beheadings take place today we realize that they are Muslim nations. We should love Muslim people because the Bible exhorts us to love our enemies.[822] However, we must not accept their faith. God says to love all sinners but we need not love their sin. The Muslim faith is built on muhammad the prophet, and allah who do not acknowledge Jesus Christ as the Son of God and as the Messiah. God opened up heaven and spoke to us by way of a voice to give us a sign to show us who His Son is that we might believe only in Him. In the Gospel of Matthew it states: "As soon as Jesus was baptized, He went up out of the water. At that moment heaven was opened, and he saw the Spirit of God descending like a dove and alighting on Him. And a voice from heaven said, 'This is My Son, whom I love; with Him I am well pleased.'"[823]

The person who was baptizing Jesus was John the Baptist. John became a witness and he gave a written record of his witness in the Gospel of John: "Then John gave this testimony: 'I saw the Spirit come down from heaven as a dove and remain on Him. And I myself did not know Him, but the One who sent me to baptize with water told me, The Man on whom you see the Spirit come down and remain is the One who will baptize with the Holy Spirit. I have seen and I testify that this is God's Chosen One.'"[824]

We know from the testimony of John the Baptist and from the testimony of God the Father that it was not mohammad in the water, it was not buddha, and it was not a Hindu god that was being

---

[821] Revelation 20:4
[822] Matthew 5:44
[823] Matthew 3:16-17
[824] John 1:32-34

baptized. It was Jesus Christ the Son of the only true God in this universe. Then Scripture tells us in 1 John: "Who is the liar? It is whoever denies that Jesus is the Christ. Such a person is the antichrist —denying the Father and the Son."[825]

Satan seeks to destroy humanity, which was created by God. He is a murderer and father of lies. Satan's lies have invaded the minds of men to create religions that do not acknowledge[826] the One and only true God and His Son the Lord Jesus Christ. These religions draw mankind into believing faiths that cannot save. There is no Savior except Jesus the Son of God.

We must stand strong in our faith even during persecution and proclaim that Jesus the Son of God is the Savior and Messiah. He is our only hope to have our sins forgiven, to have peace with God and to receive eternal life.

How will I respond when persecution comes? Am I afraid to die? Am I afraid of torture? Will I deny the true God? Will I deny my Jesus? It is easy to answer: *Of course I won't deny my Lord.* When the trials come will I stand or fall away?

OVERCOMING SIN AND PERSECUTION

We need to call on the Victor, the Lord Jesus, to overcome sin, overcome opposition, overcome the fear of death, overcome torture, overcome persecution and to help us live a godly life. Pastor Wurmbrand showed a Unites States senate sub-committee most of the deep torture wounds he had received. There were 18 deep torture wounds, where the flesh had been cut out of him. Several wounds were the size of a man's fist. He said when he was being tortured no Scripture verse could help him—he could not remember any— nothing could help him except the living Son of God, the Christ, who lived inside of him and helped him. The Son of God—the Lord Jesus Christ—is not only seated at the right hand of the Father, but He is also God and Omnipresent, which means He is present everywhere. Christ is inside of us for Scripture says: "I have been crucified with Christ and I no longer live, but *Christ lives in me.* The

---

[825] 1 John 2:22
[826] 1 John 4:3

life I now live in the body, I live by faith in the Son of God, who loved me and gave Himself for me."[827] 1 John 4 says: "You, dear children, are from God and have overcome them, because the One who is in you is greater than the one who is in the world."[828] Satan is like a roaring lion surrounding us to see how he might destroy and kill us. He wants to take away our testimonies and attacks those who live a godly life. As we yield and surrender to Jesus we will have victory in Jesus. "But thanks be to God! He gives us the victory through our Lord Jesus Christ."[829]

Then I must be taught for the coming persecution to learn selflessness, forgiveness, sacrificial and unconditional love. I heard Pastor Wurmbrand in the Peoples church of Toronto, about 40 years ago. There were nearly 2000 people in the church. He walked in without shoes. It became so quiet you could hear a pin drop. The ushers rushed to the podium to put a chair in front of the podium. He sat down quietly and opened his mouth. The Holy Spirit started to fill the auditorium as he opened his lips and then we heard him speak. He said: "Dear sisters and brothers forgive me for sitting down. I have been beaten many times and my feet are broken many times. I cannot wear shoes now and I have difficulty standing. People want me to speak about the evil Communists who beat and tortured me. I cannot do that, you see I am at fault." There were gasps in the audience. We all thought how could he be at fault? He suffered for the Gospel of Christ. Then Pastor Wurmbrand continued: "You see," he said, "they are not at fault, I am at fault, I just did not love enough."

LOVING OUR ENEMIES GREATLY

I wondered if I could love someone who cuts 18 pieces of flesh from me. I wondered about my church where people had bumped each other and they hated each other. I wondered about myself, when attacked by a sister or brother, did I love them? Did I feel it is an option to love them? Does Jesus want my obedience or do I have a choice? Must I follow what Jesus said in *Matthew 5*? There it says:

---

[827] Galatians 2:20
[828] 1 John 4:4
[829] 1 Corinthians 15:57

"But I tell you, love your enemies and pray for those who persecute you."[830] So I wondered? Am I supposed to do 4 things for a person that hates me and tortures me? Love them, bless them, do good to them and pray for them? Pastor Wurmbrand loved those people that cut 18 pieces of flesh out of him. Stephen, when he was stoned to death prayed: "Lord, do not hold this sin against them."[831] What would I have prayed? Lord help me? Get me out of this? Stop this evil? No, Stephen was more concerned about those who were killing him than his own life. Jesus said from the cross while dying a tortured death: "Father, forgive them, for they do not know what they are doing."[832] What about me? What about you?

LOVING OUR BROTHERS AND SISTERS

The Bible says we are not even Christians if we can't love our brothers or sisters! How much more our enemies. In 1 John 3 it says: "This is how we know who the children of God are and who the children of the devil are: Anyone who does not do what is right is not God's child, nor is anyone who does not love their brother and sister."[833] Also it says: "We know that we have passed from death to life, because we love each other. Anyone who does not love remains in death."[834] In 1 John 3 it also says: "If anyone has material possessions and sees a brother or sister in need but has no pity on them, how can the love of God be in that person?"[835] 1 John 4 says: "Whoever claims to love God yet hates a brother or sister is a liar. For whoever does not love their brother and sister, whom they have seen, cannot love God, whom they have not seen."[836]

---

[830] Matthew 5:44
[831] Acts 7:60
[832] Luke 23:34
[833] 1 John 3:10
[834] 1 John 3:14
[835] 1 John 3:17
[836] 1 John 4:20

SIGNS OF TRUE CHRISTIANS IN CHINA

When viewing a DVD of the Chinese underground Church made by Chinese Christians called *The Cross: Jesus In China*,[837] I saw many signs of what true Christians are like. They have:
- A personal relationship with Jesus.
- Unity with the believers.
- A deep desire to worship God.
- A great love for each other and their persecutors. They are hated yet they loved.
- Deep faith. Their persecution never stops, including jail many times. Some itinerant preachers have gone to prison 10 or more times. They face torture, beatings, electric shock and loss of life. Yet they trust the Lord and they love.
- They love not their lives unto death. Two deceased martyrs were shown in the video, with one being partially uncovered to show part of his torture wounds. Yet they love their enemies.[838]
- They accept that love means devotion, selflessness, sacrifice, and even death.
- Their path of the cross is suffering and sacrifice.
- There is deep repentance on many faces, with tears streaming down their faces.
- They have power from the Holy Spirit to witness.
- There is the power of the Holy Spirit by way of miracles, healings and driving out demons.[839]
- There is great humbleness, including great humbleness in their leaders.
- One leader could not overcome torture and he denounced Christ Jesus. He was released. In the video he was seen walking back into prison with his wife. He said he could no longer deny his Lord and would rather die in prison.
- There is deep joy. They use poetry and song to express what is in their minds and hearts. They convey through song the beauty of Jesus. Their music reflects the innocence and joy of Christians as inspired by the Holy Spirit.

---

[837] Free documentary available at: *chinasoul.org*
[838] Matthew 5:44
[839] Mark 16:17-18

- A visiting pastor was asked to give a sermon. "How long?" he asked. "An hour?" "Oh no!" "Two hours?" "Oh no!" "How long, then?" he asked. "Could you preach from early in the morning to late at night, please?" he was asked. Then the pastor realized that they did not have Bibles.

- They meet in homes, in barns, in caves, in underground tunnels and in fields, hoping to avoid detection. Yet they are busy witnessing despite the threat to their lives.

CLEANSING AND FILLING OF THE SPIRIT

Oh how my heart burns. What will we do when that kind of persecution comes us in non-persecuted countries? We must learn from our brothers and sisters in persecuted countries. Will we still follow our Lord? Will we meet in house Churches? Will we meet in the underground? We must start now to follow the Word of God in truth and in the Spirit of God.

My first step back *to live a godly life* comes with my confession to the Lord that I fell short. I need to understand His Word better, and to look at the early Church. I need to repent of my lukewarmness, of my selfishness, of my materialism, of my search for pleasure, of my pride and my unwillingness to live a life fully yielded to Jesus. I must repent of not presenting my body as a living sacrifice.[840] I must repent of not taking up the cross and following Jesus Christ.[841]

In 1 John it says: "If we confess our sins, He is faithful and just and will forgive us our sins and purify us from all unrighteousness."[842]

Once I am cleansed I then need to pray to our Heavenly Father to fill me with His Holy Spirit. We cannot overcome through our own might or power. The Lord says we can only overcome by His Spirit.[843] We need to pray and ask God the Father to give us the fullness of His Spirit.

In the Gospel of Luke it says: "Then Jesus said to them, 'Suppose you have a friend, and you go to him at midnight and say, 'Friend,

---

840 Romans 12:1
841 Mark 8:34
842 1 John 1:9
843 Zechariah 4:6

lend me three loaves of bread; a friend of mine on a journey has come to me, and I have no food to offer him.' And suppose the one inside answers, 'Don't bother me. The door is already locked, and my children and I are in bed. I can't get up and give you anything.' I tell you, even though he will not get up and give you the bread because of friendship, yet because of your shameless audacity he will surely get up and give you as much as you need.

"So I say to you: Ask and it will be given to you; seek and you will find; knock and the door will be opened to you. For everyone who asks receives; the one who seeks finds; and to the one who knocks, the door will be opened. Which of you fathers, if your son asks for a fish, will give him a snake instead? Or if he asks for an egg, will give him a scorpion? If you then, though you are evil, know how to give good gifts to your children, how much more will your Father in heaven give the Holy Spirit to those who ask Him!"[844]

Beloved sisters and brothers pray with all of your might and surrender anew to Jesus. Give up all that stands in the way of God, and ask Him to give you the filling of the Holy Spirit. This will enable you to stand in the time of persecution and to be a witness for our Lord and Savior Jesus Christ. Let it be so. *Amen.*

---

[844] Luke 11:5-13

The Coming Tsunami of Persecution

by brother Greg

"THEN YOU will be handed over to be persecuted and put to death, and you will be hated by all nations because of Me. At that time many will turn away from the faith and will betray and hate each other."[845]

Our Lord spoke these sobering words to us, as found in the Gospel of Matthew chapter 24. Something in us does not want to accept the idea that in the end times *all nations will hate and persecute Christians.* This seems like a non-reality to us and something that could never happen because we live in such religiously tolerant countries such as Canada, United Kingdom and United States. We would like to edit our Lord's Words and abbreviate them with a softer less harsh reality. Yet, this will not change the truth our Lord said would happen.

We live in cultures that turn away from pain of any kind, there are pills and remedies for even the slightest discomfort in our bodies. In such an environment persecution and suffering in our bodies for the faith of Jesus Christ seems even more absurd. There is not only a confusion over these things but there is a danger of complacency and

---

[845] Matthew 24:9-10

comfort that will have us even more unprepared for the time that will come upon us.

A TSUNAMI IS COMING

I recently watched a short documentary on the sad events of the December 26, 2004, tsunami that hit Indonesia and caused almost a quarter of a million deaths. It is well known as the *Boxing Day Tsunami.*

The video showed the Tsunami spreading to different regions, hitting the shores of heavily populated areas. What struck me was the complacency of the people in the different areas, even the amusement of it all. At one beach they see a white crescent on the distant horizon spreading across the entire large bay. People watch mesmerized as this white crescent comes nearer and nearer. When the wave swallows up two ships in the bay some of the watchers realize the magnitude of the event that is about to strike but for most it is too late. In another shoreline people smile and laugh in amusement as the entire bay is emptied of water and ships are beached. It begins as a spectacle that is full of fun and amusement as people take pictures. As the water came back in they considered it something fun to watch. When the wave struck that shoreline, many were caught unawares; their running was in vain and multitudes were screaming as they were swallowed in the waves and dragged back out to sea, never to return.

As I watched the video a great sobriety came over me—not just over the deaths of so many people—of what is about to come upon the Christians of the world, with some of us not being aware of the times we are living in. Many of us do not believe this could be the end of time.

Just as the tsunami came without warning, so will the end times persecution come upon many Christians unawares. I am not arguing for any type of position of the rapture of the church, whether pre or post, in this short article. Yet I believe firmly that we will all feel like we are in the great tribulation when this end time persecution wave hits the Church. The birth pains will become worse and worse, and many of those that have believed in a pre-tribulation rapture that would have them escape from all suffering will be 100% unprepared for what is going to come upon them.

Persecution of Christians has not diminished, but has been increasing yearly world wide.

More Christians were martyred in the twentieth century than in all previous centuries combined. Most of the Apostles (*Philip, Matthew, Mark, Peter, Paul*) were martyred. Many were martyred in the Middle Ages (*Huss, Jerome, Joan of Arc*). Between 1540 and 1570 over one million Protestants were publicly put to death in various countries in Europe. Overall, some 50 million were martyred by the Roman Catholic inquisition for *heresy* between 606 AD and the middle of the nineteenth century. Protestant reformers (*Tyndale, Latimer, Cranmer*) were martyred. Some 20 million were martyred during the 70 years of Russian atheism and Communism.

The Apostle John said to the Church in his day that they should not be surprised if the world hated them.[846] Our Lord Jesus said in the Gospel of Luke that all men will hate us.[847] But our Lord also gives us comfort in these words: "If the world hates you, keep in mind that it hated Me first."[848]

"Persecution is always meant for evil, but God always means it for good. And is it not better to suffer in this life to have an extra weight of glory in heaven?"[849]

May we prepare in our minds to suffer for the Name of Christ in our bodies.[850] May we be aware of the times and seasons that are coming upon us.

TORTURE AND MARTYRDOM

"Some Christians they proved by fire, others by the sword, others by wild beasts; yet others tasted martyrdom from cudgels and iron claws."[851] Torture not just martyrdom, has been the experience of many of God's saints in history.

Christians throughout the centuries have been subject to the worst of tortures. The evil of men has excelled in its implements of

---

[846] 1 John 3:13
[847] Luke 21:17
[848] John 15:18
[849] Paul Washer
[850] 1 Peter 4:1
[851] Antonio Gallonio (1556-1605)

torture as they punished those they deemed the worst criminals of mankind. Christians who are the light of the world and the salt of the earth are considered the dung and refuse of the earth. The most heinous acts imaginable have been the experience of those least deserving them. History will never truly tell what satan-filled men have done to the righteous of the earth. This sort of thing seems far-fetched to the modern mind yet all across the world these things still occur and will occur more at an alarming rate. An end time persecution of the Church of God is coming and will be worldwide.

Several years ago I was led on a tour of a German castle on the Rhine River. What beautiful architecture, with inlaid stone rooms, pathways and wonderful views of the German countryside! Through room after room we walked, ending the tour by going into the lower rooms of the castle. As we entered the last room I noticed right away some of the devices in the room that clearly showed me it was a room where individuals had been imprisoned. Also, more shockingly, there were implements of torture, including crowns with spikes on them and racks to stretch bodies. My mind raced through Church history to realize this room could have very well been a place were Anabaptist dissenters were tortured for their faith in Jesus Christ.

It should not surprise us that there have been so many martyrdoms in Church history, beginning with the murders of all the Apostles except the Apostle John whom they attempted to boil alive in oil—but he survived—afterwards being exiled to the prison island of Patmos. According to tradition, this is the list of the Apostles' deaths by martyrdom: Apostle Andrew, martyrdom by crucifixion (*bound to a cross*). Apostle Bartholomew, martyrdom by being flayed alive and crucified, head downward. Apostle James the Greater, martyrdom by being stabbed with a sword. Apostle James the Lesser, martyrdom by being thrown from a pinnacle of the Temple at Jerusalem, and then stoned and beaten with clubs. Apostle Mark, was dragged in the streets until his death. Apostle Jude, martyrdom by being beaten to death with a club. Apostle Matthew, martyrdom by being beheaded. Apostle Peter, martyrdom by crucifixion at Rome with his head downwards. Apostle Philip martyred. Apostle Simon, martyrdom by being sawn in half. Apostle Thomas, martyrdom by being stabbed with a spear. Apostle Paul, martyrdom by being beheaded in Rome.

One could rightly rename the first historical Book of the Church from Acts of the Apostles to *Acts of the Martyrs*.

GOD IS RAISING UP END TIME MISSIONARIES

Many of us in the modern Church age consider martyrdom something of a quick death where those involved would pass away quickly. Yet in Church history it has been the opposite, where faithful Christians have endured great torture and death at the hands of wicked men. I am writing these things not to condemn or frighten anyone but to give us the proper respect and realization of the suffering many have undergone in the Name of Christ, and will also undergo in the coming future persecution. Just as the Church began with a powerful revival of the Word of God—spread through the anointed Apostles' lips—it will end with a great revival of Gospel preaching, yet under similar circumstances of martyrdom and suffering. God is raising up end time missionaries that have no fear of death and have such a great realization of the love of Jesus Christ that they will suffer everything to spread this precious Gospel to the ends of the earth.

A LIST OF TORTURES

Here is a list of some of the various tortures used widely against Christians in church history (*These tortures were widely used in Church history and there is evidence of some of these today. Jesus will be with us in our hour of greatest need. We caution those who are young in the faith or who are not able to bear it, to go on to the next section. We ask that you please read this list reverently, as such things occurred to countless brothers and sisters in the faith of Jesus Christ throughout the last 2000 years.*) May God prepare us to suffer more to spread this great Gospel of His love:

Martyrs suspended by one foot. Nailed to the cross, head downwards. Hung up by both arms, heavy weights being attached to the feet. Christian woman suspended by the hair. Martyrs hung up by one arm only, ponderous stones being fastened to their feet. Martyr suspended by both feet, and a great stone fastened to his neck. Sometimes the blessed martyrs, after being smeared with honey were bound to stakes fixed in the ground, and then exposed to the rays of the sun to be tortured by the stings of flies and bees.

Martyr suspended by the feet, and his body and head at the same time pounded with hammers. Sometimes martyrs were bound to the circumference of great wheels, and so hurled from a height over stony places. Martyr whose limbs were interwoven in the spokes of a wheel, on which he was left exposed for days, till he died. Martyr crushed in the press, just as grapes and olives are pressed in making wine and oil. Martyr bound to four stakes and beaten with cudgels. Martyr thrown headfirst into a caldron full of molten lead or boiling oil. Martyr in a large hot frying-pan.

Martyr cast into a burning fiery furnace. Martyr who's limbs are amputated one by one. Hands and feet cut off. Sawn in two with an iron saw. Martyr tortured by having sharp reeds stuck under his finger and toe nails. Martyr thrown down naked to be devoured by wild lions. Martyr wrapped in a wild beast's hide, and so left to be torn by animals.

A DAY OF GRACE AND PREPARATION

Oh saints of God, may we weep for such faithful ones that endured so much for that precious Name of Christ that we speak of at times so freely. There is a force of evil so strong that will be fully loosed in the last days to wreak havoc on the Church of God in the earth. This time—right now—is a season of grace to spread the Gospel far and wide, and to meet regularly to encourage each other in the things of the kingdom of God. A day is coming when our freedoms will be gone in the West, Bibles will be burned, churches closed and end time suffering and martyrdom will ensue.

No matter how much persecution and torture we have to endure, we can steadfastly know that Christ is with us. He has promised to never leave or forsake us. Great shall be our consolation soon, as the Apostle Paul said of every earthly trial, "For our light and momentary troubles are achieving for us an eternal glory that far outweighs them all."[852]

---

852 2 Corinthians 4:17

For an entire life of suffering in this present age is nothing compared to the reward of eternity we will soon be enjoying in heaven. It is the martyr's crown, an emblem of beauty, righteousness and commitment for eternity.

As the martyrs' blood wets the ground, where they have put their seed—their life—there will be an abundance of new lives saved for God who see their witness. God may require of you and I such sacrifice and such a witness that many might be saved, which might include our torturers.

PRACTICAL SUGGESTIONS FOR PREPARATION

We offer a few practical suggestions:

1) To start with, read—to yourself and your family—the lives of martyrs in the Christian faith. One such book widely available is: *Foxes Book of Martyrs*.

2) Develop a theology of suffering from the Scriptures and don't allow small inconveniences and pains to disturb you. The Romanian pastor who suffered much under communism gives us some good advice: "Preparation for underground work begins by studying sufferology, martyrology. The preparation for underground work is deep spiritualization. As we peel an onion in preparation for its use, so God must *peel* from us what are mere words, sensations of our enjoyments in religion, in order to arrive at the reality of our faith. Jesus has told us that *whosoever will follow* Him will have to *take up their cross*, and He, Himself, showed how heavy this cross can be. We have to be prepared for this."[853]

3) Study the Scriptures towards the theme of martyrdom especially in the Book of Revelation. Learn to practice memorization as an underground Church pastor did while in solitary confinement: "I read the Bible from memory. To memorize the Bible is very important for an underground worker."[854]

May we also be bold to stand for the Name of Jesus Christ before others, and therefore not be ashamed before Him at His coming.[855]

---

[853] Richard Wurmbrand (1909-2001)
[854] Ibid.
[855] 1 John 2:28

A Plain Vision for Coming Persecution

by brother Brian

[EDITOR'S NOTE: It is time to be *utterly astounded* as God spoke to the prophet Habakuk. Brother Brian gives a clear clarion call to God's Remnant in many Churches and Assemblies. The message concludes with 3 distinct challenges for believers: 1) To reread the Book of Acts in a single sitting if possible. 2) Consider starting or being involved in a prayer meeting 3) And lastly to cry out to God afresh for the *true* Baptism of the Holy Spirit of God. We encourage saints to respond to this message as the Holy Spirit leads you in these 3 areas. Below is the message transcript]:

Thank you dear brother. I have that *Testimony of Algerius*[856] written down. I had actually written down his testimony at home and have it in my study. It has ministered to me time and time again. The Glory of Jesus in the Dungeon. He found *infinite sweetness in the bowels of the lion*—I don't think I will ever forget that expression.

I am very grateful to be here with you tonight. I do have a burden on my heart that I am convinced—absolutely persuaded—is from the Lord. I want you to turn with me to the Book of Habakkuk. We will begin in chapter 2.

---

[856] Algerius (AD 1557)

HABAKKUK SEES THE VISION

"I will stand at my watch and station myself on the ramparts; I will look to see what He will say to me, and what answer I am to give to this complaint. Then the Lord replied: 'Write down the revelation and make it plain on tablets so that a herald may run with it. For the revelation awaits an appointed time; it speaks of the end and will not prove false. Though it linger, wait for it; it will certainly come and will not delay.'"[857]

Now the vision that the prophet Habakkuk saw was a burden from the Lord. You notice, if you would, in the first verse of chapter 1:

"The prophecy that Habakkuk the prophet received."[858]

His burden was a vision from the Lord. A vision that God said would surely come. It wasn't that it might come to pass; it wasn't that it could come to pass. He said:

"Though it linger, wait for it; it will certainly come and will not delay."[859]

Now there are two parts to this vision that I want to share with you tonight. Then having shared the vision, I want us to see how we are to run with it because that is what He says:

"Write down the revelation and make it plain on tablets so that a herald may run with it."[860]

So first of all, the vision: what was it that the prophet Habakkuk saw? What was it that God said would surely come? He first saw a vision of coming judgment. It was judgment that was sure to come from the hand of God to Judah. According to the Word of the Lord in chapter 1, the judgment of the Lord was surely coming.

HABAKKUK PRAYS TO GOD

And the way that God was going to send judgment was not exactly what the prophet Habakkuk had in mind or had expected God to answer him in his prayer. He had been praying, verse 2:

---

[857] Habakkuk 2:1-3
[858] Habakkuk 1:1
[859] Habakkuk 2:3
[860] Habakkuk 2:2

"How long, Lord, must I call for help, but you do not listen? Or cry out to you, 'Violence!' but you do not save? Why do you make me look at injustice? Why do you tolerate wrongdoing? Destruction and violence are before me; there is strife, and conflict abounds. Therefore the law is paralyzed, and justice never prevails. The wicked hem in the righteous, so that justice is perverted."[861]

Habakkuk is praying. He is interceding for God's people. And he is saying 'How long? How long, Lord?' How long will the iniquity, the perversion, the violence, the lawlessness, the injustice in this land continue? How long will you show me all of this trouble in our nation and yet it seems like You're not doing anything about it? How long, Lord, will godly people pray revival and yet there is no revival?

He was crying out to God from an honest heart. He was praying for God to stop the sin and the decay, and to stop this dishonor and disgrace that was being brought to the Name of God through God's people. And yet it seemed like God was not answering.

How long will godly pray and there is no revival? And he is begging God to turn God's people back to Him in repentance. Brothers and sisters, how long have we prayed the same way? I know I am not the only one. How long have we prayed for revival? I remember the first conference that was held here. The burden I came to Atlanta with—with such expectation that there was a revival conference—and I knew something about *SermonIndex* so I knew this is real revival we're talking about—and fully expecting that after this conference, we're going to see a great spiritual awakening. How long have we prayed for revival yet there is no revival?

GOD DOES ANSWER PRAYER

Granted, God has moved in little pockets around the nation. He is moving, but I am talking about spiritual awakening—the kind of revival that turns the whole tide of a nation, a city or even a society. We've not seen that in this nation. We've not seen anything that compares to the great awakenings of the past nor the great revivals like the Welsh revival or the Hebrides revival. We've prayed and yet God hasn't answered like we might have expected Him to. I want to

[861] Habakkuk 1:2-4

tell you tonight that God does answer. God has heard those prayers. God heard the prayer of Habakkuk and He answers. Maybe not like Habakkuk expected Him to answer, maybe not like we expected God to answer, but God speaks and here's His answer in verse 5:

"Look at the nations and watch—and be utterly amazed. For I am going to do something in your days that you would not believe, even if you were told."[862]

Now that sounds amazing to me when God says 'be utterly amazed. For I am going to do something in your days that you would not believe, even if you were told.' But the question is what kind of work? In the next verse, God says:

"I am raising up the Babylonians, that ruthless and impetuous people, who sweep across the whole earth to seize dwellings not their own."[863]

I am going to work a work in your day and here's the work: I'm raising up the Babylonians. Who are they? These were not God-fearing people. These were enemies of God; enemy armies that God would sovereignly raise up and use as an instrument of His judgment to chasten His own people. And can you believe it? Can you believe God would do that? Maybe that's why God said 'be utterly amazed. For I am going to do something in your days that you would not believe, even if you were told.'

THE COMING PERSECUTION

Keith Green said, several years ago; when God wants to speak to His people, He will do it in three ways. First; He will touch their economy. He will touch them where it hurts, in their economy. If that doesn't work, if that doesn't turn God's people to repentance, then God will touch their ecology. Then you have floods and pestilences, hurricanes, a drought this year that has covered a huge part of this nation, tornados, hurricanes, tsunamis. Lastly though he said, God will raise up a nation to come in and invade them.

That is exactly the judgment that God is pronouncing here and that is the judgment that is soon to come upon this nation and upon

---

862 Habakkuk 1:5
863 Habakkuk 1:6

North America. God is sovereignly raising up enemy armies to invade a nation and, America, this nation, believes she's too strong for that. Her military forces are too strong for that. *That will never happen!* I want to tell you tonight, that this nation sits on the brink of utter destruction. She is ripe for the judgment of God. Judgment is at the door. America will not have a godly president to save the day, nor the nation.

National leaders and politicians will become even more corrupt. Muslims and other antichrist groups will be God's instrument of judgment and what is most surprising of all, probably, is that this holy Remnant—and she is found all over the earth, gathered in all kinds of different congregations—that has seen the King, that has come to know Jesus and is following Him wholeheartedly, she will be persecuted by people who profess to be Christians. Churches, if you will, persecuting them because they are not pledging allegiance to patriotism or anything else but the Lamb of God—and she will be arrested, we will be imprisoned, hated, beaten and even executed in this nation. I want to tell you brothers and sisters, when it happens, do not think that God's hands are tied. Don't think that this has taken God by surprise. God has actually executed the judgment however and whenever He chooses. We need to see the sovereign hand of God behind it all. I love what the brother said earlier, *the lions had to look up.* God here raised up the Babylonians, and God is a God who will allow even His people to suffer at the hands of the enemies.

JUDGMENT IS SURELY COMING

His hands are not tied. Judgment is surely coming. That is a hard message for some to embrace. Habakkuk himself is wrestling with this. He says in verse 12:

"Lord, are you not from everlasting? My God, my Holy One, You will never die. You, Lord, have appointed them to execute judgment; You, my Rock, have ordained them to punish. Your eyes are too pure to look on evil; You cannot tolerate wrongdoing. Why then do You tolerate the treacherous? Why are You silent while the wicked swallow up those more righteous than themselves?"[864]

Judgment was coming to Judah. Judgment is surely coming to North America but I want to remind you again tonight, that judgment must begin at the house of God.

"For it is time for judgment to begin with God's household; and if it begins with us, what will the outcome be for those who do not obey the Gospel of God?"[865]

Habakkuk's question in verse 13 was "Why then do You tolerate the treacherous? Why are You silent while the wicked swallow up those more righteous than themselves?"[866]   It's true that the Babylonians were more wicked than God's own people, Israel, but it's also true that Israel was sinning against much greater light. Brothers and sisters, the Muslims aren't holding a Bible in their hand, but the prosperity preacher is. The world's not holding a Bible in their hand, but I am. When God's people sin against God, they're sinning against a much greater light than the world or any other religion has.

The angry atheist doesn't claim to preach Jesus Christ nor do they rob from the people of God, but the wolf in the house of God does. The Communist doesn't claim to know Christ, but hypocrites in the house of God do. God will not always strive with such mixture in His house. There is coming a shaking. There is coming a sure and definite judgment to the house of God. A shaking where everything that can be shaken will be shaken and it will bring about a holy separation; from those who fear God and those who do not; those who know Christ and those who do not; those who have pledged their allegiance to Christ and those who haven't. It is coming. It is coming to the house of God.

JESUS CHRIST MUST HAVE PREEMINENCE

God is merciful and He is so patient. He has shown me more mercy than anybody I know. I will never give up on the mercy of God, but I will tell you this: He will not always strive with man and there is a judgment coming to the house of God. Jesus Christ is the

---

[864] Habakkuk 1:12-13
[865] 1 Peter 4:17
[866] Habakkuk 1:13

Head of the Church and He must have the preeminence in all. It's His Church, it's His body, it's His Bride—and I tell you, that any Assembly where Jesus Christ is not truly the Head is sliding rapidly to the judgment of God. Here's where we've got to make the vision plain; we've got to make it personal: do I honor Him as the Head of the house? It's not enough for us to memorize Scripture that says that Jesus Christ is the Head of the Church. It's not enough to know the Bible in our minds that says that Jesus must have the preeminence. The issue is do I honor Him as the Head? It's not enough to call Him King. Do you glorify Him as King? Do you obey Him as Lord? Do I obey Him as Lord?

There is hypocrisy in the house of God that comes under the judgment of God. We can preach—and before I could ever stand up here, God took me through weeks—because I never want to preach something I am not willing for God to do in and through me. I have asked myself these questions that I am posing to you tonight. How many of us listen to so many good messages? We even preach good Biblical messages but the issue is not can we preach them. Not, can we listen to many of them. The issue is *do we live them*? Are we the incarnation of these messages that we are receiving? There is more preaching today—good preaching—especially on *SermonIndex*; all these saints of the past. It's not the issue of how many sermons you listen to. Do you live them?

Listen, "Why do you call me, Lord, Lord' Jesus said, 'and do not do what I say?"[867] Why do you emphatically call me Lord and not obey? To live this way is to build your house on shifting sand and to have it all fall down and blown away in the coming storm.

There is lukewarmness in the house of God. This attempt to serve two masters,[868] and it will come under the judgment of God. There is coming a day where—people now are trying to combine allegiances. There will be a shaking. Christ alone or Christ not at all.

The pride of leaders and pastors who love to have the preeminence will have the rug pulled out from under them very soon, except they repent. Secret sin in the house of God; there is no fear of God and secret sin in the house of God is coming under the

---

[867] Luke 6:46
[868] Luke 16:13

judgment of God. Judgment is surely coming upon the American dream message of *Your Best Life Now*; the word of faith movement; the prosperity gospel—which is another gospel preaching another Jesus; a false gospel that promotes the love of money, self-centeredness and pride—and not only will God demand an account for the deception and dishonor to His Name in this nation, but He is especially going to demand an account of those who have spread it into the nations all across the world, and robbed the poor to line their greedy pockets. That is coming under the judgment of God.

A SHAKING IS COMING

Every house of worship where the Holy Spirit has been rejected, resisted, ignored—because we want to have Church without Him—is coming under the judgment of God. When the shaking comes, that house will shake and it will not stand. We cannot have Church apart from the Spirit of the Living God. He has been grieved. He has been resisted. He has been rejected. Listen to this Scripture from Ezekiel. We think of homosexuality and perversion—to God that was an abomination—God sent fire and brimstone on Sodom. But that was not the sin even mentioned here. These were the sins of your sister Sodom:

"Now this was the sin of your sister Sodom: She and her daughters were arrogant, overfed and unconcerned; they did not help the poor and needy."[869]

Arrogance. Pride. Overfed. We've been given so much, and yet unconcerned—as the poor and needy die outside the house of God. Have we abandoned our mission, Church of Jesus Christ? Have we forgotten the great commission to go and preach the Gospel to every creature?[870] And it's twofold: and also to make disciples of all nations teaching them to obey all that Christ has commanded us.[871] Have we forgotten that? Have we forgotten what true religion is in the house of God? Caring for the orphans, the widows in their trouble,[872] feeding the hungry, clothing the naked, ministering to the poor,

---

[869] Ezekiel 16:49
[870] Mark 16:15
[871] Matthew 28:18-20
[872] James 1:27

visiting those in prison and keeping yourself unspotted from the world. I tell you, because we have neglected this—we have not taken this seriously—judgment is coming to the house of God. But even that judgment will be an expression of God's mercy and love. The worst thing that could happen today is for God to allow Christendom to continue as She is without Him. And there is a clear distinction in 1 Peter 4 that God makes between the punishing judgment of God upon the unbeliever and the purifying judgment of God upon the believer.[873]

A PURIFYING OF THE CHURCH

The judgment that will be punishment for one will be purifying for another. For one it's punishment and utter destruction, but for the Remnant, that shaking, that persecution will be to test and try and refine His holy Remnant; His beloved Bride, His cherished Church.

Now I want you to watch this because someone inevitably says *a message of gloom and doom*. It's not gloom and doom to me. Gloom to me is for the Church to continue as She is. Hypocrisy in the house of God, hypocrisy in my heart: that's gloom. This is not a message of gloom and doom and this vision of judgment is not all that the prophet saw. He did see judgment coming. He saw the suffering of God's people coming but that's not all He saw. God says to the prophet Habakkuk: write down the vision and make it plain. Habakkuk what do you see? 'I see judgment that is sure to come. Persecution, yes. Incredible suffering of God's people, yes. A storm unlike we've ever experienced before, yes! But that's not all I see.' chapter 2 verse 14: surrounded by verse after verse of coming judgment, there's this little nugget like a nugget of gold hidden inside the side of a mountain:

"For the earth will be filled with the knowledge of the glory of the Lord as the waters cover the sea."[874]

What do you see, Habakkuk? Coming judgment but wait... I see something else. I see a coming glory. A glory that is so great that the knowledge of the glory of the Lord will cover the earth even as the

---

[873] 1 Peter 4:5, 1 Peter 4:17
[874] Habakkuk 2:14

waters cover the sea. Hallelujah! As the waters cover the sea—now where do the waters not cover the sea? Seas make up the waters. In other words, there is no place on earth where the glory of the Lord will not be known. Have you seen that, saints, through the eyes of faith? A coming glory that is a latter glory greater than the former—the greatest display of God's glory that has ever been known in the history of the world. A coming glory; where the knowledge of that glory will cover the earth even as the waters covers the sea. Why? Because in the fires of persecution, the Church gets purified. Yes, all who live godly in Christ Jesus shall suffer persecution but suffering for Christ and the sake of Christ always precedes glory. Suffering for Jesus equals glory to Jesus.

Paul the Apostle says in Romans 8:

"The Spirit himself testifies with our spirit that we are God's children. Now if we are children, then we are heirs—heirs of God and co-heirs with Christ, if indeed we share in His sufferings in order that we may also share in His glory. I consider that our present sufferings are not worth comparing with the glory that will be revealed in us."[875]

THE GLORY OF THE LORD REVEALED

Suffering. Glory! Suffering with Jesus precedes the glory of Jesus. His glory will be revealed where? According Romans 8, in the heavens somewhere? Among the stars? In some cathedral temple somewhere we have to go find? A man-made—no! In us! The glory of the Lord revealed in us! How? Through suffering. Through persecution. Habakkuk sees something else in verse 20 of chapter 2:

"The Lord is in His holy temple; let all the earth be silent before Him."[876] And the Lord, beloved, in His holy temple, through His holy temple will display His glory and the knowledge of that glory will cover the earth even as the waters cover the sea.

You remember under the old covenant when God chose to reveal His glory in the days of Moses. He commanded Moses to build the tabernacle. Moses built the tabernacle just as God had told him to do. And in that tabernacle, in the Holy of holies, the Shekhinah glory

---

[875] Romans 8:16-18
[876] Habakkuk 2:20

of God would come down. God's glory would rest among His people. God would visit His people in the tabernacle. The glory of the Lord displayed in the Holy of holies. And everybody who was there knew that the God of Abraham, Isaac and Jacob, He is God. The glory of the Lord.

But that tabernacle was one day no more and King David had a deep desire to build a house for the Lord: a temple for the Most High God. God honored that request in David but He said 'David, you're not going to build Me My house. Your son Solomon will build My temple.' King Solomon did build the temple; an incredible, magnificent temple for the Lord. You remember what happened when Solomon finished dedicating the temple to God in prayer: the glory of the Lord came down. So much so that the priests could not even enter the temple but down on their faces they went on the pavement and they worshipped God. What did they say? 'He is good; His love endures forever.' That display of God's glory was greater than the former in the tabernacle.[877]

GOD'S MANIFEST PRESENCE AND GLORY

God manifested His presence. God displayed His glory. His glory came down and was revealed through the temple but that beautiful magnificent temple of Solomon was also destroyed. God's people were taken captive for seventy years to Babylon. God then raises up a remnant. God always has a Remnant and the Remnant marched to Zion, back to Jerusalem to once again build the temple for the Lord at the command of the Lord. They were few in number but they were one in purpose and one in vision. They had come to build the house of the Lord so that the Lord could visit His people; another place for the glory of the Lord to rest—to come down among His people—that all may know that He is God. God said this: though that outward temple was not as spectacular as the previous temple (*Solomon's temple*), I will fill this temple with My glory, and the latter glory will be greater than the former glory.

What happened? Was the glory greater? It was greater because one day the Son of God Himself stepped down and He walked into

---

[877] 2 Chronicles 7:3

that temple and He opened up the Scriptures and He read. Jesus Christ stood in the temple and the Word became flesh and dwelt among us. John said "We have seen His glory."[878] The glory of the only begotten of the Father, full of grace and truth. God once again filled His house with glory and that glory was much greater than any of the former glory because this is the Son of God Himself: Jesus Christ.

Displaying and seeing the glory of God in the face of Jesus. We beheld His glory. Our Lord went to the cross, died on the cross for our sins, was raised again on the third day, ascended into heaven and He is now seated at the right hand of the Father. That temple in Jerusalem was destroyed in 70 AD. Not one stone found left on top of another. I still hear the Spirit of the Lord: "Heaven is My throne, and the earth is My footstool. What kind of house will you build for Me? says the Lord. Or where will My resting place be?"[879] God longing to visit His people. Where is the place once again where God will display His glory? Habakkuk said "The Lord is in his holy temple; let all the earth be silent before Him."[880] and through that holy temple the knowledge of the glory of the Lord covers the earth even as the waters cover the sea. But where is that temple? Stephen said in Acts 7: "The Most High does not live in houses made by human hands."[881] Where is that temple? The answer is given by the Apostle Paul:

"Don't you know that you yourselves are God's temple and that God's Spirit dwells in your midst? If anyone destroys God's temple, God will destroy that person; for God's temple is sacred, and you together are that temple."[882]

The prophet says 'I see the Lord in His holy temple' and the Apostle Paul says *'yes, the temple of God is holy and which temple you are.'* You see it, brothers and sisters, that's the vision. The vision of God's coming glory is the coming of the greatest display of the glory of God ever in the history of the world. I want to tell you that this is the Church's finest hour. I believe it with all of my heart. We are

---

[878] John 1:14
[879] Acts 7:49
[880] Habakkuk 2:20
[881] Acts 7:48
[882] 1 Corinthians 3:16-17

living in incredible days. God Almighty wanting to display His glory once again to such a degree: that glory will be greater than the former glory. It has to be if the knowledge of it will cover the earth as the waters cover the sea. He wants to do it where? Through His Church, through His body, through His temple which is us.

Coming judgment, yes. Coming persecution, yes. Suffering; yes. But a glory of God and to God who makes it all worth it. I agree with the Apostle Paul: the sufferings of this present time are not even worthy to be compared to the glory which shall be revealed in us. There is the vision but, how do we run with it?

HOW TO RUN WITH THE VISION

He said write the vision that He may run who reads it. In other words, do something with this vision. It demands a response, a practical response. Run with the vision. Someone who is running is either running away from something or they are running in pursuit of something. I want to say to you tonight to run with this vision is to run in pursuit; not of something but Someone.

Hebrews chapter 12. Run with the vision but how? Run pursuing Someone:

"Therefore, since we are surrounded by such a great cloud of witnesses, let us throw off everything that hinders and the sin that so easily entangles. And let us run with perseverance the race marked out for us, fixing our eyes on Jesus, the pioneer and perfecter of faith. For the joy set before Him He endured the cross, scorning its shame, and sat down at the right hand of the throne of God."[883]

This is a pursuit, namely, of Jesus Christ Himself. You want to run with the vision? Pursue Christ with all your heart. Fix your eyes on Christ, the author and finisher of our faith. Let Jesus fill your vision. Go after Him. Let Him be your chief delight, your highest ambition, your most passionate pursuit—your greatest desire should be the Lord Jesus Christ Himself. Otherwise, you're not running the race! You're not running with the vision. Make it plain. Make it personal. How is it with you? What is your greatest passion? What's your most passionate pursuit? What do you talk about the most?

---

[883] Hebrews 12: 1-2

Who do you talk about the most? Jesus Christ? Or your Bible translation? Jesus Christ? Or your particular doctrine, theology, eschatology...? Jesus Christ? Or your ministry? Jesus Christ or your gifts? Jesus Christ or your head-covering? Jesus Christ or your children, your family...? Jesus Christ or your denomination? It can be a number of things, brothers and sisters, and they're not all bad. Everything should pale in comparison with our love for Him. Love for Christ; the pursuit of Christ. I tell you, this Remnant that God is raising up that is scattered all over the earth shares one thing in common: to you who believe, He is precious! Christ is precious! Hallelujah!

WHEN CHRIST IS EVERYTHING TO YOU

When He's precious to you like that, you are willing to suffer the loss of everything and to count it but dung—rubbish—for the sake of knowing Christ more. There is so much more of Jesus to know than I know and that you know. Are you willing? Are you willing to suffer the loss of all things for the sake of Him? Knowing Him, following Him, being closer to Him.

Algerius said in that dungeon *the One who I once followed afar, I now see. He holds my hand. He's with me.*[884]

When Christ is everything to you, something else happens. You run with this vision in pursuit of Christ, something else happens. You will hate sin with a passion. You will loath it. You will hate it with a passion. Notice he says in verse 1:

"Let us throw off everything that hinders and the sin that so easily entangles. And let us run."[885]

Again, the Lord made so clear to me: make this plain. Is there sin in your life? Make it personal. Is there sin in your life? Are you regarding iniquity in your heart? When Christ is precious to you, you will hate sin! You will get dead-serious about repentance. Not just confessing your sin but forsaking it!

I was walking this trail I always walk to pray, the other day. The Lord was showing me *to you who believe, He is precious.* Blessed are

---

[884] Algerius (AD 1557)
[885] Hebrews 12: 1

the pure in heart. Worshipping Jesus as I'm walking along and someone's dog had vomited right there in the middle of the trail. I looked at that and obviously you're repulsed by that. The Holy Spirit reminded me *that's what sin looks like to me.* I said Jesus *make sin look like that to me.* Repulsive.

This pursuit of Christ is a pursuit of holiness. Remember brothers and sisters, without holiness, no one will see the Lord. The Lord is in His holy temple, let all the earth be silent.

Not just running now—we're running in pursuit of Christ, we're running in pursuit of Him—but we're running with purpose. The Apostle Paul says:

"Do you not know that in a race all the runners run, but only one gets the prize? Run in such a way as to get the prize."[886] In other words, run to win. Run on purpose. The Apostle Paul ran with purpose. He says in verse 25:

"Everyone who competes in the games goes into strict training. They do it to get a crown that will not last, but we do it to get a crown that will last forever. Therefore I do not run like someone running aimlessly; I do not fight like a boxer beating the air. No, I strike a blow to my body and make it my slave so that after I have preached to others, I myself will not be disqualified for the prize."[887]

He ran on purpose. Paul was so concerned about coming to the end of His race and finding out that he had run it in vain. He would not be distracted from His purpose. He's running with the vision. His eyes are on Christ. He disciplined his body. He didn't let food, sleep, leisure and entertainment master him nor distract him from this vision of Christ. He wouldn't be distracted from what Christ had clearly called him to do. He wouldn't waste time. He wouldn't become spiritually lazy. I get embarrassed of myself when I'm talking about persecution. I'm reading *Foxes' Book of Martyrs* and all of this— and I see a spiritual laziness that I'm prone to—areas of my life where I'm not dying now. There is a lot of spiritual laziness and undiscipline in the house of God. Are we running with purpose? Are we running with our eyes fixed on Christ? And what was his purpose? Verse 23:

"I do all this for the sake of the Gospel."[888]

---

[886] 1 Corinthians 9:24
[887] 1 Corinthians 9:25-27
[888] 1 Corinthians 9:23

That's his purpose and he wouldn't stray from it. Paul was passionate and determined not to run in vain. His purpose was the Gospel. He wouldn't waste time. He took every open door; every opportunity that he had everywhere the Spirit led him. He was sitting ready to preach the Gospel. He said 'I am not ashamed of the Gospel.'[889]

HAVING COMPASSION FOR THE LOST

My son Luke reminded me the other day of a quote he had read by *D.L. Moody*: "I don't find anywhere that God says the world is going to grow better and better. I look upon this world as a wrecked vessel and God has given me a lifeboat, and said to me 'Moody, save all you can!'"[890] You know, Moody didn't stray from that purpose. Brothers and sisters, you and I have a purpose. It has to do with the Gospel of Jesus Christ. Are you running with it? The messenger who runs with the vision is a messenger who is running with Good News. Christ died for our sins. He rose from the dead. He lives and He is coming again. Repent and believe the Gospel. That's the man, that's the woman, that's the child of God who's running on purpose. They have not lost sight of the true Gospel of Jesus Christ. I want to ask you again: what are you doing with the news that has been placed at your hands? Are you running with the vision? Have you gotten away from the true Gospel of Jesus Christ? He came to save souls; to seek and to save that which was lost. The sins of Sodom, again I tell you: the poor and needy were dying outside her doors and she was unconcerned.

Any Christianity that doesn't carry the compassion of Christ to the lost is a dead religion. It's not true Christianity. Get back to your calling, brothers and sisters. Who are you praying for that's lost? Who are you reaching out to with the Gospel of Jesus Christ? Who are you discipling? There is at least one person who is younger in the faith than you are that you can disciple. If you do not know one, you need to pray for someone, lead them to Christ, and disciple them. Get

[889] Romans 1:16
[890] D.L. Moody (1837-1899)

back to your purpose. Get back to your calling. What has God called you to do? Get back to it.

Don't stray from your purpose. Run on purpose. Why? Because one day, very soon, we must all appear before the judgment seat of Christ. We will give an account to what we have done in this body.[891] Did I run on purpose? Pity the man—God forbid—you come to the end of the race, you see the glory of Jesus, you stand at the judgment seat of Christ and it's suddenly revealed to you, you ran in vain. You wasted time. You went this way, that way, the other—you didn't run on purpose. You run pursuing Christ, you run on purpose. That purpose is the Gospel.

THE PRAYERLESS CHURCH AND THE COMING STORM

Can I tell you another purpose? It's a God-given purpose to all of us who are believers: Prayer. You run with this vision by prayer—everything by prayer. Listen carefully to a verse that the Spirit of God has arrested my heart with. He continues to bring it back to my remembrance—it seems like every day now, 1 Peter 4:7:

"The end of all things is near. Therefore be alert and of sober mind so that you may pray."[892]

If the Apostle Peter said that when the Spirit of God moved him to write this, how much closer are we to the end of all things? The end of all things is at hand, therefore be serious and watchful in your prayers. Because the end of all things is at hand, get serious about prayer. Get back to our knees. Get back to our purpose, Church. My house shall be called a house of prayer.[893] The prayerless church will not be ready for this soon coming storm, I assure you. The most effective ministry of preparation we have is prayer. Our Lord Jesus commanded it. Not only that, He set the example for us. The most trying hour ever that the Lord faced on this earth was in that dark night in Gethsemane. When the cross was set before Him, but it was not just the physical cross: the cup was set before Him. That cup meant He would take upon Himself the sins of the whole world. In that cup was the wrath of God. Talk about a crisis hour, talk about a

---

[891] 2 Corinthians 5:10
[892] 1 Peter 4:7
[893] Matthew 21:13

difficult hour that none of us can even come close to understanding or comprehending—how would He prepare for it? Let's follow in His steps. How did He prepare? He went to prayer.

He says to His disciples "You stay up and stay awake with Me. Watch and pray"[894] because they were also about to face a very difficult, trying, testing time—an hour that was set before them.

The only way for you to be prepared is pray! Stay awake and pray. Jesus went a little further, fell on His face and prayed. He comes back and finds His disciples sleeping, wakes them up again, goes back and prays again so fervently that He sweats as it were, droplets of blood. He prayed and He prayed and He prayed.

When the hour came, He was prepared. His disciples slept when they should have been praying. What is the result? One denies Him, one betrays Him, and they all forsook Him and fled. How will you stand in the coming persecution when you're prayerless? The prayerless church will not stand in the coming storm. I assure you, the most—single most—vital, important meeting of the Church is the prayer meeting. I believe that. I am one hundred percent persuaded of that and I am not just preaching it—that's what we live in Barnsdall. Why? Because we're nothing without God. We started in a barn, coming together and saying 'What are we going to do brother Brian?' 'I don't know.' Down to our knees and we prayed. We never lost sight that Saturday night, is prayer: prayer meeting. Nothing can substitute that. There is nothing more important. I feel tonight, as the richest man on the face of the earth. You know why? Because I have a little flock in *Barnsdall* who, right now, they're not listening to the message; they're watching it, the volume is down, they're praying corporately. 'Brother Brian, we're going to pray for you till it goes off air. We're not going to stop praying.'

They didn't just start tonight. Nor did they start today. Sunday morning, I had finished preaching—one brother stands up: 'This is what we're going to do. Remember when brother Brian's son was sick? He was fighting cancer. God taught us to fight and pray. Brother Brian is going to Atlanta on Thursday. We're going to start to fast and pray. Who'll take the first hour? Who'll take the second hour?' One hand goes up; one after the other. Then from Thursday, around the

---

[894] Matthew 26:41

clock, twenty-four hours all the way up to tonight: somebody has been praying for this conference and for me. Glory to God! That means more to me than anything. They told me that and I went to thank them and broke down weeping; I couldn't contain myself. That's the greatest gift any preacher, any pastor, can ever have.

But why? It's because God has revealed to us: *In everything by prayer.* That's such a small flock. We have two prayer meetings on Saturday night; small prayer meetings. Small people—nobodies. But a great big God shows up every time at prayer meeting. Sometimes you have to pray through but He comes. And the result; sinners have come to Christ as a result of calling upon God on Saturday night. They've come to Christ on Saturday morning. As a result of that prayer meeting, marriages have been restored, relationships have been reconciled, people have been healed miraculously. Most of all God manifests His presence on Sunday. He meets with us. He continues to surprise us. Week, after, week, after week—brothers who are now standing in the pulpit preaching: if you had told them a year ago they would be preaching—nobody would have believed you. That's what God does when His people pray.

The greatest way to prepare—the greatest preparation we have—for persecution, or anything for that matter, is to call upon the Lord in prayer. Pray! Make the vision plain. Make it personal.

PRAYER MEETINGS CRITICAL

So I ask you very plainly, very straight-forwardly, are you part of a vibrant prayer meeting right now? At least once a week? Are you part of a prayer meeting? If not, why not? You know, what the Lord showed me, brothers and sisters? This coming persecution: it's not enough that I stand. Do we have any kind of love for our brothers and sisters? It's not enough that I stand. My brother, he must stand. I want him to stand. I want my sister to stand.

They denied Christ; they fell asleep instead of praying. We have got to stay on our knees and see our dependence upon God and pray together. Are you part of prayer meeting? If not, you need to start one! Somebody says *I can't find anybody to pray with me.* You start one. I assure you, God has seven thousand that have not bowed their knee to baal, and you need to find them. Ask Him for one—two—

just one or two to join with you. If they will not join right away, you start the prayer meeting and the Father, Son and Holy Spirit will show up and meet with you in that prayer meeting, and He will draw one or two. Start the prayer meeting! Let nothing substitute it! Nothing at all! That's one meeting we will not miss! If you have to miss Sunday morning, so be it! Wednesday? So be it! Do not miss Saturday night!

HAVING THE POWER OF THE HOLY SPIRIT

They don't want to miss Saturday night. They saw God bring my son through cancer and get totally healed—from calling upon the Lord. That's the Lord's doing—miraculous testimonies that God has done in people's lives. Are you part of a prayer meeting? Get serious about prayer because without it—and this is what I am coming to the final part of running with the vision—there is no power. Prayer precedes the power of the Holy Spirit, the power of God. I want to tell you that we must have the power of the Holy Spirit. Self-confidence, grit-teeth, sheer determination and even sincere promises will fail in the coming storm and persecution. Those who have waited upon the Lord in prayer—who put no more confidence in the flesh, who have believed and received the promise of the Father, who have been baptized in the Holy Spirit—they will not waiver. They will be His witnesses. They shall prophesy. They shall preach boldly. They shall praise the Lord at all times. Through them—the holy Remnant —the knowledge of the glory of the Lord will fill the earth even as the waters cover the sea.

What sets them apart? The same thing that set the Apostles in the early Church apart: the Baptism of the Holy Spirit. The Spirit of the living God will be with them, in them and upon them. I know, believe me I know, there is so much of the counterfeit of the Baptism of the Holy Spirit today. There is an overwhelming abundance of the counterfeit of the Baptism in Christendom today. Then there are others who simply resist and reject and ignore any work and ministry of the Holy Spirit altogether. There are those who are even afraid to say *Baptism of the Holy Spirit*. I don't want to join or be a part of either group. I am not saying that condescendingly; I used to be in one of those groups. I don't want to be a part of either one, or join either one; nor am I afraid to say *Baptism of the Holy Spirit*. Why? Because that is the promise of the Father. Speaking of Jesus; "He shall baptize you with the Holy Spirit and fire." That is what I want. That is what I need, a continual filling of the Spirit of God—continually. The promises are for you and your children and as many as the Lord our God shall call.

The evidence—that so many would disagree on—is, let's come back to Acts 1:8, the Words of Jesus:

"But you will receive power when the Holy Spirit comes on you; and you will be My witnesses."[895]

THE EVIDENCE OF THE BAPTISM OF THE SPIRIT

What is the evidence of the Baptism of the Holy Spirit? Power! Power to become holy—because He is the Holy Spirit—power to be witnesses of Christ! You know better than I because I don't know Greek, but I know this Greek word for *witnesses* is *martus*. The same word for martyrs. The same word in other parts in the Scripture where they actually use the word *martyr;* Acts 22:20, the Apostle Paul speaking of Stephen:

"And when the blood of your martyr [*martus*] Stephen was shed."[896]

Revelation 2, Jesus speaking of Antipas:

"I know where you live—where Satan has his throne. Yet you remain true to My Name. You did not renounce your faith in Me, not even in the days of Antipas, My faithful witness [*martus*], who was put to death in your city—where Satan lives."[897]

"I saw that the woman was drunk with the blood of God's holy people, the blood of those who bore testimony [*martus*] to Jesus."[898]

Witnesses. Martyrs. A holy people endued with power from on-high who did not love their lives to the death. How? You tell me, how did that great cloud of witnesses who have gone before us—some of them sawn in two, some of them ripped apart by lions in an arena as the crowd cheered, jeered, mocked, some of them burned at the stake

---

[895] Acts 1:8
[896] Acts 22:20
[897] Revelation 2:13
[898] Revelation 17:6

—they never denied Christ; never stopped loving their enemies; never stopped preaching; never stopped praising the Lord even in the midst as their bodies burned.

How? "Not by might, nor by power but by My Spirit says the Lord." That's the only way, brothers and sisters. Lydia Perpetua—a 22-year-old mother—had her baby boy taken away from her, thrown into prison, thrown into an arena of wild beasts and finally was martyred at the end of the sword of a gladiator in that arena. While she was laying there before she died, cried out 'Give up the world. Stand fast in the faith. Love one another. Don't let our suffering become a stumbling block to you.' How did a 22-year-old mother do that? "Not by might, nor by power but My Spirit says the Lord"[899]— she was filled with the Holy Spirit. There is no other way.

Allan Cameron, a Scottish covenanter, while being held in prison, they bring to him the head and the hands of his son. They cruelly asked him, if he knew them. He said 'Yes, I know them. I know them' as he kissed them 'they are my son's—my own dear son's. It is the Lord, it is the good will of the Lord who cannot wrong me nor mine, but has made goodness and mercy to follow us all of our days.' How did he do it? 'Not by might, not by power but My Spirit says the Lord.' You must be filled with the Holy Spirit. We must be endued with power from on-high. We need the Spirit of the Living God.

REREADING THE BOOK OF ACTS

Brothers and sisters, what do we do about our lack of love—our lack of faithfulness, our lack of wholeheartedness, our lack of boldness, our lack of holiness, our lack of joy, our lack of prayer, our lack of power in witness? 'Not by might, nor by power but My Spirit says the Lord.'[900] I want to plead with you making this vision plain. Put away the modern books on the Holy Spirit. I walk into a Christian bookstore today and I get nauseated. Put away the modern books on the Holy Spirit. Even turn off the computer. Set aside the CDs. Pick up this Book (*the Bible*). Read the Book of Acts one more

---

[899] Zechariah 4:2
[900] Zechariah 4:6

time. Better yet, read it in one sitting, at the most two sittings. Do as I have done myself; read the Book of Acts and ask 'What is missing in my life?' What is missing in the Church today? What is missing? This is it! You must be filled with the Holy Spirit! You must be endued with power from on-high. That's what I want! Not what you see around—what did Jesus have? What did the Apostles have? What did the early Church have? That's what I want. That's the answer to our lack.

So I want to ask you: if you are thirsty, if you are serious about coming to Jesus for cleansing and freedom from all sin, if you are willing to be broken bread and poured out wine, to serve others— He's not going to fill anybody that's all about themselves, full of themselves, not willing to be poured out—if you're willing to surrender all to Jesus, and you simply ask Him in faith, He will fill you with the Holy Spirit!

Are you willing to obey every Word He says? He will fill you with the Holy Spirit. Regardless of what your doctrine or teaching is, no God-fearing, Bible-believing, blood-bought saint of God can ignore, neglect, the command of Ephesians 5:18, which says clearly:

"Do not get drunk on wine, which leads to debauchery. Instead, be filled with the Spirit."[901]

Continually—be ye being filled with the Spirit—that is a command. We cannot ignore it. The result? Ephesians 5:19;

"Speaking to one another with psalms, hymns, and songs from the Spirit. Sing and make music from your heart to the Lord, always giving thanks to God the Father for everything, in the Name of our Lord Jesus Christ."[902]

What I am saying to you is that someone who is filled with the Holy Spirit will praise the Lord at all times. They will sing to Him. They will praise Him. They will worship Him at all times. I want to tell you brothers and sisters, we're not called in these days just to hold down the fort. No! You're not called to go and stack-up food and hide somewhere. No, we are called to go in the power of the Holy Spirit on purpose; reaching the lost world, making disciples, joining the Lord Jesus in building His Church—because it's through that temple

[901] Ephesians 5:18
[902] Ephesians 5:19-20

that glory of the Lord will cover the earth even as the waters cover the sea.

I come to a close. Back to Habakkuk. I want you to see this as we close, that there is a progression in the Book of Habakkuk. Only three short chapters. In chapter 1, he's wrestling with the vision. In chapter 2 he receives the vision. In chapter 3, he's running with the vision. In chapter 1—just as you and I must move from Romans 6 to Romans 7 to Romans 8, we must also move from Habakkuk 1, to Habakkuk 2 to Habakkuk 3. There's a progression. He's wrestling with the vision. The suffering, the persecution, judgment to come, but ultimately he's wrestling with the God who's calling His people to suffer. Habakkuk's very name means *wrestle* or *embrace*.

THE EMBRACING OF MARTYRDOM

Number 1: Are you willing to embrace a God who calls you to martyrdom? Are you willing to embrace a Christ who calls you to take up a cross and die for His glory? That's the only true and living Christ there is. 'If any man be My disciple, let him take up his cross daily and follow Me.' Some of you may be wrestling right now.

Habakkuk says 'we shall not die...' yes. And you need to make the resolve if you are wrestling. 'Lord, by faith, and by Your grace, I am willing to embrace the cross.' Get on the cross. Die to this self-life, *because I want nothing more than You—and You to be glorified.*

Chapter 2, he receives the vision. That vision is that in the midst of all this suffering—again, the knowledge of the glory of the Lord covering the earth even as the waters cover the sea—the Lord in His holy temple. He receives that by faith. God wants to glorify Himself through His Church. Receive that vision.

In chapter 3, he runs with it. How does he run with it? Chapter 3 is an entire chapter of prayer. It's Habakkuk's prayer. Yet, even in this prayer, there is a progression. The prayer begins in verse two with:

"Lord, I have heard of Your fame; I stand in awe of Your deeds, Lord. Repeat them in our day, in our time make them known; in wrath remember mercy."[903]

---

[903] Habakkuk 3:2

NEVER LET GO OF THE MERCY OF GOD

We pray. You run with the vision by prayer, but don't give up on the mercy of God. Judgment has to come to the house of God. In wrath, remember mercy. Still pray for the mercy—above all, mercy upon us. His mercy endures forever. Never let go of the mercy of God. In wrath, remember mercy. Never let go of praying 'God, revive Your work. Revive!' Yes, this is revival but it means persecution, and in the fires of persecution the Church gets purified.'

This prayer progresses. It's petition now but what happens, as he prays—like always happens if you really pray—he now sees the Lord. Once he sees the Lord, there's no perplexity. There are no more questions. There is no more wrestling. He sees the Lord, he comes to the end of the chapter and he says this, verse 17:

"Though the fig tree does not bud and there are no grapes on the vines, though the olive crop fails and the fields produce no food, though there are no sheep in the pen and no cattle in the stalls, yet I will rejoice in the Lord, I will be joyful in God my Savior. The Sovereign Lord is my strength; He makes my feet like the feet of a deer, He enables me to tread on the heights."[904]

The progression: from petition to praise. This is the Remnant God is raising up in spite of circumstances, in the midst of persecution, in the midst of pain and in the midst of suffering. Praise the Name of the Lord with all of your heart because He is worthy of praise!

No more questions because he's not looking at the Babylonians now, he sees God. He doesn't see the persecutors anymore, but the Lord. His eyes are upon the Lord. When will the glory of the Lord cover the earth as the waters cover the sea? When His people rise up in the power of the Holy Spirit to praise Him at all times! Brothers and sisters, let's run with the vision. Let's pursue the Person of Jesus Christ with passion unlike we've ever pursued Him before. Are you willing to suffer the loss of everything to gain Him, to know Him more—let's run on purpose. Let's run on purpose with this message of the Gospel of Jesus Christ. Join with someone building the true

[904] Habakkuk 3:17-19

body of Christ. Making of disciples, preaching the Gospel, run on purpose, start the prayer meeting. Start praying. Get to prayer! Run on purpose. Seek God to be filled with the Holy Spirit.

FILL US WITH THE HOLY SPIRIT

I simply want to ask you plainly tonight: if you're one like myself, who is seeing your lack, you see your need, and even tonight you say the Holy Spirit has been speaking to you—you say 'God, I need You to fill me afresh with Your Holy Spirit. Baptize me with Your Spirit. Baptize me with Your presence, with Your love... Lord God, all of You —I want more of You.' The Holy Spirit always glorifies Christ. *More of You Jesus. More of You. Fill me Lord.*

You don't have to wait for weeks. I don't believe that. If you meet the conditions—you're thirsty—Jesus said 'out of your innermost beings will flow rivers of living water.' I simply want to ask you to join me in asking God to do something within our own hearts. Join the Apostle Paul in that prayer of his in Ephesians 3 that says "He may strengthen you with power through His Spirit in your inner being,"[905] Let the rivers of living water flow for Your glory. Fill us with all the fullness of God, so we can love our enemies, so that we can preach the Gospel with power and anointing, so that we can praise You at all times in the midst of every circumstance. Fill us with the Holy Spirit. That is my prayer. If that is your desire tonight, that is your prayer—as we enter into a time of worship—I want to invite you to come to the altar. You cry out to God. You pray. You cry out to God 'This is my need. Here is my lack. Lord, You gave a promise. This is the promise of the Father. He said it's for me, for my children and as many as You shall call.

Brothers and sisters, as we heard already; if you being evil know how to give good gifts to your children, how much more will the Heavenly Father give the Holy Spirit to those that ask Him. He is willing. He is more willing to give than you are to receive. If you are willing to meet those simple requirements: *I'm thirsty. Jesus I come to You first for cleansing. I'm willing to surrender all, I'm willing to be poured out, I'm willing to go wherever You tell me to go, do whatever You*

---

[905] Ephesians 3:16

tell me to do, say whatever You tell me to say. I'm going take You at Your Word and promise. Fill me with the Holy Spirit.

I believe we should go out of this place in the power of the Holy Spirit. One of the evidences of that will be that we will be a people who praise the Lord at all times. In every circumstance, even if the fruit is not on the vine and the fig tree does not blossom, and there are not cattle in the stalls. We will rejoice in the Lord. Amen?

Please stand to your feet as we pray. Allow us the time not to rush in the presence of God, but to praise Him, to call upon Him in prayer. Brothers and sisters, when you know God has answered your prayer, rise to praise Him. Praise Him tonight with all of your heart.

Father, I ask You in the Name of Jesus to do what only You can do. No man can impart anything, God, apart from You. We come to You. We come directly to You, our Father and our God. The One we can call Abba. We cry out to You Abba Father, we come to You tonight Father, and You know the condition of each and every heart here tonight. You know the condition of each and every heart listening online. Perhaps there are people right in their own houses right now who are seeing their lack, seeing their need, their desperate need to be filled, baptized with the Holy Spirit—would You meet us tonight, Father?

We don't have time to waste. We don't have games to play. We don't have to figure out or explain it all. It's very simple: We lack. We can do nothing apart from You. You made a promise and we come to You tonight, Father to fill us afresh with Your Holy Spirit. Would You do that, Father, as we enter into a time of worship and praise. I pray God, tonight, You pour out upon us a spirit of praise, that we would go forth praising Your glorious, magnificent Name; the Name of Jesus—the Name that is above every other name. We love You Lord and we glorify You tonight in Jesus' Name, Amen.

Appendix II

Select Teachings for Gospel Fellowships

Chinese House Churches Interview

by brother Denny

[EDITOR'S NOTE: This interview was conducted by brother Denny with two brothers who worked and are involved with the rural Chinese underground house Churches where God is doing a vibrant work. He has been building a pure pristine Book of Acts fellowship in House Church networks all over rural China. There is a simplicity to the move of God yet such fervency, love, and desire born in the hearts of these believers. We need to break out of the simple 1 hour church meeting patterns, and start to serve the Lord with full commitment like many of these precious brothers and sisters in the Lord. For many of us the questions and truths that are revealed are very important for us to hear as we gather under the Headship of Jesus Christ in local areas. Below is the interview transcript]:

Brother Denny: Let's move on to another important question. How do the Chinese Christians evaluate American Christianity?

Brother Ren: They feel like the Church in the West is playing games. They are troubled with all the laughter in the meetings. They are broken and weeping in their Assemblies, and we are telling jokes.[906] This brings very different results. They feel we are bound by

---

[906] James 4:9

traditions and programs and therefore cannot follow the Holy Spirit's leadings. We have to make sure we have that direct line to the Holy Spirit and seek to hear His voice. We can never overemphasize the difference between the followers of Jesus in the West and in China. These followers in China hear their Master's voice, and they follow Him. This is actually a very simple theology.

The Christians in the West have been able to eliminate Christ and His direct presence in their midst. I have a feeling sometimes that the whole Christianity in the West could be going for years before they discover that Jesus has not been with them for a long time.[907] He has gone somewhere else. He is not with them anymore.

Brother Paul: The personal message I got from brother Yun is that of Jesus asleep in the boat. His whole point was that so many people in missions, in churches, and in ministries start out with the power of God and great visions. But, then people think, *Okay, we can row it ourselves now. Thank you very much.* And Jesus goes to sleep in the boat. Great storms arise. They have to wake Jesus up before it is too late to calm the storm.[908] Make sure Jesus isn't asleep in your Church, in your family, or in your life.

ON THE HOLY SPIRIT

Brother Denny: What does the Chinese Church believe about the Holy Spirit? It seems very evident that they are a powerful people. How does this work out in their theology of the Spirit?

Brother Paul: They believe it is God's command to every believer to be baptized by the Holy Spirit.[909] They also believe that we must have continual fillings[910] as our life goes on in the Lord Jesus. This is the primary reason for all the amazing things that we have shared in the meeting. Imagine how different the American Christians would be if millions of them would be filled with the Spirit.

---

[907] Revelation 3:20
[908] Mark 4:35-41
[909] Acts 1:5
[910] Ephesians 5:18

ON HOLY LIVING

Brother Denny: What does the Chinese Church believe about holy living? This is an area of much confusion here in America. The professing church is filled with worldliness.

Brother Paul: They are conservative Christians. They order their lives according to the Word of God. Many do not have Bibles, but those who do study much to see what God says about living a Christian life. Their women are modest, in spirit[911] and in their clothing.[912] The Chinese culture is different from American culture, but what they wear is modest.

They are all poor, so they have no problems with fashion. This matter of holy living is a real problem to them when they try to relate to Christians from the West. They struggle when denominations try to claim them as *one of us*, when they are very different.

ON DIVINE HEALING

Brother Denny: Some of the testimonies about healing are amazing. They cause me to sit in astonishment as I hear them. Could you elaborate on the subject of healing a bit more? How often do things like what we heard tonight happen? What is their theology of healing?

Brother Ren: First, let me answer the theology part of the question. They have a very simple theology about healing. They believe that God is a healer.[913] It is simply one of the many manifestations of His holy character. In America, you believe that God can heal. In China, they believe He does all the time. It is according to your faith and ours. You receive what you believe. The people are poor and cannot afford to go to the doctor. Because of this, they have to trust in God in ways that American's do not. Healings happen all the time, but people also have sickness that they have to deal with. Poverty and persecution brings extra hardships

---

[911] 1 Timothy 2:10
[912] 1 Timothy 2:11-15
[913] Exodus 15:26

upon them, and thus they get sick more often. Sometimes God heals, and sometimes He does not. God is sovereign.[914]

Brother Denny: Could you also comment on some of the other miracles that you share tonight? It is hard for us to relate to so many supernatural happenings. How does this affect the Church there?

Brother Paul: They believe in a miracle working God. At first, in the beginning of the revival, everyone was astonished as well. As God began to work many miracles, the Church just began to expect miracles. It is not a distraction as it is in the West. Miracles happen at a meeting, and the preacher just goes right on preaching the Gospel. There is an expectation that God will confirm His Word with miracles.[915] Eighty percent of the Church has experienced miracles of some sort or another. Because of this, they expect them. They never glorify the miracles; they glorify God. The gift of miracles is in the Bible, and God works through this gift to honor His Name.

Brother Denny: Have you ever heard of someone being raised from the dead?

Brother Ren: Oh yes, it happens quite often. Many times when someone is killed, or dies from persecution, the leaders will go where the body is to pray and find out if God would have the person live again.

ON TRUE UNITY

Brother Denny: I have often said in my preaching, "When persecution comes, true unity will come with it, because there will be no mixture with the world." In light of this, what do they believe about unity? We have all this ecumenical confusion here in our land.

Brother Paul: Again, their theology is very simple. Their unity is based on the essentials of the faith and true marks of discipleship. They say, "Disciples witness, and are persecuted because they witness."

This is where the lines of unity are drawn. There are differences among them, but they do not allow these to divide them in the war

---

[914] Job 1:21
[915] Romans 15:19

for souls. They believe there is more that unifies them than there is that separates them.

Brother Denny: Could you comment on the name given to these Chinese Christians. I am referring to the name *house Churches*. What is the significance of this name?

Brother Ren: The name signifies several different things. First, the name is given because they meet in houses. There are several reasons for this, and I will comment on them in a moment. The second reason has to do with a distinction between them and the registered churches, which meet in buildings. The last reason is the most important one, they call themselves house Churches out of conviction. They meet in homes because they believe it is more Biblical.[916] It is also true that they have to because of persecution, but the primary reason is evangelical in nature. Even if the government of China allowed them liberty to meet openly, they would still meet in houses. Meeting in homes is one of the greatest keys to the tremendous growth of the Church. The more meeting places, the more they can win the lost to Christ. In addition, when they meet in houses, it does not cost them any money. Finances often slow Church growth.

ON CHURCH MEETINGS

Brother Denny: Could you tell me what the Church services are like when they meet together and feel free? I know there are times when they have to be quiet, but what is it like when they are free?

Brother Ren: The Chinese Christians are a lively, responsive congregation when they gather in freedom. They sing some hymns and some choruses, and the singing is wholehearted. During the preaching and open testimonies, there are lots of amens and hallelujahs. They meet in forests and caves to do this so they will not be heard.[917]

---

[916] Philemon 1:2
[917] Hebrews 11:38

ON REVIVAL THEOLOGY

Brother Denny: You mentioned in your presentation that revival has been continuing for decades. Can you give me some reasons why it does not grow cold or stop?

Brother Paul: As I see it, there are two reasons. First, the Church is busy fulfilling God's purposes for it on the earth. That purpose is evangelism. As God's people do His work, He continues to pour out His Spirit upon them. This is a secret to ongoing revival. The Chinese Church has a powerful vision of the Great Commission.[918] They believe it is the Church's responsibility to preach the Gospel to their generation.[919] The second reason flows out of the first.

Because of their persistence in preaching the Gospel, they are persecuted repeatedly. This persecution brings purifying, and that brings more anointing. These two work together to create an atmosphere of revival.

Brother Ren: There is another reason why they still have revival. The Church leaders are careful to give the Holy Spirit His place in directing the work. They allow God's Spirit free course to move how and where He will. They see the American church as one that is too organized. The leaders have a saying about revival that I feel is helpful. They call it, *How to kill a revival.*

- Man wants to organize it to suit his understanding.

- Then after he has it organized, he then secures himself a position in it.

- Once this is done, the Spirit is grieved, and slowly withdraws.

- Then the Revival becomes a history class, and everyone talks about it in the past.

ON END TIMES THEOLOGY

Brother Denny: Could you comment on the eschatology of the house Churches? What is their end time theology?

Brother Paul: Their theology is again very simple. They believe that Jesus Christ is coming again. He is coming for His Bride who

---

[918] Luke 24:46-47
[919] Mark 16:15

has made herself ready. As far as the details of how all this will happen, there are some differences. These differences do not divide them. The strongest point of their theology has to do with evangelism.

They believe the Gospel must be preached among all nations, and then shall the end come. They get this from Matthew 24.[920] Because of this belief, they have strong convictions about evangelism. They believe that if you are not actively busy preaching to others, you are hindering the second coming of Christ, and you need to repent.

ON DISCIPLESHIP AND TRAINING

Brother Denny: For my last question, let's talk a little about the leaders of this movement. The Church is growing at a very fast rate, and yet it is underground. Therefore, it would be hard to give much formal training to the leaders. From an American perspective, many would believe you cannot lead a Church until you have had much formal training. Obviously, this training is not happening in China, yet the Church is thriving. How can this be? Can you explain some of preparations the leaders receive?

Brother Ren: Most of the top leaders are very poor. The strongest point of their character is love. They pour out their lives for the persecuted sheep in China both in labors and by subjecting themselves to the dangers of imprisonment. One wrong move and they sit in a prison cell for five or ten years. This is love as many in America have never known. They do train their leaders. The training, however, is very simple. They train them in three major areas. Let me state them briefly.

- They teach them how to be a disciple of Jesus Christ and walk with Him daily. Then from that walk, they must learn how to witness for Christ in a dangerous hostile environment.

- They teach them how to die daily[921] and how to die really. These are both very important because of the persecutions leaders face.

---

[920] Matthew 24:14
[921] 1 Corinthians 15:31

- They teach them how to escape the police when they are caught, and how to escape from prison if God says *Run*.

The Word of God is very important to these leaders. They have memorized and internalized many chapters of the Bible. They cannot carry a Bible around in their hands, so they make sure that they can carry one in their heart. The fire of the Holy Spirit is also very important in ministry.[922] These men are constantly being empowered by the Spirit. This is leadership in China, and this is how the Church spreads so rapidly.

Brother Denny: Thank you for taking the time to share with me. I am deeply challenged by the answers to my questions. I know the hearts of the people who will read this article. They will be thrilled and humbled by our Chinese brethren. May God help us. We lack in so many of these areas, but we want to change.

This concludes the interview about the Chinese house Churches. What can I say? Zion in America must reckon with Zion in China. "This God is our God for ever and ever."[923] When Communism closed the doors to China in 1949, there were one million believers in China. Now, fifty years later, there are eighty-million disciples of Jesus Christ. There are also many true Christians in the registered churches. Christ is building His Church in China, and the gates of hell are not prevailing against her.[924] Praise ye the Lord. Dear brothers and sisters, let us repent of our lukewarmness[925] and unbelief[926] and let us believe God for mighty things. The persecution will come. Most Christians in America acknowledge this. We need to get prepared.

---

[922] Matthew 3:11, 1 Thessalonians 5:19
[923] Psalm 48:14
[924] Matthew 16:18
[925] Revelation 3:16
[926] Hebrews 3:12

God's New Thing
by brother David

[EDITOR'S NOTE: This message[927] was preached at a *SermonIndex Revival Conference* event in Wales in the Moriah Chapel church where the famous Welsh revival began in 1904. This message given by David Legge in that historic pulpit calls for a glorious new work of the Spirit of God in our day. Such a work will glorify the Lord Jesus Christ as the true Head of the Church and Lord of all creation. May we be challenged afresh to accept and look forward to God's work in these last days. The following is the text transcription of the message]:

I want you to turn with me to Isaiah's prophecy chapter 43 please, Isaiah chapter 43. Now let me give a little bit of introduction to this message by saying that I believe, with all my heart, that God has been very real and very operative in this Conference, I know He has in my own heart—particularly today—but even leading up to these meetings as I sought God over messages. There are messages that I had on my heart, that other men have preached. This message that I'm about to preach, I know has been on the heart of some of the other men. Now that, to me, is a positive sign that God's Spirit is at work. We are one body, and it is one Spirit that indwells us. But this message is—and I don't like measuring messages, but as far as burden goes (*and preachers here will understand what I mean when I say*

---

[927] This message was transcribed into text by *Andrew W.* of *preachtheword.com* where you can access all of *brother David's* written and preaching ministry.

burden)—as far as burden goes, this is the greatest as far as I am concerned, for me.

Abba Father, Holy Father, in Jesus' Name, Your Holy Child Jesus, we ask for the unction to function in the power and demonstration of the Spirit of the Living God. You are the God of Abraham, Isaac, Jacob. You are the God and Father of our Lord Jesus Christ. You are not the God of the dead, but the God of the living. O, Living God of the living, reveal Yourself tonight. You have called upon us and said: 'Give me your heart.' Lord, I believe that some have given You their heart, but Lord—could we be bold enough to say to You this evening: 'Lord, give us Your heart?' In Jesus' Name, Amen.

Isaiah 43 then, and we're going to begin reading at verse 16, and I'm preaching to you on *God's New Thing*. Isaiah 43 verse 16: "This is what the Lord says—He who made a way through the sea, a path through the mighty waters, who drew out the chariots and horses, the army and reinforcements together, and they lay there, never to rise again, extinguished, snuffed out like a wick: 'Forget the former things; do not dwell on the past. See, I am doing a new thing! Now it springs up; do you not perceive it? I am making a way in the wilderness and streams in the wasteland. The wild animals honor me, the jackals and the owls, because I provide water in the wilderness and streams in the wasteland, to give drink to My people, My chosen, the people I formed for Myself that they may proclaim My praise.'"[928] *Amen.*

THE TERM REVIVAL

The term *revival*, I think, is often understood as *a rediscovery of old truth.* I believe that is correct, and there are many examples from the Scriptures and indeed from church history that would bear this out. Perhaps the most obvious example, to my mind at least, is the rediscovery of the Book of the Law in the old temple in Ezra and Nehemiah's day. When the people discovered what God's Law actually said, they were broken and they were cut to their heart—because they realized how far away they had gotten from their God. There was a great move, a reformation, we would say *a genuine revival*

---

[928] Isaiah 43:16-21

and people actually put into practice certain things that had never been fully practiced truly among God's people.

It is a grave mistake to think that those rediscovered old truths will wear the same clothes of those who once espoused them.

So a rediscovery of old truths brought subsequent repentance and obedience to the Word of God. It is true that revival is when old paths of the Word of God, the precepts and the principles of the Bible that never change from generation to generation, are rediscovered—and, as we've heard already, repentance toward God is exercised in a new obedience to what God's Word asks of us. But— and this is the emphasis of my message tonight—though that is the case, nevertheless it is a grave mistake, I say again a grave mistake, to think that those rediscovered old truths will wear the same clothes of those who once espoused them.

1904, praise God. 1905, praise God. In Ulster we are celebrating this year the 150th anniversary of the 1859 revival that you enjoyed here as well and, we heard today, America and Canada and spread to many parts of the world. It is great, and I commend your celebration of God moving in the past. There is, from that, a genuine longing for God to do it again—but I wonder, I ask my own heart, and I ask you tonight: if at times our reminiscences of past revivals are more of a nostalgic romanticism about how things used to be done? 'The good old days,' 'old-time religion,' rather than a genuine longing for God to do something again—even if it may not resemble the thing that we loved Him for doing in the past.

READY FOR GOD'S NEW THING?

I hope you're getting this. Let me put it in a question to you: are you ready and willing for God to do a new thing? Now, if we are not, we may miss what God is going to do—or, could I be bold enough to say, what God has already started doing. Now, don't misunderstand what I'm saying—if anyone knows me, and I know most of you don't, but you will know that I stand firmly on the principles of God's Word. We do need to rediscover the same truths as were rediscovered in past revivals, but let me be absolutely clear: it is wrong—wrong!— to expect God to revive in an identical manner! Also, I think it is wrong for us to desire God to reproduce an identical revival. Now, let me give you two reasons for that at least: one is from a human perspective, and the other is from the divine. From the human perspective, it is wrong to desire God to reproduce an identical revival because what sufficed to revive in 1859 and 1904 and 1905 does not suffice to revive the Church in the world of the 21st century. We need something new! We need something fresh! But from the divine perspective: God is the God of the original! He is the God of the new thing! Though obviously, if you study revival, you will know there are great similarities shared in every revival—not least, the fundamental doctrinal truths celebrated—but each is original in its own right, and each has had features and peculiarities that were special to it.

Now, we must face facts, that our God is the God of the new thing! I want to show you this from Scripture. Such was the case in Isaiah's day. Look with me please at verses 16 and 17 again: "This is what the Lord says—He who made a way through the sea, a path through the mighty waters, who drew out the chariots and horses, the army and reinforcements together, and they lay there, never to rise again, extinguished, snuffed out like a wick."[929] Now, what Isaiah is saying there is simply that the past can teach us, and we must study the past—but we must not be bound to the past, or bound by the past, we must always be looking forward to what God is yet to do. The Lord, in Isaiah's day, wanted them in the present to live in the reality of the past—and the incident that he is referring to in verses 16 and 17 is the exodus of the children of Israel out of bondage in Egypt towards the promised land.

God's people often do miss what God is doing, and we might well ask the question: Why?

Now, you must understand the Hebrew mind: The exodus was the greatest miracle, and is still regarded as the greatest miracle among the people of the Jews. Yet God is saying in Isaiah's day, verse 18, "Remember not the former things." Now, that's staggering. In verse 9 he says the same concerning former things, and he's referring to the exodus acts of God once again. In verse 19 He says: "Behold, I will do a new thing"—literally it could be translated, *I am going to do a new thing.*

---

[929] Isaiah 43:16-17

GOD'S NEW THING IN ISAIAH'S DAY

Now, what is the new thing that God specifically is talking about here in Isaiah's day? Well, the children of Israel are in bondage to Babylon, and God is telling them that there's going to be a national liberation, and it will be patterned on the exodus. It will spring, it will sprout like a seed which is germinated, and its time has come. God is saying: 'Shall you not see it?', but I think that could be translated, 'Do you not see it?' The reason why He's saying: 'Do you not see it?', the import of it is, 'You can't miss it! You can't miss what I'm going to do!' But wait, here's the point: they were missing it. They were missing it!

God's people often do miss what God is doing, and we might well ask the question: Why? We're going to get the answer, but before that look at verse 19, the second part, speaking of these great acts of God that are going to happen in Isaiah's day, deliverance from Babylon: "See, I am doing a new thing! Now it springs up; do you not perceive it? I am making a way in the wilderness and streams in the wasteland."[930] The acts of God are going to bring the whole world into harmony for the children of God. Now this, ultimately, will not be perfected until the Messianic day when, as we read in chapter 11, even the animal kingdom will come into the great benefits of what it is for God to rule and reign in His universe. Ultimately many of these events that we read of in Isaiah will not be fulfilled in completeness until our Lord's return, and then they will surpass the exodus—Hallelujah!

But what I want you to see tonight is—and this is my point—in some immediate sense these journeying people of God in bondage in Babylon, God says: "You're going to be met by a transformed world. It shall spring forth, you will not be able to miss it! I will make a road in the wilderness and rivers in the desert." This was Isaiah's emphasis: you are in danger, children of God, of missing what God was doing there and then, and is about to do—why? 'Because you are focusing on what I did in the past.' God says: "Do you not see what I am about to do?"

---

[930] Isaiah 43:19

Now there are many lessons we can take out of this tonight, but one of them is this: God is always doing something—always. I emphasized this in my last message about having a perception of God: he who comes to God must believe that He is—and that *is* can mean *active*. We must believe that He is instrumental in our universe. Even when it looks as if nothing is happening—and there are times when we would be forgiven, would we not, to think that God is doing nothing; especially when we compare what's happening now with what happened in the past! But we need to rediscover this knowledge that God is doing something now!

GOD DOING NOTHING?

In the Book of Habakkuk, the prophet was told: "Look at the nations and watch—and be utterly amazed. For I am going to do something in your days that you would not believe, even if you were told."[931] The tense is right in the Amplified Version of the Bible: "I am working a work in your day—I'm doing it now, and you cannot see it, but if you were told it, it would blow your mind!" Now, in Habakkuk's day, He was raising up the Babylonians—that's a strange work in itself, is it not? It was unexpected. Think of it: God chastising His people for wickedness, and how is He doing it? He's raising up an even more wicked nation to rebuke His own people.

Incidentally Paul, when he was in Pisidian Antioch in Acts chapter 13, when he was in the synagogue he quoted that verse from Habakkuk chapter 1 verse 5. He applied it to the judgment that was coming on Israel because they had rejected God's Messiah—and was that not a new thing, because what was God now doing? He was turning to the Gentiles, He was leaving the Jews in blindness for a season—but nevertheless, it is the rebuke of God upon them, because they did not recognize His new work, His new thing. God is working today, God is working in Wales, God is working in Scotland, God is working in England, God is working in Ireland! Jesus said: "My Father is always at His work to this very day, and I too am

---

[931] Habakkuk 1:5

working."[932] But here's my message, brothers and sisters: if we have a preconceived idea of how He must work, we might miss Him.

THE PHARISEE REVIVAL MOVEMENT

God's new thing was in Isaiah's day, but secondly I want you to see that God's new thing was in Messiah's day. Probably the dominant theme of the Gospels is Christ-rejection by the Jews. He came unto His own, His own things, and His own people received Him not. Why? We could give many reasons, but if we could give one it would be this: He did not live up to their expectations! Right? It was a new thing that threw the scribes of Scripture off the scent completely! The biggest opponents to the new thing were the Pharisees! Now please hear me: the Pharisees were a revival movement, did you know that? Did you know that?

You see, great liberalism had come into Judaistic theology; through the Sadducees who did not believe in resurrection, did not believe in the spirit realm, did not believe in angels and so forth; and other influences. So the Pharisees grew up as a sect who wanted to revive the Torah Scriptures, and they wanted to bring every facet of Jewish life into harmony with the law of God. It might surprise you even further to know that our Lord Jesus sided with them often theologically. He said in Matthew 23 verse 1: "Listen to the Pharisees, for they sit in Moses' seat. Do what they teach, but not what they do." In Matthew's Gospel and in Luke's Gospel He agreed with them on what is the substance and great law of God: "To love the Lord your God, and to love your neighbor as yourself."[933] Paul the apostle, when he was before the Sanhedrin, you remember what happened there, don't you? He sided with the Pharisees over the issue of the resurrection. Now he had a reason to do it, to get them at one another when they were against him—but nevertheless, theologically, he stood on the same grounds.

Do you know that a *back to the Bible* movement can be as dead as the Pharisees? The Pharisees knew their Bibles, but they did not know their God.

---

[932] John 5:17
[933] Matthew 22:37-39

The tragedy was, for the Pharisees, they had the letter of the law without the power of the Spirit. They recognized false doctrine a mile off, but they did not recognize their God when He showed up in the flesh. In fact, the Lord Jesus said: "You study the Scriptures diligently because you think that in them you have eternal life. These are the very Scriptures that testify about Me."[934] You know the Bible inside out, back to front, and yet you've missed Me whom the Bible is all about!

OPPOSING THE WORK OF THE SPIRIT

It is amazing how it can often be the most Biblically literate who oppose an obvious work of the Spirit of God—and often they oppose it on doctrinal grounds. That is what happened to our Lord, to the point that they actually accused Him of demon-possession by Beelzebub, and ultimately it led to His crucifixion. To a large extent, legalism motivated Christ-rejection. Legalism is manifest in self-righteousness and over-obsession with tradition, and a very overt and acute judgmentalism. But do we understand that it was the spirit of legalism that motivated the unpardonable sin? Do you know what I believe the unpardonable sin was? There was the witness of the Spirit to Messiah in Jesus Christ, unbelief on the part of the Jewish nation at that time was the unpardonable sin.

Revival movements—and I love this movement, and I love this convention, and all these conventions—but they must beware, because it is not the Biblically illiterate, it is not the halfhearted or the spiritually lazy who struggle in this area; it is often the highly motivated that will do everything correctly and Biblically who often confine God to their understanding, and who often miss God when He reveals His arm! Don't misunderstand what I'm saying: we need discernment more than ever in this day and age, but understand this —legalism is equally as dangerous as any false doctrine. The poison of legalism is that it confines God to work in a way that I am comfortable with. The legalist's God is too small!

God is neither predictable nor controllable, and that was the offense of Christ: He broke the mould. His disciples were a new

---

[934] John 5:39

breed, and the old wineskins of the religious forms of Judaism were bursting under the pressure of the exuberance of the new wine! Now, I have to say, sadly—and I know very little, but I feel this in my heart —that this may, this very same thing, may be true of movements that have grown out of revival. Let me quote you an author, he says: "Most significant movements start by being a little wide, settle down to respectable middle age—and then, rejoicing in their respectability, relax into a creeping death."[935] Now you can think of many a denomination, many an institution, a para-church organization, and most of them started out from a move of God—but where are they this evening? But even those who still, in a measure, are on fire for God—do they not expect or even, God forbid that we should say it, require God to do it the same way again? That in itself can be a hindrance, and it may be such groups that will oppose the new thing when it comes.

Listen to the same author: "The hostility to revivals is never to the idea of revival, which is ardently prayed for, but to God's answer to our prayers and the unexpected form it may take. To recognize a divine visitation we must view it through twin lenses of discernment and humility. It is easy to recognize it in books, or in retrospect since we are usually accepting the view of the writer of a particular history, but to recognize it when it occurs is more different. During the revivals of the past 300 years many Christians were too confused by their wrong expectations to perceive what God was doing."[936] Vance Havner put it like this: "Evangelicals have all the answers, but they make the wrong conclusions."[937] Evangelicals have all the facts, but they make the wrong conclusions.

SECOND GUESSING GOD

Whenever we think we can second-guess God, I find in my own experience, He scraps the blueprint and surprises us again. I think it's the same with revival—He scraps the blueprint and surprises us again. We know from creation that our God is a God of ultimate variety, and I believe that He is the same in revival. He did a new

---

[935] John White
[936] Ibid.
[937] Vance Havner (1901-1986)

thing in Isaiah's day, He did a new thing in Messiah's day—and let us see that He did a new thing in the days of Pentecost. Turn with me to Joel chapter 2 please, Joel 2 verse 28: "And afterward, I will pour out My Spirit on all people. Your sons and daughters will prophesy, your old men will dream dreams, your young men will see visions. Even on My servants, both men and women, I will pour out My Spirit in those days. I will show wonders in the heavens and on the earth, blood and fire and billows of smoke. The sun will be turned to darkness and the moon to blood before the coming of the great and dreadful day of the Lord. And everyone who calls on the Name of the Lord will be saved; for on Mount Zion and in Jerusalem there will be deliverance, as the Lord has said, even among the survivors whom the Lord calls."[938]

This is the last days, these are the days we are living in—and half of these Words were fulfilled on the Day of Pentecost, God's new thing—and many of them will be fulfilled when our Lord Jesus returns. So let us turn to Acts chapter 2, please, to see the fulfillment of Joel's prophecy. Acts chapter 2, God's new thing, verse 1: "When the day of Pentecost came, they were all together in one place. Suddenly a sound like the blowing of a violent wind came from heaven and filled the whole house where they were sitting. They saw what seemed to be tongues of fire that separated and came to rest on each of them. All of them were filled with the Holy Spirit and began to speak in other tongues as the Spirit enabled them. Now there were staying in Jerusalem God-fearing Jews from every nation under heaven."[939] Now, see the response please, to God's new thing, verse 6, utter confusion! "When they heard this sound, a crowd came together in bewilderment, because each one heard their own language being spoken."[940]

In verses 7 and 8 there is utter amazement, marveling and, indeed, questioning. Verse 7: "Utterly amazed, they asked: 'Aren't all these who are speaking Galileans? Then how is it that each of us hears them in our native language?'"[941] Look at verse 11, the second half, and verse 12—people are perplexed: "'We hear them declaring the

---

[938] Joel 2:28-32
[939] Acts 2:1-5
[940] Acts 2:6
[941] Acts 2:7-8

wonders of God in our own tongues!' Amazed and perplexed, they asked one another, 'What does this mean?'"[942] Look at verse 13, there is ridicule, misunderstanding and mockery: "Some, however, made fun of them and said, 'They have had too much wine.'

Then Peter stood up with the Eleven, raised his voice and addressed the crowd: 'Fellow Jews and all of you who live in Jerusalem, let me explain this to you; listen carefully to what I say. These people are not drunk, as you suppose. It's only nine in the morning! No, this is what was spoken by the prophet Joel.'"[943] The Authorized Version says in verse 16: "This is that, this is that which was spoken by the prophet Joel."

Peter, who was so involved as an instrument in ushering in God's new thing, Peter himself stumbled at the offense of it.

Now, this is the point of Peter as he preached to these Jews: you're familiar with the prophecy, but you have failed to recognize the fulfillment! God's new thing in Isaiah's day, in Messiah's day, in the days of Pentecost—but come with me again to the Apostolic day in general. The first Christians were Jewish, you do know that? At the beginning it was assumed that the special character of their ceremonies and their identity, uniquely, would continue. There was great confusion when Gentiles started being born again—a new thing! It challenged them, and it raised questions like: must these Gentiles become Jews and observe Judaism if we are to accept them? Or, how should we as Jews relate to Gentiles, because we have strict social and dietary laws? And God spoke—and thank God, He still speaks—God spoke to Peter. He was on a housetop in Acts chapter 10, and God gave him a vision in a place called Joppa. He saw a sheet falling down from heaven of unclean animals, unclean in the dietary laws of Judaism, and God said to Peter: "Do not call anything impure that God has made clean."[944]

STUMBLING AT THE OFFENSE OF A NEW THING

You remember, don't you, that Peter had been given the keys to the kingdom. It was Peter who was going to open the kingdom of

[942] Acts 2:11-12
[943] Acts 2:13-16
[944] Acts 10:15

God to the Gentiles. Peter reported back to the Jews that, according to the circumstances regarding Cornelius, Peter said: "I saw the Holy Spirit fall upon them as He did upon us at the beginning." But what happened? Judaisers entered into the Church, we read about them in Galatians. Their message is found in Acts 15 verse 1, and they said that the Gentiles had to be circumcised if they were to be saved. This is the tragedy of that matter: Peter, who was so involved as an instrument in ushering in God's new thing, Peter himself stumbled at the offense of it.

Turn with me to Galatians chapter 2, verse 11 of Galatians 2—I hope you don't mind reading the Bible! Galatians chapter 2 verse 11: "When Cephas," Paul says, "came to Antioch, I opposed him to his face,"—imagine!— "because he stood condemned. For before certain men came from James, he used to eat with the Gentiles. But when they arrived, he began to draw back and separate himself from the Gentiles because he was afraid of those who belonged to the circumcision group. The other Jews joined him in his hypocrisy, so that by their hypocrisy even Barnabas was led astray. When I saw that they were not acting in line with the truth of the Gospel, I said to Cephas in front of them all, 'You are a Jew, yet you live like a Gentile and not like a Jew. How is it, then, that you force Gentiles to follow Jewish customs?'"[945]

GOD ALWAYS UPSETS THE STATUS QUO

Now, listen carefully to what I'm saying: Peter was the instrument to open the kingdom of God to the Gentiles, and yet he stumbled at the offense of God's new thing. Revival always upsets the status quo! Now, we must understand the hurdle it was for the Jews to accept Gentiles—but this was God's new thing and, in fact, more accurately it was God's new man. "For He Himself is our peace, who has made the two groups one and has destroyed the barrier, the dividing wall of hostility."[946]

Jonathan Edwards, the great puritan theologian of revival, said this: "A work of God without stumbling blocks is never to be

---

[945] Galatians 2:11-14
[946] Ephesians 2:14

expected."[947] God is always pushing our boundaries. Shock and awe will always play some part in what God does, and we must not contain God to our sphere of knowledge of Him, or our expectations from Him! Our convictions ought never to become restrictions of what God does in our lives and in our Churches!

God was the God of a new thing in Isaiah's day, in Messiah's day, in the Day of Pentecost, in the Apostolic day, and in the historical revival days. One author says: "From a safe distance of several hundred years or several thousand miles, revival clearly looks invigorating. But when we actually look at a revival (either through close historical study or firsthand investigation) we find something not nearly so clear as we imagined. There is sin and infighting and doctrinal error. And if we find ourselves in the midst of revival, rather than being invigorated, we may be filled with skepticism, or disgust, anger or even fear." Why? Because we fear what we do not understand!

REVIVAL IS MESSY

Why does our expectation not match the reality? Why is revival sometimes so messy? Because revival is war—of course, it's the Lord that has the victory—but that's why it's so untidy at times. When there is unusual emotion expressed—there was a question about this on the panel—where there is apparent disorder we start to fear. Some of the phenomenon we do not understand, we fear. Much opposition to revival is based on a wrong notion of order. Someone has said: "If we insist that revival must be decent and orderly, as we define those terms, we automatically blind ourselves to most revivals. Revival stirs our hearts when we read about it, but would we perceive it as of God if it broke out noisily in one of our own services or meetings?"

The revival that we have heard so much about these couple of days that accompanied Evan Roberts was denounced by a Congregational minister—Peter Price was his name—as a sham and a mockery. I'm quoting him now, "a sham and a mockery, a blasphemous travesty of the real thing." What made this all the more sad was the fact that Prices' own church had been blessed with revival.

---

[947] Jonathan Edwards (1703-1758)

The additions of hundreds of converts a few months previously in 1904 were to his church. Now Price clearly objected to some of the style of Evan Roberts, and I'm sure all would agree that Evan Roberts was not perfect—but unfortunately Price overplayed his opposition and could not see the hand of God in what he disagreed with. Warren Wiersbe once said: "It never ceases to amaze me that God blesses people I disagree with."

Dr Forbes Winslow, who was a psychiatrist in Evan Roberts' day, took a different line of attack against Roberts, and I'm quoting him, he said: "I would have men like Evan Roberts locked up as a common felon, and their meetings prohibited like those of the socialists and anarchists as being dangerous to the public"—even though four doctors had signed a certificate of Roberts' physical and mental health. It was jibes like those, and the cruel attack of his brother in Christ, Peter Price, that broke the evangelist. By the spring of 1906 he began to retire from public life.

There are stories about Whitefield and Wesley 200 years previous to the Welsh revival. They were opposed because they preached in the open-air, and not in a church building. Whitefield, in a place called Cambuslang in Scotland where there was a great move of God, Whitefield had tracts written against him, and he was accused as 'a limb of antichrist' for being in the church of England. In the 1940s Duncan Campbell was accused of hypnotizing people in the Scottish islands, and he was opposed by other ministers because of his teaching on the Baptism of the Holy Spirit. Listen to what Arthur Wallace says: "If we find a revival that is not spoken against, we had better look again to ensure that it is revival."

GOD WANTS TO DO A NEW THING TODAY!

God did a new thing in Isaiah's day, He did a new thing in Messiah's day, He did a new thing in the days of Pentecost, He did a new thing in the days of the Apostles, and He did a new thing in the days of historical revival—Oh, He wants to do a new thing today! I believe that He has started a new thing! But someone will ask: how do we know the genuine article? Oh, that is a question. Not everything that is new is true. Jonathan Edwards, in a paper entitled *The Distinguishing Marks of a Work of the Spirit of God*, expounds 1

John chapter 4 and verse 1—and I'm almost finished, please turn with me to it. First John chapter 4 verse 1, the great puritan theologian on revival said in that paper: "How can one spot a genuine as from a false prophet?" I believe the distinction is the same with genuine revival and false so-called moves of God. "Dear friends, do not believe every spirit, but test the spirits to see whether they are from God, because many false prophets have gone out into the world."[948]

Jonathan Edwards expounds 1 John chapter 4, the whole thing, and we haven't got time to read through it—read through it when you go home—but here's how he differentiates between the genuine and the false: One, does the preaching in the movement affirm the historic Jesus as the crucified and risen Messiah? Is it Christ-centred? Two, does it oppose sin and worldly lusts? Three, does it awaken respect for Scripture by affirming its truth and its divine source? Four, does it awaken an awareness of the shortness of life and the coming of judgment? Five, does it awaken genuine love, both towards God and one's neighbour? Six, does it produce converts with good fruit in their lives?

Someone has said: "It will be from such an orchard, the orchard of 1 John 4, that the fruit of any new thing will come forth from"—but ultimately, time and truth go together. Time will tell, but these timeless truths will be evident! Now, that said, with all the scriptural knowledge, with all the discernment that we can get: when God does a new thing, His new thing, it will be new! "'For My thoughts are not your thoughts, neither are your ways My ways,' declares the Lord."[949]

A SOLEMN WARNING OF FIGHTING AGAINST GOD

I have discharged the burden: do we not need for God to do something new? Do we not need for God to do a new thing in our day and generation? But saints beware, revival movement beware when it comes, lest you be found, or I be found, to fight against God.

Let us pray. While all our heads bowed please, we are in God's presence, and I have felt God's presence nearer to me today than I

---

[948] 1 John 4:1
[949] Isaiah 55:8

think I ever have. While your head is bowed, ask yourself: are your expectations on the altar, your expectations of what revival must be, should be, and will be? Now I am a grasshopper in the presence of giants here tonight, giants of men in the Spirit who have experienced revival—I have not. But I trust them in the Spirit when I say and ask —if it might seem bold to ask it—are you restricting God to what He did before? Are you limiting God to something that He has done in the past? Will you hear His voice? "Remember not the former things. You can't miss what I'm doing now if you would look at it."

Father, I am sorry that I'm so weak, and just maybe not getting this across the way it should be or it must be. O God, O God, You're doing a new thing, You're calling a Remnant of people from many lands, and You have a burning in their heart from the Holy Spirit. O God, there's something new that we believe is going to happen. We don't want sham, we don't want false fire, we don't want counterfeit, we want the real thing —and yet Lord, let none of us limit You. O God, let us not miss it. "Pass me not, O gentle Savior, Hear my humble cry; While on others Thou art calling, Do not pass me by."

Submission and Leadership
by brother Zac

[EDITOR'S NOTE: As you gather together under the Headship of Jesus Christ may you be open to the Lord, by His Spirit, to see godly leaders raised up that are humble and serve the body of Christ. Not leaders that seek their own honor or use believers to exalt themselves. Rather, servant leaders who emulate Jesus Christ and desire others in the body to come to full maturity in the Lord. Hence, in the end, leaders raise up other leaders, for that is the goal; *true servanthood's aim is for others*. To submit to such leaders who share in the character of the early Apostles and the Lord will be of great benefit and blessing to gatherings. Un-submission leads to carnality and is the first sin of the devil[950] who did not submit to God's authority over him. Though in the early stages of a gathering a leader might not be gifted or called, so always believers must defer and exalt the Lord Jesus Christ as the ultimate leader over the Church Assembly.]

The laws of the Kingdom of God are quite opposite to the laws of earthly kingdoms—as different as Heaven is from earth.[951]

On earth, leaders who exercise authority over others are considered to be superior, and those who have to submit, inferior. It is exactly the reverse in the body of Christ. The laws of the body call us to:

---

[950] 1 Timothy 3:6
[951] Isaiah 55:8,9

"Honor Christ by submitting to each other";[952]
"Serve each other with humble spirits";[953]
And "through love, serve one another."[954]

Every member is called to submit to and serve the other. "How is this possible?" one may ask, "Are not the younger ones called to submit to the elders?"

Such a question arises because submission is often misunderstood to mean obedience alone. We can submit to others by denying ourselves also. This is how Jesus lived. He denied His rights constantly in His relationships with others. This is the primary meaning of submission. And this is what each member of the Body is called to do.

Jesus has shown us the glory of submission, and so we should rejoice to walk this pathway all through our lives.

SUBMISSION TO DIVINELY APPOINTED AUTHORITY

God is the ultimate authority in the universe. There is no doubt about that whatsoever. But God also delegates authority. Government rulers, parents and Church leaders have authority in society, homes and churches.

The Church is not, as some consider it, a democracy where everyone is directly responsible to God alone. No. There are leaders appointed by the Lord in the body, whom we should submit to and obey. This is the will of God and clearly taught in Scripture.

Just as the Word of God commands people to submit to rulers, wives to husbands, children to parents, and servants to masters, so also it commands subjection in the Church.

For example, the Bible teaches that man is God's delegated authority over woman. Even though redeemed men and women are equally members of the Body of Christ, yet God commands woman to be in subjection to man in the Church.[955]

Similarly, God has placed elders to give leadership to local Churches. Where elders are truly placed of God in a Church, they are

[952] Ephesians 5:21 (*The Living Bible*)
[953] 1 Peter 5:5 (*The Living Bible*)
[954] Galatians 5:6
[955] 1 Corinthians 11:3, 1 Corinthians 14:33-35, 1 Timothy 2:11-13

the Lord's delegates and wield something of His authority. The Lord told the disciples whom He sent out, "The one who listens to you listens to Me, and the one who rejects you rejects Me."[956]

The Word of God has commands such as:

"Obey your leaders, and submit to them; for they keep watch over your souls, as those who will give an account. Let them do this with joy and not with grief, for this would be unprofitable for you."[957]

"Now we ask you, brothers and sisters, to acknowledge those who work hard among you, who care for you in the Lord and who admonish you. Hold them in the highest regard in love because of their work. Live in peace with each other."[958]

"You know that the household of Stephanas were the first converts in Achaia, and they have devoted themselves to the service of the Lord's people. I urge you, brothers and sisters, to submit to such people and to everyone who joins in the work and labors at it."[959]

"The elders who direct the affairs of the Church well are worthy of double honor, especially those whose work is preaching and teaching."[960]

"In the same way, you who are younger, submit yourselves to your elders."[961]

God places us as members of Christ's Body in fellowship groups (*Churches or teams of Christian workers*). Therein, we are called to submit to the spiritual leaders God appoints over us, and to move with them as a team. In individual matters, it comes to us through our spiritual leaders.

In Acts 16:9-10, we read that Paul alone received guidance from God as to where he and his team of workers were to proceed next. His team, comprising of Silas, Timothy and Luke, followed him, fully believing that God was leading, for they were working under Paul's leadership. It was not necessary for them to obtain separate guidance

---

[956] Luke 10:16

[957] Hebrews 13:17 (*New American Standard Bible*)

[958] 1 Thessalonians 5:12-13

[959] 1 Corinthians 16:15-16

[960] 1 Timothy 5:17

[961] 1 Peter 5:5

from God for their move, for it was a team matter and God had already spoken to their leader.

In the human body too, certain members are so placed that they have to move when certain other members move. For example, the little finger on my right hand is an independent member that can move by itself, in direct obedience to signals from the head. At the same time, being a member of my right arm, it has to move along with that arm when the arm moves. It cannot detach itself from my arm at such times and refuse to move, for God has placed it as a part of the *team* of members that constitute my right arm. It does not have to move when my left arm moves, for it is not a member of that team, but it does have to move with its own team.

If God has placed us in a Church fellowship, or in a team of Christian workers, we are obliged to submit to the leadership that God has placed over us and to follow them in team matters. The only thing that we need to be sure of is that God has placed us in that team. Once that matter is settled, there is no question but that God expects us to submit to and obey our leaders. Many problems in Christian work are solved once this Scriptural principle is understood.

Consider the example of the Son of God Himself. As a young lad, we read that He lived in subjection to Joseph and Mary.[962] Jesus was perfect. Joseph and Mary were not. Yet the Perfect One lived for years in subjection to imperfect human beings, because that was God's will for Him. The Father's will settled all matters with finality for Jesus. If His Father wanted him to live in subjection to Joseph and Mary, He would do just that—and that too, for as long as His Father wanted Him to.

A time did come later on in Jesus' life, when (*after His Baptism*) He ceased to be subject to them—when His Father called Him to leave His home and move out into His ministry as the Son of God. Thereafter, His answer to His mother Mary was, "What do I have to do with you."[963] But as long as His Father kept Him in subjection to Joseph and Mary, He joyfully submitted.

---

[962] Luke 2:51
[963] John 2:4

So we see, from the example of the Perfect Son of God too, that the only important question is, "Is it God's will that I should be in this fellowship?" If the answer is 'Yes,' then it becomes our duty to submit to God-appointed leadership.

Rebellion against authority was the first sin committed in the universe, when Lucifer, the head of the angels, rebelled against God's authority over him.

In the world today, there are two spirits operating—the Spirit of Christ leading people to submit to divinely constituted authority, and the spirit of Satan leading people to rebel against such authority.

The spirit of rebellion is rife today in society, in the home and in the Church too. This is a clear indication of the world rapidly drifting away from God, and being increasingly controlled by Satan. We are called as members of Christ's body to stand against this satanic principle and to follow Christ's example of submission.

We can never lose out by submission to God-appointed leadership. On the other hand, we have a lot to lose by rebellion.

Submission to divinely appointed leadership is God's method of leading us on to spiritual maturity. We shall remain spiritually stunted if we do not submit where God calls us to.

Many a believer has never learned in experience the reality of God's sovereignty because he has never known what it is to be checked and thwarted in his plans as a result of a humble submission to his spiritual leaders. No one can serve God effectively or be a spiritual leader himself who has never known submission to others at any time in his life.

Submission is not something disgraceful and oppressive, as the Devil whispers in our ears. On the contrary, it is the means by which God protects us spiritually. In the early years of our Christian life, when we are still ignorant of the ways of God, we can be saved from many a pitfall ourselves and also be protected from leading others astray in our youthful zeal, if we submit to our spiritual leaders. Those years spent in submission can also be the time when God teaches us the laws of His Kingdom and thereby makes us spiritually wealthy, so that we can have a ministry to others.

How much we lose when we evade the pathway of submission!

LEADERSHIP IN THE BODY OF CHRIST

God Himself calls some members of the body of Christ to exercise spiritual leadership over others.

One of the first things that all such leaders must recognize is that Christ is the only Head of the body. Headship is never delegated by Christ to anyone. Individual domination in a local Church (*or group of Churches*) or in a fellowship of Christian workers, is therefore a positive violation of the sovereign Headship of Christ.

This is why the leadership prescribed for the New Testament Church is through a body of elders (*plural not singular*). The elders together are to exercise spiritual authority.[964]

In Matthew 18:18-20, Jesus said that where two or three gathered together in His Name, He would be present in their midst giving them authority to bind and to free. The immediate context of the passage (*see v.17*) seems to indicate that Christ was referring primarily (*though not exclusively*) to the elders of the Church (*being at least two or three in number*) exercising this authority. One person by himself apparently could not exercise such authority. (*Otherwise it would have been meaningless for Christ to specify: Two or three.*)

We are not living today under Old Testament conditions. In those days, God often appointed one man to lead His people—e.g. Moses, Joshua, David, etc., Those leaders were all types of Christ. Now that Christ has come, He alone is the Head of the people of God. And He works through corporate leadership in the body.

In the early days of the Christian era, the Lord did give a special authority to the eleven Apostles and to the Apostle Paul over the Churches, but that was because the Apostles were the foundation stones of the Church[965] and were the channels through which God gave His written Word to the Church. Such a situation does not exist today, and so it would not only be foolish but audacious for anyone to justify his authoritarian actions by reference to Paul's action as an apostle. It is more likely that such a person may be like Diotrephes rather than like Paul.[966]

---

[964] Acts 14:23, Acts 20:17, 1 Timothy 5:17, Titus 1:5, James 5:14, 1 Peter 5:1
[965] Ephesians 2:20, Revelation 21:14
[966] 3 John 9

Diotrephes was a self-appointed 'apostle' who wanted to take the lead single-handed in the Church. He is denounced in no uncertain terms by John.

Wherever a man today seeks to give single-handed leadership to God's people, he stands in great danger of leading them back to Old Testament conditions spiritually. This must be borne in mind especially by those with strong leadership capabilities.

No doubt, God does even today, form teams of Christian workers where a Timothy and a Titus work under a Paul. But this should only be in the initial stages of the formation of the team. As time went by, even Timothy and Titus were considered by Paul as fellow-workers of equal standing and not as junior helpers. The divinely ordained plan for leadership in the Body of Christ is through a group of elders (*whether for a Church or for a team of workers*). This is a provision that God has made for the safety of the Church—to prevent any one person's point of view from becoming too dominant.

It is easy for those with great vision and ability to get impatient with the slowness of others with whom they have to share leadership in Christian work. They may then be tempted to assert themselves, and override others, claiming that they are doing so for the ongoing of the work of God. But such a violation of God's order will finally lead to the stunting of the growth of other members of the Body of Christ.

Look around and see the condition of churches and organizations where there is one strong authoritarian leader, and you will invariably find that the Christians therein are spiritual dwarfs. Such one-man leadership may appear to be dynamic with an abundance of programs, but the Christians who are led do not grow. This is not God's intention for Christ's Body. He would rather have fewer programs and projects, and more spiritual growth among the members.

QUALIFICATIONS FOR LEADERS

Only God can appoint a man to be a spiritual leader. If our appointment to an office is merely by man, we can never exercise Christ's authority. Herein lies the foolishness of those who seek to be voted into positions of Christian leadership—and do not seek to be appointed by God.

A spiritual leader must lead his flock in the way of the Cross. This implies that he must be one who is faithfully walking the way of self-denial himself.

Then again, no one can be a leader in the body of Christ who does not long to be a servant of others, as Christ Himself was. Jesus said, "The kings and great men of the earth lord it over the people; but among you it is different. Whoever wants to be great among you must be your servant. And whoever wants to be greatest of all must be the slave of all. For even I, the Messiah, am not here to be served, but to help others."[967] Paul, the great Apostle, who had an authority exceeding anyone else's, was a servant of others.[968] This is another of the primary qualifications for spiritual leadership.

A spiritual leader is called to exercise authority over those whom God places under him, and at the same time to be a brother to them and a fellow-member in the same body. It is this delicately balanced relationship of leader-brother that is often so difficult to maintain. We tend to be unbalanced one way or the other. We shall need much grace from the Lord constantly if we are to maintain this balance. Hence the absolute necessity for the leader to live close to God in a *face-to-face* relationship. This was the secret of Moses' effective leadership of 3 million of God's people in the most adverse of circumstances for 40 years.[969]

Spiritual authority, being God-given, is not something that we have to assert over others or even force others to submit to. We should never compel others to listen to us or to obey us. God Himself will deal with those who resist His representatives. The servant of the Lord does not ever have to strive with men[970]—for if God is behind our authority, why should we seek to defend our position. God will Himself defend us and establish our authority. If we are seeking to assert our authority ourselves, it must be because our authority is not God-given at all.

---

967 Mark 10:42-45 (*The Living Bible*)
968 2 Corinthians 4:5, 1 Corinthians 9:19
969 Deuteronomy 34:10, Numbers 12:8
970 2 Timothy 2:24-25

A spiritual leader should not defend himself or seek to justify and vindicate himself, when attacked or slandered. The Bible says, "Christ is your example. Follow in His steps—He never answered back when insulted; when He suffered He did not threaten to get even; He left His case in the hands of God Who always judges fairly."[971] The Son of God, the greatest authority, refused to strive with men and to assert His rule over them. He left it to God to defend Him and to vindicate Him. This is the path that all under-shepherds in the Church must tread. As a spiritual leader, if you live under God's authority yourself, you can safely leave everything in His Hands. You can afford to ignore slander and criticism and backbiting against you, for God's promise is that He Himself will defend His servants against such attacks.[972] Oswald Chambers has said that when someone flings mud at us, if we try to wipe it off, we will stain our clothes. But if we leave it alone, it will dry up in due course and fall off by itself; and there will not be any stain. This is the wisest way to deal with slander.

Watchman Nee, out of the many years of experience that God gave him in the exercise of spiritual leadership in China, gives us some wise counsel in his book, *Spiritual Authority*. He says:

"It is not the violent or the strong but a man like Paul whose bodily presence is weak and whose speech is of no account[973]—whom God will establish as an authority. People usually assume such things as the following to be the necessary requirements for an authority: splendor and magnificence, strength of personality, bearing or appearance, and power. To be an authority, they reason, one must possess a strong determination, clever ideas, and eloquent lips. But it is not these that represent authority; instead they stand for the flesh. No one in the Old Testament exceeded Moses as a God-established authority, yet he was the meekest of all men. While he was in Egypt he was quite fierce, both in killing the Egyptian and in reprimanding the Hebrews. He dealt with people by his own fleshly hand. So at that time God did not appoint him as an authority. It was only after he had become very meek—more than all men on earth[974]—that God used him to be an authority. The person least likely to be given

[971] 1 Peter 2:21-23 (*The Living Bible*)
[972] Isaiah 54:17
[973] 2 Corinthians 10:10
[974] Numbers 12:3

authority is often the very one who considers himself an authority. Likewise, the more authority a person thinks he has, the less he actually does have.

"Authority is set up to execute God's order, not to uplift oneself. It is to give God's children a sense of God, not to give a sense of oneself. The important thing is to help people to be subject to God's authority. To be a delegated authority is not at all an easy thing, because it requires the emptying of oneself.

"Authority is not a matter of position. Where spiritual ministry is lacking, there can be no positional authority. Whoever has spiritual service before God has authority before men. Who, then, can fight for this authority, for there is no way to strive for ministry? Just as ministry is distributed by the Lord, so authority is also decided by Him. We should not attempt to outdo the authority of our ministry. Many brothers mistakenly imagine that they can take up authority at random, not knowing that one's authority before men is equal to one's ministry before God. If authority exceeds ministry, it becomes positional, and is therefore no longer spiritual.

"Those who seek to exercise authority should not be given authority, for God never gives authority to such persons. But strange to say, he who senses his incompetency is the one to whom God gives authority. A man needs to fall before God before he can be used; whenever he lifts himself up he is rejected by God.

"How serious will be the judgment upon those who grab God's authority with their carnal hands. May we fear authority as we fear the fire of Hell. To represent God is not an easy thing; it is too great and too marvelous for us to touch. We need to walk strictly in the way of obedience. The path for us is obedience, not authority; it is to be servants, not to be heads; to be slaves, not to be rulers. Both Moses and David were the greatest of authorities, yet they were not people who tried to establish their own authority. Those today who desire to be in authority ought to follow their footsteps. There should always be fear and trembling in this matter of being an authority."[975]

The Church today suffers because of a great dearth of spiritual leaders. There are many who hold titles and exercise their authority officially. But spiritual leadership is scarcely to be found. Jesus once

---

[975] Watchman Nee (1903-1972)

looked out at the crowds that came to Him and felt great pity for them, "Because their problems were so great and they didn't know what to do or where to go for help. They were like sheep without a shepherd."[976] The situation is just the same today.

We desperately need leaders in the Church, who have the heart of a shepherd and the spirit of a servant, men who fear God and tremble at His Word.

---

[976] Matthew 9:36 (*The Living Bible*)

Baptism of the Holy Spirit
by brother Denny

[EDITOR'S NOTE: In our day, the importance of experiencing the true Spirit Baptism is paramount. Because of satanic counterfeits, the true body of Christ has been alarmed and made hesitant to call out to the Lord for a fresh infusion of God's Spirit in a public meeting or private prayer time. We believe that as believers gather it is essential to pray for endowments of the Holy Spirit. If the presence of God is not with the Church, She will never further the purpose of God in the earth. The Gospels and the Book of Acts teaches the Baptism of the Holy Spirit.[977] If we say we believe the Bible then we must also believe in this Baptism. The Book of 1 Corinthians teaches us that the Holy Spirit gives diverse gifts and that not all receive the gift of speaking in tongues.[978]   May God protect, shield and keep saints from the counterfeit. This article emphasizes faith in receiving the Holy Spirit. This must also be balanced with asking the Lord verbally for the Spirit (*see Luke 11:5-13*). Below is the text transcription of the message]:

I don't know, maybe this week is like what Ezekiel was talking about there back in the Old Testament. Remember when he talked about this river flowing out from under the throne of heaven? And he went so far and he was in to his ankles, and then he went so far and

---

[977] Matthew 3:11, Mark 1:8, Luke 3:16, John 1:33
[978] 1 Corinthians 12:10

he was in up to knees, and then he went so far and he was in up to his waist, and then he was swimming! Do it, Lord, do it.

Let's stand for a word of prayer. Can we do that?

Lord we love You this morning. We come to You in Jesus' Name. We thank You for loving us. We don't really understand it, but we thank You that You do, You love us. Father, we come to You this morning because we have no where else to go. We come to You this morning because we don't have anything to say. If You don't give us something to say, Lord, we know. We come to You this morning because without You we can do nothing, and so we pray that You will again this morning, and throughout the day, anoint this day with Your presence. Anoint this preacher with Your anointing, Lord, with Your message for the day. Anoint the ears of our heart, Lord, the eyes of our understanding this day. We pray in Jesus' Name, Amen.

This morning I want to speak on the Baptism of the Holy Spirit, and New Testament reality. What is the effect of the anointing of the Holy Spirit in a believer's life? The prophet Samuel was speaking prophetically to Saul during the time he was to be anointed king. He said these words to Saul. He said, "The Spirit of the Lord will come powerfully upon you, and you will prophesy with them; and you will be changed into a different person."[979] That's powerful. The Spirit of the Lord is going to come upon you, Saul, and you will prophesy, and you shall be turned into another man. That puts the whole thing in a nutshell, doesn't it? The one hundred and twenty in the upper room, and the Apostles, I'm sure that they could say those very words. "When the day of Pentecost came, the Spirit of the Lord came upon us, and we prophesied and we were turned into another man."[980]

WITHOUT PENTECOST

Before that, they had dull apprehensions of the truth that Jesus was speaking to them. Before that, they had a weak vision, seeing very dimly the things that Christ was trying to describe to them that would happen in the future. Before that, they were a feeble bunch, with a feeble faith. Before that, they were weak in their brotherly love

---

[979] 1 Samuel 10:6
[980] Acts 2:1

one for another, and their resolutions were short lived. They were fearful, they were doubters, they were running scared, and I think we could probably say just to describe just an overall description of them —I mean, they were very sincere. These were the men that had enough insight to see way beyond those Pharisees who knew their Bibles inside and out. They had enough insight to say, "We have found the Messiah."[981] They were full of religious zeal. They were seeking the highest that they knew.

They were not evil, wicked men, but they were moving in the natural rather than in the spiritual. I think that's a good description. They had open hearts, they had found the Messiah, they had forsaken all, they treasured His Word, but yet they moved in the realm of the natural so much of the time. That's a good description of them.

Maybe it's a good description of us also. We are here, we love to be here, we love the Word, we're exited about what's happening here, but if we give an overall evaluation of our day-to-day life, we move in the natural, rather than the spiritual, most of the time. I mean, Peter was so bold when Christ began to prophesy to them, and tell them that He was going to go to the cross, and shed His blood, which would be the redemption of all mankind. Peter was so much in the natural and so out of tune in the spiritual that Christ had to say to him, "Get behind me, Satan! You are a stumbling block to me; you do not have in mind the concerns of God, but merely human concerns."[982]

CHANGED INTO ANOTHER MAN

They moved in the realm of the natural so much of the time, but after Pentecost, they were changed into another man. Peter was changed into another man after Pentecost. They began to move in the realm of the Spirit. Their character was transformed. They were different men. Their words became quick and powerful, life changing words. Their words cut to the heart.

Imagine just a little bit with me this morning the day after Pentecost. Yesterday was a busy day, Peter was busy all day long.

[981] John 1:41
[982] Matthew 16:23

There was a lot going on during the day of the Pentecost. I'm not sure how many people he baptized himself, but I'm sure when he laid his head down to go to sleep, at the end of that day, the day of Pentecost, he was very weary in body. He woke up the next morning, he heard the Lord speaking in him, *Good morning, Peter.* With the ears of his heart he heard the voice of His Savior the Lord Jesus Christ who told him, "I will not leave you as orphans; I will come to you,[983] Peter. I will come to you." That was the day after Pentecost. Imagine when they all got together, and began to share,

"I'm just so different, I'm just so different!"

"I am, too! I mean the Lord is just speaking inside of my heart!"

"It's that same way with me!"

"Oh, praise God, this is wonderful!"

"Yes, it is! I wonder what it all means?"

"I do too!"

You know those conversations went on the day after Pentecost. Maybe they dropped down on their knees together and started praying, *Oh, Lord, now we understand what You were talking about, Lord! We don't know what we're doing. Lead us, oh God. Oh, please help us to know that to do. Give us Your guidance Lord. Thank You that You didn't leave us comfortless; You didn't leave us as an orphan, but You did come to us.*

MORE THAN A DOCTRINAL STATEMENT

You know Him, He is with you, but He shall be in you. Now do you think that the Lord Jesus was giving those Apostles a doctrinal teaching when He said those words to them, or do you think he was trying to help them to understand that they would have a totally different experience after that day? How many of you think he was giving him a doctrinal statement?

Now it is a doctrinal statement, don't misunderstand me. It is a doctrinal statement, but that is not all it is. "I will not leave you as orphans; I will come to you."[984] Just picture that. He's been with them for three and a half years. Every problem they had, they just

[983] John 14:18
[984] John 14:18

went and said, "Lord what should we do?" It was all cared for. Every question they had, they just went to Him and said, "Well Lord, we don't understand this, could you explain it?" and He gave them the answer. Every situation that they faced: "We have all of these people who need to eat, we don't know what to do with them," He took care of it. But now they were standing on the Mount of Olives and He just disappeared out of their sight. But now it's the day after Pentecost and they understand. He didn't leave us comfortless.

A HOLY PEOPLE FOR GOD

What is the effect of the anointing of the Holy Spirit in the life of the believers? That He, God, would raise up, by that anointing, holy people, with holy hearts, living holy lives, filled with holy character, who walk with a Holy God, and speak holy words, that are anointed by the Holy Spirit.

Brethren, that is what the anointing of the Holy Spirit is all about. That is what it's all about. That is what is in the longing heart of God for His people. God is an awesome, Holy God. One-half a second glimpse of this Holy God that we've been talking about all week long—one-half of a second glimpse of Him would bring every one of us down on our face in utter abandonment, and it's the longing of the heart of God that His great Name would be sanctified among the heathen by the way that His people move and live and act and speak in this world around us.

That's the longing of his heart, and it was the joy that was set before the Lord Jesus as He despised the shame and endured the cross. Don't you think for a minute, brethren, that Jesus went through all of that so that He could buy a one-way ticket to heaven for you and me. He didn't go through all of that so that we could live our own selfish lives all of our days, and end up in glory for all of eternity after that. Brethren, that's not what Jesus went to the cross for. He went to the cross that He might raise up, through the anointing that was poured out because of that cross, a holy people anointed with the Holy Spirit, speaking holy Words!

We all know that, that's nothing new to us. That's not a new revelation, but it's good for us to consider again and again. To explain the whole plan of God in a very simple nutshell: that Anointing was given to make us like Jesus, and you can spend the rest of your life figuring out what all of that means—Amen? To make us a "chosen people, a royal priesthood, a holy nation, God's special possession, that you may declare the praises of Him who called you out of darkness into his wonderful light."[985] That is what the anointing of the Holy Spirit is all about, brethren, to cause us to glorify God; to cause us to love God with all of our heart and mind and soul and strength; to turn our hearts away from selfishness, to love your neighbors as yourself. This is what the anointing of the Holy Spirit is all about; that we henceforth no longer live unto ourselves but unto Him.

TWOFOLD PURPOSE OF THE BAPTISM

As I see the Baptism of the Holy Spirit I see a twofold purpose of the Baptism of the Holy Spirit. Number one, to empower us to be New Testament Christians, emphasizing the *be*, and number two, to empower us to do exploits in building God's kingdom while we are here upon this earth. That combination, brothers, is pretty powerful when you put the two together. To be New Testament Christians, doing exploits of kingdom building while we are here upon this earth, that is what the anointing is all about.

Brethren, New Covenant reality comes through, and by, the overwhelming presence of the living God coming upon us and abiding. Think about that. New Covenant reality comes through, and by, our being overwhelmed by the presence of the living God and abiding in that Presence. That's the only way it comes.

Consider this morning Christ the Anointed One. I told you earlier this week that we would come back to that word. I want to consider Christ the Anointed One this morning. He is the mediator of the New Testament. He is the mediator of the New Covenant. He through the anointing, mediates, dispenses, and gives forth the reality of the New Covenant in our hearts and our lives. That's where it comes from. He is the mediator. Just like this natural world we live in, there is a mediator of the will. When someone dies, there is an executor that has been appointed, that executor is the one who

---

[985] 1 Peter 2:9

mediates the will to those who are written in the will. He dispenses to those the things that are written in the will, and the Lord Jesus Christ, the anointed One, He as mediator, gives that which was written in the will. He mediates the reality of the New Covenant. Consider these words.

The Bible speaks of spiritual warfare. In Ephesians chapter 6 it speaks of spiritual mindedness. In Romans chapter 8 it speaks of a spiritual walk. The Bible speaks about spiritual weapons in 2 Corinthians chapter 10 and spiritual gifts in 1 Corinthians chapter 12. The Bible speaks of spiritual fruit in Galatians chapter 5, and spiritual armor in Ephesians chapter 6, and it speaks of a glorious spiritual ministry in 2 Corinthians chapter 3.

Now all of these things are only reality in a believer's life if they are overwhelmed with the presence of the Living God. Those spiritual realities, they don't mean very much at all if we are not going to live in the power of the Holy Spirit. None of these can happen without the anointing, brethren, it makes no sense at all. They're far away somewhere—these are only far away concepts if we are not filled with the Spirit of God.

I guess the burden that I have this morning is simply this: Here we have this New Testament, and all of the beautiful things that are written in it. But what does it do for us if we're not going to walk in the anointing of the Spirit of God?

LOOKING AT WHAT THE BIBLE SAYS

God began to lay all of these things on my heart. I don't know if I can tell you when, but I began to give them to the people, week after week, not in condemnation, but to lay them out and say to the brothers and the sisters, "Brothers, this is it! Look at it! Look what the Bible says! Look what the New Testament says! Let's go for this! Let's go for this kind of life! Come on, let's go!" But all the while doing that and saying those words, as the weeks and months go by and turn into years, it takes a while to get through, realizing that so many of the people do not live anywhere near this. They don't live anywhere near this, and if you're a minister in this room, you know that's the way it is. You know it.

Slowly it dawned upon me as I prayed. You know, when you minister to your people, and you know you're giving them solid meat, good stuff, things that could change their life, and you don't see them changing, you have to then say, "What's wrong, here? Is there something wrong with me?" And I'm sure that there's something wrong with me. But slowly it dawned upon me as I prayed about it (*I pray about it much*), that these people can't do this stuff. They've never been empowered by the Holy Spirit. They can't do this stuff.

I'm getting up on Sunday morning, preaching out of Ephesians, chapter 3, "Strengthen you with power through His Spirit in your inner being."[986] I would finish my sermon, and go sit down and everybody just sat there, and they didn't even say anything. At first I thought, "Hey, maybe I didn't do that right." No, one's saying anything. I try to figure it out, but I think I figured it out. They're just sitting there thinking, "Oh! I am no where near that! I have nothing to say! I'm just going to sit here." It began to dawn upon me: These people can't do this. They've never been empowered with the Holy Spirit! They've never been overwhelmed with the Spirit of the living God. They've never been strengthened with might by His spirit in the inner man. They don't know the reality of Christ dwelling in their hearts by faith. They are not comprehending the breadth and the depth and the lengths and the height. They do not know the experiential knowledge of the love of Christ which passes knowledge and can't be explained! They need the Holy Spirit to make it a reality, and, brothers, so do you. To make it a reality, you need the Holy Spirit.

What a miserable way to be a New Testament Christian! Without reality. But that's reality in many, many people's lives. They're just kind of gazing in there, *Oh, that's beautiful. My, yes. Look at all of it! Wow, that's glorious, but we can't get it.* Dear brothers, these things are made real in the life of the believer by the power of the Holy Spirit and there's no other way—no other way!

---

[986] Ephesians 3:16

CRUCIFIED WITH CHRIST

Here are the Words of the New Testament, "I have been crucified with Christ and I no longer live, but Christ lives in me."[987] Isn't that a beautiful verse? Wouldn't that be a beautiful life, to walk through life in the reality of that? "I am crucified through Christ, nevertheless I live. Yet not I but Christ liveth in me, the spirit of wisdom and revelation in the knowledge of Him." Do you know what that verse means, brethren? That's talking about the spiritual revelation of the Lord Jesus Christ! It's talking about a spiritual revealing of Christ and His glory, and His majesty, and His character, and His beauty being imparted to my heart and my life, but it won't be imparted if I don't see it, and I won't see it if I don't live in the unction of the Holy Spirit. It's just some nice story, otherwise. Just some nice story about a nice man.

Listen to the Words of the New Testament, "Transformed into His image with ever-increasing glory."[988] Oh, you want to be changed this morning, brethren? You want to be changed? "Changed from glory to glory, even as by the Spirit of the Lord." See these verses? They're the New Testament! We read them all of the time! *God wants them to be a reality to us.* That verse, if I understand that verse at all, what that verse is saying to me is this: That I should be living in the unction of the Holy Spirit, and under that unction, I should open up this Bible with an open face beholding as in a glass, the glory of the Lord in the pages of this Book. And as I gaze by the Spirit on the glory of the Lord in the pages in this Book, I am changed into this very image. Isn't that a right interpretation of those verses?

NORMAL NEW TESTAMENT CHRISTIANITY

You might say, "Well, brother Denny, you're going way over our heads today." I may be going over our heads, but this is normal New Testament Christianity, and if it's going over our head we need to come to grips with he fact that we're anemic. I mean, we sing the song, "Oh, to be like Thee, blessed Redeemer, Oh, to be like Thee."

---

[987] Galatians 2:20
[988] 2 Corinthians 3:18

That song doesn't become a reality in our life. We aren't changed into the image of Christ if we aren't going to live in the power of the Spirit of the Living God. And that's why men can go for twenty years, and still there's not much about them. Twenty years? Why? Well, they read their Bible, they go to church, you know, all of that stuff. But there's not abiding anointing in their life, and because there isn't, they don't have much imparted as the weeks go by and the years go by, they stay relatively the same.

"Where the Spirit of the Lord is, there is freedom."[989] That is the power to do God's will. Beautiful verse, that verse speaks victory. That verse speaks of being more than conquerors. Amen? Where the Spirit of the Lord is, we are more than conquerors. Christ in you, the hope of glory. See these verses. Oh listen, I could do this for a long time, I mean my heart is full of all of these verses. I've been reveling in the revelation of the New Covenant. But, how about it—theological statement or living reality? Christ in you, the hope of glory. Paul says, "The mystery that has been kept hidden for ages and generations, but is now disclosed to the Lord's people."[990] A mystery. Christ can live in you, and that is the hope of glory. You want your one-way ticket to heaven in your back pocket? That's how you keep that one way ticket in your back pocket. Christ living in me, in reality, the hope of glory.

"If the Spirit of Him who raised Jesus from the dead is living in you."[991] That word *living* means to make a home. It doesn't mean to visit every now and then. *Living in you*, He that raised up Christ from the dead shall also quicken your mortal bodies. How is the resurrection going to take place? By His Spirit that lives in you. Christ in you, in reality, is the hope of glory. That's the reality of the hope of the resurrection. "It is God who works in you to will and to act in order to fulfill His good purpose."[992] What a beautiful way to live! With God living inside of me, motivating me, inspiring me, empowering me, leading me to be motivated to want to do, and empower me to do His good pleasure. That's beautiful! I can handle that kind of Christian life, how about you? Amen! Lord, I'll vote for

---

[989] 2 Corinthians 3:17
[990] Colossians 1:26
[991] Romans 8:11
[992] Philippians 2:13

that one! "Dead to sin but alive to God in Christ Jesus"[993]—and I could just go on, and on, and on. There are so many of them. It's the reading of the will, brethren! It's what Jesus bought and paid for by His death, and through the resurrection. It's the will and Testament of Jesus Christ.

THE IN-CHRIST EXPERIENCE

This is the *in-Christ* experience in the life of a believer that we are talking about here. The in-Christ experience in the life of a believer. You know all of those verses in the Bible, *In Him*. In whom? *In Christ*. This is the in-Christ experience in the life of a believer. The anointing of the Holy Spirit is the in-Christ experience in the life of a believer. That's it. To be in Christ is to be in the anointing. To be in the anointing is to be in Christ. Why? He is the anointed. That's what His Name means. He is the Anointed. He is anointed now, brethren. To be in the anointing is to be in Christ. We are the body of the Anointed One. Can I say it that way? That's right, isn't it? "Now you are the body of Christ, and each one of you is a part of it."[994] Paul says, "You are the body of the Anointed One." You can stay on that verse for about two weeks. "You are the body of the Anointed One."

Or, let me say, *Are you the body of the Anointed One?* He has no hands but our hands. He has no body to live out His glorious holiness through, but our bodies. Are you the body of the Anointed One? These are good questions to consider this morning. These are good questions. I mean, it changes things quite a bit. We can't sit in here this morning and say, "Yeah, the worldly church out there—it's apostate. And they're this, and they're that, and they're worldly, and they're departing." We can't sit here this morning and throw any stones, brethren.

Are you part of the body of the Anointed One? These are probing questions this morning. Probing questions. These are deep realities we're speaking about, brethren. Realities. You begin to see them rising up out of the Book of Hebrews if you read it about thirty times. You know the Book of Hebrews? You know, our High Priests are more

---

[993] Romans 6:11
[994] 1 Corinthians 12:27

excellent priests with the mediator of the New Covenant, a spiritual priesthood? The minister of the heavenly sanctuary? That's our Christ. The ministry of the heavenly sanctuary. Have you been into the throne room lately? Don't you know you have a Minister of the heavenly sanctuary? We have our Aaron, bless God! We have Him! Paul said to the Hebrews, "We have much to say about this, but it is hard to make it clear to you because you no longer try to understand."[995]

A NEW TESTAMENT IMPERATIVE

Dear brothers, what I'm speaking about here is not a New Testament option. This is a New Testament imperative. It is not an option. Sometimes, somehow, I think that we have gotten that in our mind. "Oh well, the preachers must have this—they need to be anointed. Yes, they need to be men of God, they're our preachers." No, this is a New Testament imperative for every child of God. I think we skipped the Book of Acts and moved—ran into the Epistles, and we're miserably stumbling around in there, trying to figure out what this Christian life is all about. We skipped the Book of Acts, brethren, and the New Testament is just kind of a phase to us. We bounce around in there, and try over here. "That's not the way," so you try over this way. We're just bouncing around in there, and we've skipped the Book of Acts. We cannot simply go our way living a carnal, subnormal Christian life anymore. We can't do it. It's time to have Judgment Day early.

Have you been immersed in the overwhelming presence of the Living God since ye believed? Remember I told you the other day that interesting little bit of information about the word Christ—sixty times in the Gospels. Five-hundred times from Pentecost, onward. Christ, the Anointed, all through the New Testament, five-hundred times. That phrase is used in the New Testament from Pentecost onward five-hundred times: The Anointed!

Yet the people of God are not anointed! How can this be? Christ was anointed with the Holy Spirit for His earthly ministry.[996] But

---

995 Hebrews 5:11
996 Luke 3, Matthew 3

Christ is also anointed with the Holy Spirit for His heavenly ministry. Turn to Acts 2. Hold your place there, and turn to Psalm 133 for a moment. Psalm 133 says, "How good and pleasant it is when God's people live together in unity!"[997] And may I put it into the New Testament context, for brethren to dwell together in the unity of the Spirit. The word behold means, *Stop, and gaze upon that.* Now verse 2, "It is like the precious ointment upon the head that ran down upon the beard, even Aaron's beard, that went down to the skirt of his garment."[998]

You get that picture? Aaron was anointed with the precious ointment. They poured it on his head, and I think it's very clear just from looking at that Scripture that they didn't do it like this. What do you think? They dumped it on him, and it went down onto his head, and went down over his beard, and started dripping down off of his beard, and started landing on his shoulders, and flowed and ran down all the way to the hem of his garment. Get the picture?

OUR HEAVENLY AARON

Now let's look at the heavenly Aaron for a moment. Acts chapter 2, verse 33. Peter must have got this in the spirit of revelation, because I know he did didn't study for that sermon that he preached on the day of Pentecost. He didn't meditate on that one ahead of time, but in his explanation to all of these people that are trying to figure out what is going on and why these men, these women, these one-hundred and twenty that came out of the upper room seem like they're drunk in the middle of the day, speaking all kinds of languages and all these people from all different countries from all over the known world are hearing these words in their own language.

Peter stands up to try to explain to them what's going on, and of course he begins by telling them "No, this is what was spoken by the prophet Joel,"[999] and he quotes the verses there out of the Book of Joel. Then he goes on to preach about Christ, the Christ. And he says in verse 32, "God has raised this Jesus to life, and we are all witnesses of it. Exalted to the right hand of God, He has received from the

---

997 Psalm 133:1
998 Psalm 133:2
999 Acts 2:16

Father the promised Holy Spirit."[1000] Received? Same word. Same thing. Received, baptized, filled, fallen upon—all of those are the same word. "Jesus *received* the promise of the Holy Spirit, and has poured out what you now see and hear."[1001]

Now just picture our heavenly Aaron. He's been to the cross, He despised the shame, He shed His blood for the sins of humanity, He bore our sins in His own body on the tree, He died for you and I, they laid Him in the grave, three days later he came up from the grave, He was raised from the dead according to the Spirit of Holiness, He walked with them for forty days, then He ascended back up to the Father, and only told them, "Wait for the promise of the Father—it's coming." So, the Head of the body is in heaven, and the Father pours the oil upon the head of the Son in heaven. And the oil runs down over His head, down upon His beard, and it begins to drip down upon the rest of His body. "Suddenly a sound like the blowing of a violent wind came from heaven and filled the whole house where they were sitting,"[1002] and the body of Christ was baptized with the Holy Spirit. That is the Christ which is mentioned five-hundred times from Pentecost to the end of the Bible.

THE HOLY SPIRIT IS A GIFT

Yesterday, we finished our meeting encouraging you in a waiting, believing, faith-filled expectancy. Remember, I warned you that you can get off and go into extremes and all of that, and I encouraged you yesterday that this whole matter is a matter of faith. It is the gift of the Holy Spirit. It is the promise of the Father. And may I say today, it's already given; believe it! The Christ is anointed. Believe it, receive it! By grace through faith, it's done! And I say that, having said everything that I said yesterday, having agreed with everything that Brother Manny said last night that, yes, we need to be clean, yes, our heart needs to be yielded if we're going to move in the flow of the anointing of the Christ. It's absurd to think that we could if we're full of selfishness. But if our heart as we sit here today is clear—I'm not

---

[1000] Acts 2:32-33
[1001] Acts 2:33
[1002] Acts 2:2

saying you have to be a perfect person. You just have to have your heart clear, and your will yielded, saying, *God—anything.*

Brother, it's yours. It's there. It's here. It's a reality. But like everything else in the Christian life, if you don't believe it, you won't enter in—a waiting, believing, faith-filled expectancy. Do you believe it? We're really accountable now, aren't we?

Let's kneel together for prayer. Can we do that?

"He is here, Hallelujah, He is here, Amen,

He is here, Holy, Holy, I will bless His Name again,

He is here, listen closely, hear Him calling out your name,

He is here, you can touch Him, you will never be the same."

Ah, brethren, do you believe that little song this morning? *He is here, you can touch Him.* By faith, by grace through faith, you can touch Him. I want you to pray this little prayer this morning if your heart is clear. If it is not, I plead with you, let it go. But if you heart is clear, I want you to pray this prayer with me:

My dear Heavenly Father, I am Your son. I know that You love me. My heart is clear, washed in the precious blood of Your Son. My will is yielded. I'll do anything You say. My dear Father, I am Your son. By faith this morning, fill me with Your Spirit, Lord. I receive the anointing which is already given. By faith, I receive the anointing, and I thank You for it, Father. In Jesus' Name, Amen.

Without the Holy Spirit of God

by brother Chadwick

[EDITOR'S NOTE: Christianity was birthed in the Holy Spirit. Jesus our Lord taught it was essential to rely and wait for the power of the Spirit. We sadly see many abuses of Spirit-led living in modern Christendom but this should make us all the more hungry for the true manifestation. We are impotent without the infilling power of the Spirit. When we have God in the midst everything changes. We will not be able to stay quiet, we will speak boldly for our Lord that bought us with such a great price.[1003] The underground Church in China chooses their leadership from those who are the hungriest after God. Are you hungry for the living God? For His power displayed in your life?]

The Church knows quite well both the reason and the remedy for failure. The human resources of the Church were never so great. The opportunities of the Church were never so glorious. The need for the work of the Church was never so urgent. The crisis is momentous; and the Church staggers helplessly amid it all. When the ancient Church reproached God with sleeping at the post of duty, God

---

[1003] 1 Corinthians 6:20

charged His people with being staggering drunk.[1004] The Church knows perfectly well what is the matter. The Church has lost the note of authority, the secret of wisdom, and the gift of power, through persistent and willful neglect of the Holy Spirit of God. Confusion and impotence are inevitable when the wisdom and resources of the world are substituted for the presence and power of the Spirit of God.

Proofs abound. The New Testament furnishes examples of Churches filled with the Spirit and Churches without the Spirit. The differences are obvious. The Church of which Apollos was minister had not so much as heard that the Spirit was given.[1005] The Church in our day has no such excuse. Ours is the sin of denial. He has been shut out from the place in which He is indispensable. Religion has been reconstructed without Him. There is no denial of the supernatural, but it is insisted that the supernatural must conform to natural law. It is admitted that truth is inspired, but its inspiration must develop along the lines of natural selection and growth. Religion cannot be allowed to have come upon any other lines than those of literature, philosophy, and ethics. The Christian religion has simply the honor of being less faulty than the rest. Jesus Christ must be accounted for in the same way.

CHRISTIAN BELIEVERS WITHOUT THE SPIRIT

The Church still has a theology of the Holy Spirit, but it has no living consciousness of His presence and power. Theology without experience is like faith without works: it is dead.[1006] The signs of death abound. Prayer-meetings have died out because men did not believe in the Holy Spirit. The liberty of prophesying has gone because men believe in investigation and not in inspiration. There is a dearth of conversions because faith about the new birth as a creative act of the Holy Spirit[1007] has lost its grip on intellect and heart. The experience of the Spirit Baptism is no longer preached and testified, because Christian experience, though it may have to begin in the Spirit, must be perfected in the wisdom of the flesh and the culture of

---

[1004] Isaiah 51:17
[1005] Acts 19:2
[1006] James 2:17
[1007] John 3:6-7

the schools. Confusion and impotence are the inevitable results when the wisdom and resources of the world are substituted for the presence and power of the Spirit.

The cravings lost religious men represent must be met by the experience of Pentecost. Modernism and mysticism are also the products of a religion that is not baptized of the Holy Spirit. Sacerdotalism is another. These things flourish on impoverished soil and dunghills. They are the works of the flesh, and the product of spiritual death. The answer is in the demonstration of a supernatural religion, and the only way to a supernatural religion is in the abiding presence of the Spirit of God.

The Church is the creation of the Holy Spirit. It is a community of believers who owe their religious life from first to last to the Spirit. Apart from Him there can be neither Christian nor Church. The Christian religion is not institutional but experimental. It is not an ordained class, neither is it in ordinances and sacraments. It is not a fellowship of common interest in culture, virtue, or service. Membership is by spiritual birth.[1008] The roll of membership is kept in heaven. Christ is the gate.[1009] He knows them that are His, and they know Him.[1010] The church roll and the Lamb's book of life are not always identical. "Therefore I want you to know that no one who is speaking by the Spirit of God says, 'Jesus be cursed,' and no one can say, 'Jesus is Lord,' except by the Holy Spirit."[1011] And confession of the Lordship of Jesus Christ is the first condition of membership in His Church.[1012] The command to tarry in the city until there came clothing of power from on high[1013] proves that the one essential equipment of the Church is the gift of the Holy Spirit. Nothing else avails for the real work of the Church. For much that is undertaken by the Church He is not necessary. The Holy Spirit is no more needed to run bazaars, social clubs, institutions, and picnics, than He is to run a circus. Religious services and organized institutions do not

---

[1008] John 3:3
[1009] John 10:7
[1010] John 10:14
[1011] 1 Corinthians 12:3
[1012] Romans 10:9
[1013] Luke 24:49

constitute a Christian Church, and these may flourish without the gift of Pentecostal fire.[1014]

THE LIFE OF THE BODY OF CHRIST

The work of the Spirit in the Church is set forth in the promises of Jesus on the eve of His departure, and demonstrated in the Acts of the Apostles. The Gospels tells of "all that Jesus began to do and to teach until the day He was taken up to heaven,"[1015] and the Acts of the Apostles tells of all that He continued to do and to teach after the day in which He was received up. The Holy Spirit is the active, administrative Agent of the glorified Son. He is the Paraclete, the Deputy, the acting Representative of the ascended Christ. His mission is to glorify Christ by perpetuating His character, establishing His kingdom, and accomplishing His redeeming purpose in the world. The Church is the body of Christ,[1016] and the Spirit is the Spirit of Christ.[1017] He fills the body, directs its movements, controls its members, inspires its wisdom, supplies its strength. He guides into the truth, sanctifies its agents, and empowers for witnessing.[1018] The work of the Church is to "minister the Spirit,"[1019] to speak His message, and transmit His power. He calls and distributes, controls and guides, inspires and strengthens.

The Spirit has never abdicated His authority nor relegated His power. Neither Pope nor Parliament, neither Conference nor Council is supreme in the Church of Christ. The Church that is man-managed instead of God-governed is doomed to failure. A ministry that is college trained but not Spirit-filled works no miracles. The Church that multiplies committees and neglects prayer may be fussy, noisy, enterprising, but it labors in vain[1020] and spends its strength for naught. It is possible to excel in mechanics and fail in dynamic. There is a superabundance of machinery; what is wanting is power. To run an organization needs no God. Man can supply the energy,

---

[1014] Matthew 3:11
[1015] Acts 1:1-2
[1016] 1 Corinthians 12:27
[1017] Romans 8:9
[1018] Acts 1:8, Mark 13:11
[1019] 2 Corinthians 3:6
[1020] Psalm 127:1

enterprise, and enthusiasm for things human. The real work of a Church depends upon the power of the Spirit.

The Presence of the Spirit is vital and central to the work of the Church. Nothing else avails. Apart from Him wisdom becomes folly, and strength weakness. The Church is called to be a "spiritual house"[1021] and a holy priesthood. Only spiritual people can be its "living stones,"[1022] and only the Spirit-filled its priests. Scholarship is blind to spiritual truth till He reveals. Worship is idolatry till He inspires. Preaching is powerless if it be not a demonstration of His power. Prayer is vain unless He energizes. Human resources of learning and organization, wealth and enthusiasm, reform and philanthropy, are worse than useless if there be no Holy Spirit in them. The Church always fails at the point of self-confidence.

When the Church is run on the same lines as a circus, there may be crowds, but there is no Shekinah.[1023] That is why prayer is the test of faith and the secret of power. The Spirit of God travails in the prayer-life of the soul. Miracles are the direct work of His power, and without miracles the Church cannot live. The carnal can argue, but it is the Spirit that convicts. Education can civilize, but it is being born of the Spirit that saves. The energy of the flesh can run bazaars, organize amusements, and raise millions; but it is the presence of the Holy Spirit that makes a temple of the living God. The root-trouble of the present distress is that the Church has more faith in the world and the flesh[1024] than in the Holy Spirit, and things will get no better till we get back to His realized presence and power. The breath of the four winds would turn death into life and dry bones into mighty armies, but it only comes by prayer.

RELIGIOUS FORM AND THE WAY OF THE SPIRIT

The Acts of the Apostles gives us an account of a Church destitute of the Spirit. The picture corresponds in many particulars with that of the Church in the Apocalypse that had lost its Christ. The Church in Laodicea was rich and respectable, prosperous and

---

[1021] 1 Peter 2:5
[1022] Ibid.
[1023] The manifest presence of God (see Exodus 13:20-22).
[1024] 1 John 2:16

influential, complacent and confident, but was blind to the tragedy on the doorstep.[1025] Their worship was faultless in form and passionless in spirit. There was no heresy in their creed, but there was no fire in their souls. The Spirit of Christ was outside.[1026] Ephesus and Laodicea have much in common, for where Christ is dishonored there can be no Pentecost.

The Church at Ephesus had the advantage of a distinguished and brilliant preacher. He was a man of great scholarship, who had won distinction at a great university. No preacher can have too much learning, and the Bible gives due recognition to the fact that Apollos was "a learned man."[1027] In addition to the wisdom of the schools he had, "a thorough knowledge of the Scriptures." Some preachers have finished their ministerial training with the confession that they had learned less about their Bibles than about any other subject; but this man had been taught the Scriptures and "instructed in the way of the Lord."[1028] His teaching was Scriptural, orthodox, careful. To scholarship he added passion. This accomplished scholar, Scriptural in doctrine and careful in exegesis, literally "boiled over in spirit."[1029] Enthusiasm does not often accompany scholarship. It is bad form among cultured people. Religious fervor generally declines with the advance of education. Much learning has a tendency to make cold, dry preachers. This was a rare type of college-made preacher. His fervor survived success in study, and he came through his course intense and scholarly, fervent and accurate, faithful and accomplished, courageous and cultured.

It seems hardly credible that such a minister should lack the very things essential for the work of the Christian ministry. He had neither Gospel nor power. In his preaching there was no Cross, no Resurrection, no Pentecost. He preached Jesus, but he did not know Christ crucified. Peter the fisherman was worth a thousand of him. Eloquent, learned, Scriptural, impassioned, faithful and courageous, Apollos had no Gospel. Carefully trained, well-instructed, a courageous learner, and an effective teacher, he had no vision. Skilled

---

[1025] Revelation 3:17
[1026] Revelation 3:20
[1027] Acts 18:24
[1028] Acts 18:25
[1029] Ibid. *"Spoke with great fervor."*

in definition, powerful in debate, earnest in advocacy, he had no power. The colleges had given him of their best, but they left him ignorant of things vital and destitute of the Holy Spirit.

Like priests, like people.[1030] Like minister, like members. Truth comes through personality; and the level of a preacher's experience determines both the range and level of the sermon. It also determines the level to which he can help others. John's Baptism in the pulpit resulted in a corresponding religion in the pew. It was a cold-water Gospel and a cold-water piety. To Paul's keen eye there was something wanting. They were sternly devout, orderly, reverent; but it was not Christian worship and experience. Their heads were bowed and their faces gave evidence of discipline, but they were not radiant. Their lives were marked by strict integrity, for John's cold-water religion was severely moral. They were as fervent as they were upright, and as religious as they were conscientious. Their religion was marked by a spirit of deep penitence and godly fear. They were upright in life, fervent in religion, devout in spirit, faithful in service; and yet, without the Holy Spirit. Their religion was a strict, external observance; not an indwelling Presence. They lived by rule, not by illumination. God saves from within; they disciplined themselves from without. Religion to them was a joyless burden, for they carried their God on their backs instead of in their hearts.

THE DIFFERENCE HOLY SPIRIT FIRE MAKES

Pentecost transforms the preacher. The commonest bush ablaze with the presence of God becomes a miracle of glory. Under its influence the feeble become as David, and the choice mighty "like the angel of the Lord."[1031] The ministry energized by the Holy Spirit is marked by aggressive evangelism, social revolution, and persecution. Holy Spirit preaching led to the burning of the books of the magic art,[1032] and it stirred up the opposition of those who trafficked in the ruin of the people. Indifference to religion is impossible where the preacher is a flame of fire. To the Church, Pentecost brought light, power, joy. There came to each illumination of mind, assurance of

---

[1030] Hosea 4:9
[1031] Zechariah 12:8
[1032] Acts 19:19

heart, intensity of love, fullness of power, exuberance of joy, No one needed to ask if they had received the Holy Spirit. Fire is self-evident. So is power! Even demons know the difference between the power of inspiration and the correctness of instruction. Secondhand gospels work no miracles. Uninspired devices end in defeat and shame. The only power that is adequate for Christian life and Christian work is the power of the Holy Spirit.

The work of God is not by might of man or by the power of men, but by His Spirit.[1033] It is by Him the truth convicts and converts, sanctifies and saves. The philosophies of men fail, but the Word of God in the demonstration of the Spirit[1034] prevails. Our wants are many and our faults innumerable, but they are all comprehended in our lack of the Holy Spirit. We want nothing but the fire.

The resources of the Church are in "God's provision of the Spirit of Jesus Christ."[1035] The Spirit is more than the Minister of consolation. He is Christ without the limitations of the flesh and the material world. He can reveal what Christ could not speak. He has resources of power greater than those Christ could use, and He makes possible greater works than His. He is the Spirit of God, the Spirit of truth, the Spirit of witness, the Spirit of conviction, the Spirit of power, the Spirit of holiness, the Spirit of life, the Spirit of adoption, the Spirit of help, the Spirit of liberty, the Spirit of wisdom, the Spirit of revelation, the Spirit of promise, the Spirit of love, the Spirit of meekness, the Spirit of sound mind, the Spirit of grace, the Spirit of glory, and the Spirit of prophecy. It is for the Church to explore the resources of the Spirit. The resources of the world are futile. The resources of the Church within herself are inadequate. In the fullness of the Spirit there is abundance of wisdom, resources, and power; but a man-managed, world-incorporating, priest-pretending church can never save the world or fulfill the mission of Christ.[1036]

[1033] Zechariah 4:6
[1034] 1 Corinthians 2:4
[1035] Philippians 1:19
[1036] Matthew 28:18-20

Loving Your Brothers and Sisters

by brother Edgar

THE LORD Jesus put special emphasis on loving our brothers and sisters. Jesus prayed in the garden to His Father; "that all of them may be one, Father, just as You are in Me and I am in You. May they also be in Us so that the world may believe that You have sent Me."[1037] Jesus gives the purpose for love in the body of Christ: "That the world might believe!" Jesus gave a very specific commandment in John 15: "My command is this: Love each other as I have loved you. Greater love has no one than this: to lay down one's life for one's friends."[1038] In John 13, Jesus said: "A new command I give you: Love one another. As I have loved you, so you must love one another. By this everyone will know that you are My disciples, if you love one another."[1039]

While we have these clear commandments from the Lord we find it difficult to get along with sisters and brothers. They behave differently, have different opinions, look differently, speak differently, have a different education, and a different status. There are real or perceived inequities based on our opinions and judgments. Even in

---

[1037] John 17:21
[1038] John 15:12-13
[1039] John 13:34-35

the early Church in the Book of Acts we find disagreement. In Acts chapter 6 there was dispute and murmurings.[1040] Other passages in the New Testament refer to biting and devouring, pride,[1041] provoking, envy,[1042] anger,[1043] unforgiveness,[1044] bitterness,[1045] and division[1046] in the body of Christ. Satan will use any openings to try and destroy a gathering of believers through these sins which so easily beset us. The Apostle John reminds us: "Dear friends, let us love one another, for love comes from God. Everyone who loves has been born of God and knows God. Whoever does not love does not know God, because God is love."[1047]

"If someone says, 'I love God,' and hates his brother, he is a liar; for he who does not love his brother whom he has seen, how can he love God whom he has not seen?"[1048]

"Whoever hates his brother is a murderer, and you know that no murderer has eternal life abiding in him. By this we know love, because He laid down His life for us. And we also ought to lay down our lives for the brethren."[1049] Jesus explains in Matthew 5: "You have heard that it was said, 'Love your neighbor and hate your enemy.' But I tell you, love your enemies and pray for those who persecute you, that you may be children of your Father in heaven. He causes His sun to rise on the evil and the good, and sends rain on the righteous and the unrighteous. If you love those who love you, what reward will you get? Are not even the tax collectors doing that? And if you greet only your own people, what are you doing more than others? Do not even pagans do that? Be perfect, therefore, as your heavenly Father is perfect."[1050]

We are to love our sisters and brothers regardless of whether they look different, speak different or have different opinions. The

---

[1040] Acts 6:1
[1041] Mark 7:22
[1042] 1 Timothy 6:4
[1043] Colossians 3:8
[1044] Mark 11:26
[1045] Ephesians 4:31
[1046] Jude 1:19
[1047] 1 John 4:7-8
[1048] 1 John 4:20
[1049] 1 John 3:15-16
[1050] Matthew 5:43-48

commandment to love applies whether they are nice, whether they have invited others to their house and not us, or whether they speak about us. Jesus is clear; we are to love even those who do not appear to love us.

"What does love look like? It has the hands to help others. It has the feet to hasten to the poor and needy. It has eyes to see misery and want. It has the ears to hear the sighs and sorrows of men. That is what love looks like."[1051]

"You will find as you look back upon your life that the moments when you have truly lived are the moments when you have done things in the spirit of love."[1052]

Here are 3 principles that will help us love our sisters and brothers in our gatherings of believers:

I.) Every sister or brother is made in the image of God. In Genesis, God said: "Let Us make mankind in Our image, in Our likeness."[1053]

II.) Every sister or brother has a soul with a greater value than this world. Scripture says; "What good is it for someone to gain the whole world, yet forfeit their soul?"[1054] God sent His Son Jesus to die for us. Jesus the Son of God would not have come to die for us if our soul was worth nothing. Our soul has a great value because Jesus died for us.

III.) Every sister or brother can do at least one thing better than I can. God has given each of us one or more spiritual gifts and responsibilities that set us apart from our brothers and sisters. According to 1 Corinthians 12, the Holy Spirit has given each one in the body of Christ a particular function. What would the ear do without the eyes? The body of Christ would be blind. What would the feet do without the hands? What would the heart do without the bowels? There is a task for each member of the body.[1055]

So, the three points that help us esteem each other better and learn how to love are:

[1051] Augustine of Hippo (A.D. 354-430)
[1052] Henry Drummond (1851-1897)
[1053] Genesis 1:26
[1054] Mark 8:36
[1055] 1 Corinthians 12:15-20

A.) Each person is made in the Image of God. B.) Every soul has a value greater than this world. C.) Everyone can do at least one thing better than I can.

Look at your sisters and brothers and see their strength and not their weaknesses. Think of whatsoever is lovely. Look at your sisters and brothers and see their beauty and not their faults. Esteem them better than yourself and you will learn to love and become *one.*

THE MISUSE OF AGAPE LOVE

One of the areas of danger in gatherings of believers is the misuse by men, women and youth of the blessed gift of *agape* love God has given all that are born again.

God has given true believers an unselfish, unconditional and sacrificial love which is called agape love. God exemplified this love first, by offering up His Son on a cross, to die for us that we might be able to live eternally in heaven and have peace with God the Father.[1056] When we are born again by repenting[1057] and accepting Jesus as our Savior,[1058] this unselfish love is given to us by God, to love Him, and to love and win others for Christ Jesus. This love is so very attractive and draws men, women and children into the fellowship and under the sound of the Gospel.

HOUSE CHURCHES AND TEMPTATION

1 Corinthians 13 tells us that without love we are nothing.[1059] We must share the love of the Lord Jesus.

Many house Churches do not have much room. There is close contact and touching at times. Satan conspires with our old flesh to bring about temptation. Such temptations come to our mind, emotions, feelings and desires. The temptations are then used by Satan to entice our flesh, further resulting in sinful thoughts and sinful behavior, to destroy the fellowship. He is the father of lies and a

---

[1056] John 3:16
[1057] 2 Peter 3:9
[1058] Ephesians 3:17
[1059] 1 Corinthians 13:2

murderer. Satan encircles us like a roaring lion seeking whom he may devour. The act of *agape* love, the kindness, the joy, the selfless sharing of one self with others becomes a temptation for the carnal Christians and for visitors who are not yet born again. As lonely and rejected people come to the house fellowship they may attempt to establish contacts and relationships that are of the flesh, the world and Satan. *Lust takes* and *love gives*.

The leaders and elders must hold each other and the fellowship accountable that no immoral behavior is permitted to be part of the fellowship.[1060] If you permit it Satan will destroy the fellowship.

CORRECTION IN GOD'S HOUSE

Firstly at all cost a sin must be brought out into the light[1061] and there should be forgiveness sought by all involved.[1062] If one is not truly repenting and humbling themselves then Scripture provides the way for correction when the laws of God are broken resulting in the expulsion of the sinner for a period of time. Please read 1 Corinthians Chapter 5, where an immoral man is given to Satan for a time:

"It is actually reported that there is sexual immorality among you, and of a kind that even pagans do not tolerate: A man is sleeping with his father's wife. And you are proud! Shouldn't you rather have gone into mourning and have put out of your fellowship the man who has been doing this? For my part, even though I am not physically present, I am with you in spirit. As one who is present with you in this way, I have already passed judgment in the Name of our Lord Jesus on the one who has been doing this. So when you are assembled and I am with you in spirit, and the power of our Lord Jesus is present, hand this man over to Satan for the destruction of the flesh, so that his spirit may be saved on the day of the Lord. Your boasting is not good. Don't you know that a little yeast leavens the whole batch of dough? Get rid of the old yeast, so that you may be a new unleavened batch—as you really are. For Christ, our Passover lamb, has been sacrificed. Therefore let us keep the Festival, not with

---

[1060] 1 Thessalonians 4:3-4
[1061] 1 John 1:6
[1062] Matthew 18:15-17

the old bread leavened with malice and wickedness, but with the unleavened bread of sincerity and truth.

"I wrote to you in my letter not to associate with sexually immoral people—not at all meaning the people of this world who are immoral, or the greedy and swindlers, or idolaters. In that case you would have to leave this world. But now I am writing to you that you must not associate with anyone who claims to be a brother or sister but is sexually immoral or greedy, an idolater or slanderer, a drunkard or swindler. Do not even eat with such people. What business is it of mine to judge those outside the Church? Are you not to judge those inside? God will judge those outside. 'Expel the wicked person from among you.'"[1063]

EVIDENCE OF TURNING FROM SIN

In time, and where there is evidence, that the sinner has repented and changed his or her behavior, the brother or sister should be forgiven and reintroduced to the fellowship. This is described in 2 Corinthians 2:

"If anyone has caused grief, he has not so much grieved me as he has grieved all of you to some extent—not to put it too severely. The punishment inflicted on him by the majority is sufficient. Now instead, you ought to forgive and comfort him, so that he will not be overwhelmed by excessive sorrow. I urge you, therefore, to reaffirm your love for him. Another reason I wrote you was to see if you would stand the test and be obedient in everything. Anyone you forgive, I also forgive. And what I have forgiven—if there was anything to forgive—I have forgiven in the sight of Christ for your sake, in order that Satan might not outwit us. For we are not unaware of his schemes."[1064]

When a brother or sister, who has sinned, is reintroduced to the fellowship, there needs to be evidence, that they have repented and turned from their sin:

"If we confess our sins, He is faithful and just and will forgive us our sins and purify us from all unrighteousness."[1065]

[1063] 1 Corinthians 5
[1064] 2 Corinthians 2:5-11
[1065] 1 John 1:9

"Produce fruit in keeping with repentance."[1066]

If others have been hurt there should be the asking of forgiveness by the sinner. Scripture says:

"Leave your gift there in front of the altar. First go and be reconciled to them; then come and offer your gift."[1067]

If the person the sinner is seeking forgiveness from does not want to forgive, then that does not prevent the sinner from rejoining the fellowship, as he or she has tried to seek forgiveness. The person who has been harmed and does not want to forgive needs to be counseled to forgive, as God has forgiven, to reestablish unity.

If any harm has been done, the sinner must make restitution where possible. This shows that he or she has truly repented. Consider Zacchaeus when he repented: he gave away half of what he owned to the poor and paid back 4 times the amount that he cheated out of people.[1068]

Lastly, if there are any accusations against elders in the fellowship, Scripture says:

"Do not entertain an accusation against an elder unless it is brought by two or three witnesses."[1069]

We must always act with love for this is the heart of our Father in heaven. We love our sisters and brothers unconditionally but we are not permitted to tolerate open sin in our fellowships. Some might say this is not loving and not merciful. God loves all the world but He does not want His Flock ravished by the evil one through sin. We act in love and we will love those that have strayed dealing with them in kindness and gentleness. "Brothers and sisters, if someone is caught in a sin, you who live by the Spirit should restore that person gently. But watch yourselves, or you also may be tempted."[1070]

[1066] Matthew 3:8
[1067] Matthew 5:24
[1068] Luke 19:5-10
[1069] 1 Timothy 5:19
[1070] Galatians 6:1

Appendix III

Gospel Fellowships
Additional Resources

Statement of Faith for Gospel Fellowships

[EDITOR'S NOTE: After the Lord's clear leading to use the name *Gospel Fellowships* there was a word search preformed on the internet and this statement of faith from one of the larger Chinese house Church networks called: *China Gospel Fellowship* was found. This was a surprise and great blessing for before we were never aware of this underground house Church name. After reading their statement of faith, there was an immediate burden to make this statement of faith available to *Gospel Fellowships* and to any other house Churches or groups that would like to identify with the statement. We believe it is a tremendous way for believers to be in unity worldwide with precious brothers and sisters in China who are experiencing a great expansion of the Church and revival. Below is the statement of faith found on the *China Gospel Fellowship*[1071] page]:

Having grown up in hardship and sufferings, the Chinese house Church has constantly been accused of being a cult by people who are unaware of the truth and who have ulterior motives. For the purpose of making known the true faith of the Church, some house Church leaders joined together on behalf of all house Churches and composed the Statement of Faith of Chinese house Churches in November 1998. The following is the complete statement.

[1071] One of the largest house Church networks in China with over 8 million members.

INTRODUCTION

In order to establish a common, legitimate criteria of faith for house Churches in China, in order to lay a foundation on which overseas Christian Churches can enjoy fellowship with us in unity, in order to help our government and people to understand our faith, and in order to draw a clear distinction between us and heresies and cults, a group of key leaders from several major Chinese house Church movements met together in a certain location in north China in *November 1998*. They prayed together, studied the Bible together, and together drafted the following statement of our faith.

1. THE BIBLE

We believe that all 66 Books of the Bible are God-breathed.[1072] They were inspired by God through the Holy Spirit to the prophets and Apostles who composed them.[1073] The Bible is complete and inerrant truth. It has the highest authority. Nobody is allowed to distort it in any way.[1074]

The Bible clearly states God's purpose of redemption of mankind.[1075] The Bible is the highest standard of our Christian life and ministry. We are against any denials of the Bible; we are against any teaching or theories that regard the Bible as out of date, or as erroneous; we are also against the practice of believing only in selected sections of the Scripture.[1076] We want to emphasize that the Scriptures must be interpreted in light of their historical context and within the overall context of scriptural teachings. While interpreting the Bible, one must seek the guidance of the Holy Spirit and the principle of interpreting the Scripture by the Scripture.[1077] The interpretation should be coherent and consistent, but not based on isolated verses. Biblical interpretation should take into account the

---

[1072] 2 Timothy 3:16
[1073] Hebrews 1:1, 1 Peter 1:10
[1074] Romans 3:4, Revelation 22:18-19
[1075] John 3:16, 2 Peter 3:9
[1076] Psalm 19:7–9, Acts 20:27
[1077] 1 John 2:27, 1 Corinthians 2:13

orthodox faith that has been taken as the heritage of the Church down through history. We are against interpretation of the Scripture merely according to one's own will, or by subjective spiritualization.[1078]

2. TRIUNE GOD

We believe in the only one true God,[1079] the eternally self-existing triune God who is the Father, the Son and the Holy Spirit.[1080] While sharing the same nature, the same honor and the same glory, the Father, the Son and the Holy Spirit are distinct persons who have differently functional roles in the work of redemption. The Father planned salvation; the Son fulfilled salvation; while the Holy Spirit applies the salvation.[1081] However, the Father, the Son and the Holy Spirit are not separate and independent of each other. They are one in unity. The Son reveals the Father;[1082] the Holy Spirit reveals the Son; [1083] the Father, the Son and the Holy Spirit are together worshipped and praised. We pray to the Father through the Holy Spirit in the Name of the Son.[1084]

We believe that God created the universe and all things, and He created man in His own image.[1085] God has all things in His own control and sustains all things.[1086] He is the Lord of human history. The almighty God is a righteous, holy, faithful and loving God. He is omniscient,[1087] omnipresent[1088] and omnipotent.[1089] He manifests His sovereignty throughout human history.[1090] The Son and the Holy Spirit are eternal: the Son has the relationship of Son to the Father,

---

[1078] 2 Peter 1:20
[1079] John 17:3, Ephesians 4:5
[1080] Matthew 28:19, 2 Corinthians 13:14
[1081] Ephesians 1:5
[1082] Luke 10:22
[1083] 1 Corinthians 2:10, 1 Corinthians 12:3
[1084] 1 Corinthians 1:2
[1085] Genesis 1:27
[1086] Hebrews 1:3
[1087] Psalms 147:5, Hebrews 4:13, Psalms 139:4
[1088] Acts 17:24, Jeremiah 23:23-24, Psalms 139:7-12
[1089] Matthew 19:26, Jeremiah 32:27, Psalms 147:5
[1090] Revelation 4:11, Proverbs 16:4

but is not created;[1091] the Holy Spirit is sent by the Father and the Son.

God is spirit. He has no visible form or shape. Christians should worship Him in spirit and in truth.[1092] Christians have no other object of worship apart from this triune God. We reject wrong explanations of the trinity, such as: one body with three forms (like water, ice and vapor), or one body with three identities (like the sun, light and heat; or the son, the father and the husband).

3. CHRIST

We believe that Jesus is God's unique Son, that He is the Word who became flesh and came to this world.[1093] In His perfect humanity He was tempted yet never sinned.[1094] He gave Himself to the death on the cross, and shed His blood to redeem everyone who has faith in Him from sin and death.[1095] He rose from death, ascended to heaven, was seated at the right hand of the Father, received Holy Spirit from the Father, and sent the Spirit to those who believe in Him.[1096] At the end of the age, Jesus is going to come back to judge the world.[1097]

Christians receive the status of sonship from God, but they remain human; they never become God.[1098]

Nobody knows the exact date of Jesus' return, but we are confident that Jesus will return, and we can also know some of the signs of His return.[1099]

We are against any teaching that says Jesus has come the second time in His incarnated form.[1100] We are opposed to anyone who

---

[1091] John 1:1-3, Proverbs 30:4, Hebrews 1:3
[1092] John 4:24
[1093] John 1:14, John 3:16
[1094] Hebrews 4:15
[1095] Matthew 20:28, Galatians 3:13, 1 Peter 2:24
[1096] Acts 2:33
[1097] 1 Thessalonians 1:7-8
[1098] Romans 8:15
[1099] Matthew 24-25
[1100] 2 Thessalonians 2:3

claims himself to be Christ.[1101] Any teaching that claims Jesus has already returned is a heresy.

4. REDEMPTION

We believe if a person has confessed his sin and repented,[1102] if he has believed in Jesus as the Son of God who died for our sin on the cross and resurrected from death on the third day[1103] to pardon our sins,[1104] and if he has received the Holy Spirit[1105] that God has promised, then he is born again and saved.[1106] It is by grace and through faith that we are saved.[1107] By faith we are justified; by faith we receive the Holy Spirit, and by faith we become the sons of God.

We believe that God can keep His children completely in Jesus Christ,[1108] while the believers are obligated to hold on to their faith firmly till the end.[1109]

We believe that the indwelling of the Holy Spirit is an evidence of salvation, and that the Spirit of God testifies with our spirits that we are children of God.[1110]

We are against the practice of taking any specific phenomenon or personal experiences as common criterions of salvation for all.

We are against any doctrine that teaches a saved person is allowed to freely sin under God's grace.[1111] We are against the teaching of multi-salvation (that one can lose but then gain back his salvation many times); we are also against salvation by keeping the law.[1112]

[1101] Matthew 24:4-5
[1102] Mark 1:14-15, Luke 13:3, Acts 2:38
[1103] 1 Corinthians 15:4
[1104] Ephesians 1:7
[1105] Ephesians 1:13
[1106] John 3:3
[1107] Ephesians 2:8
[1108] Jude 1:24, John 10:28
[1109] Hebrews 3:14
[1110] Romans 8:16
[1111] Romans 6:1-2, Titus 2:12
[1112] Galatians 2:21

5. THE HOLY SPIRIT

We believe the Holy Spirit is the third person in the Godhead. He is the Spirit of God,[1113] the Spirit of Christ,[1114] the Spirit of truth,[1115] and the Spirit of holiness.[1116]

The illumination of the Holy Spirit convicts man of his sins, brings him to the knowledge of truth, leads him to faith in Christ and therefore to being born again and salvation. The Holy Spirit leads believers into the truth, teaches them to understand the truth, and guides them to submission to Christ as well as to the fruitfulness of the abundant life. The Holy Spirit bestows upon believers all kinds of power, and witnesses the powerful deeds of God with signs and wonders.[1117] The Holy Spirit searches all things.[1118]

In Christ, God grants a diversity of gifts of the Holy Spirit to the Church so as to manifest the glory of Christ.[1119] With faith and desire, Christians can experience the pouring down of the Holy Spirit on them and be filled with the Holy Spirit.[1120]

We deny any doctrine that teaches the cessation of signs and wonders or the termination of the gifts of the Holy Spirit after the age of the Apostles.

We don't forbid the speaking of tongues,[1121] neither do we force people to speak in tongues, or insist that speaking in tongues is the evidence of salvation.

We refute the view that the Holy Spirit is merely a kind of inspiration instead of being a personal member of the Godhead.

[1113] 2 Corinthians 3:17
[1114] Romans 8:9
[1115] John 16:13
[1116] Romans 1:4
[1117] Romans 15:19
[1118] 1 Corinthians 1:20
[1119] 1 Corinthians 12:14
[1120] Joel 2:28, Ephesians 5:18
[1121] 1 Corinthians 14:39

6. THE CHURCH

We believe that the Church is composed of all who are called by God in Jesus Christ.[1122]

Christ is the Head of the Church. The Church is the body of Christ,[1123] the house of God, and the pillar and foundation of truth.[1124]

The Church is both regional and universal. It consists of all Churches of sound faith currently existing around the world, as well as the Churches of the saints down through history.

The Church should be governed according to Biblical principles. Its spiritual ministry should not be controlled or dominated by secular powers.

Brothers and sisters in the Church are members of one body, with each fulfilling its roles.[1125] The body builds itself up in love, and grows into Him who is the head. The universal Church should reach unity in the faith and in the Holy Spirit, and be united into one in Christ.[1126]

The purpose of the Church is to proclaim the Gospel, to teach and shepherd believers, to build and send missionaries, to denounce heresies and uphold truth, and to defend the Word. As Christians gather together in the Name of the Lord, the number of people meeting together or the location of the meeting should not be limited. Each believer is a priest,[1127] and each has the right and obligation to preach the Gospel to the ends of the earth.[1128]

We are against the alliance between the Church and politics, or any politics intermingled into the Church. We are against the Church's dependence on foreign political powers for its growth.

We are against the Church's participation in any activities that undermine solidarity of national people groups or the unification of the state.

[1122] 1 Corinthians 1:2
[1123] Colossians 1:18
[1124] 1 Timothy 3:15
[1125] Romans 12:4
[1126] Ephesians 4:13
[1127] 1 Peter 2:9
[1128] Mark 16:15

7. THE LAST DAYS

We believe Christ will return, but no one except the Father knows the date of His return.[1129] On the day when Christ returns, He will come in glory and power on the clouds with the angels. On that day, the angels will blow the trumpet, and those who were dead in Christ will rise first. After that, all born again Christians who are still alive will also be transformed. Their bodies will all be glorified, and they will all be caught up together in the clouds to meet the Lord in the air.[1130]

The saints will then reign together with Christ for a thousand years,[1131] during which Satan will be cast into the Abyss. When the thousand years are over, Satan will be released temporarily and will go out to deceive the nations until he is finally thrown into the lake of burning sulfur.[1132] After that, Christ will sit on the great white throne to judge men from each nation, tribe and people. Everyone will rise from the dead and be judged before the throne. If anyone's name is not found written in the Book of life, he will be thrown into the lake of fire. The former heaven and earth will be consumed by fire. Death and Hades will also be thrown into the fire.[1133]

Those whose names are found written in the Book of life will enter into the new heaven and the new earth, living there with God forever.[1134] We believe that while waiting for the coming of the Lord, believers should serve the Lord with great diligence, preach the Word of life,[1135] and bear abundant fruits in their words, actions, faith, love and holiness. We also believe that those who do this shall receive all kinds of rewards.[1136]

As for whether the rapture happens before, during or after the great tribulation, we recognize that each denomination has its own conviction, and therefore there is no absolute conclusion in regard to

---

[1129] Matthew 24:36
[1130] 1 Thessalonians 4:16-17
[1131] Revelation 20:4
[1132] Revelation 20:10
[1133] Revelation 20:11-15
[1134] Revelation 21:1-3
[1135] 2 Timothy 4:2
[1136] James 1:12, Revelation 22:12, Matthew 25:21

this. The duty of each Christian is to be alert[1137] and prepare himself for the coming of the Lord.[1138]

CONCLUDING EXHORTATIONS

We give our thanks and praise to our almighty heavenly Father who has led us to draft this Statement of Faith. Our desire is that the Holy Spirit will move brothers and sisters in more Churches to accept and identify themselves with this Statement, and to read the Statement in the Churches so as to strengthen the faith of the believers in resisting heresies and cults, so that together we can welcome the great revival of the Church.

May the Lord bless the Church in the world.

May the Lord bless the peoples of all Nations.

May praises and glory be unto our true and triune God. Amen!

[1137] 1 Thessalonians 5:6
[1138] Matthew 25:1-13

Chronological Bible Reading of Scriptures

THERE IS a great need in the body of Christ for consistent reading of the Holy Scriptures in their entirety, book by book, chapter by chapter, verse by verse. In this case we are encouraging a chronological reading of the Scriptures. Most of the confusion is created when certain teachers, groups, or denominations take singular verses out of context and compare them with others. Though it is a good spiritual principle to compare spiritual truths with spiritual truths,[1139] yet this must all be done in the larger context of God's Word. Therefore we are encouraging all of God's saints to have a consistent discipline of reading through the whole Scriptures once a year as a supplemental reading plan.

This plan takes just 10-25 minutes of your day to read through the given chapters. One recommendation is to mark or underline one verse that stood out to you that you can apply into your life or memorize.[1140] In your reading, see the person of the Lord Jesus Christ in all the chapters for our Lord said that the Scriptures testified of Him.[1141] Learn of the character of God and spend time praying to the Lord what you have learnt. Also, we recommend that believers

---

[1139] 1 Corinthians 2:13
[1140] James 1:22, Psalm 119:11
[1141] Luke 24:27

spend extra time reading through the *Book of Acts* on an ongoing basis for it is a clear blueprint for the Church and need for the Holy Spirit.

Lastly, we highly recommend you spend much more time in the Scriptures on your own where the Holy Spirit is leading you to meditate on.[1142] Let this plan be a possible solution for you to ensure you are reading through all the Scriptures at least once per year. You can check the boxes ☐ beside each passage as a checklist.

READING SCHEDULE

Jan 1: Genesis 1-3 ☐
Jan 2: Genesis 4-7 ☐
Jan 3: Genesis 8-11 ☐
Jan 4: Job 1-5 ☐
Jan 5: Job 6-9 ☐
Jan 6: Job 10-13 ☐
Jan 7: Job 14-16 ☐
Jan 8: Job 17-20 ☐
Jan 9: Job 21-23 ☐
Jan 10: Job 24-28 ☐
Jan 11: Job 29-31 ☐
Jan 12: Job 32-34 ☐
Jan 13: Job 35-37 ☐
Jan 14: Job 38-39 ☐
Jan 15: Job 40-42 ☐
Jan 16: Genesis 12-15 ☐
Jan 17: Genesis 16-18 ☐
Jan 18: Genesis 19-21 ☐
Jan 19: Genesis 22-24 ☐
Jan 20: Genesis 25-26 ☐
Jan 21: Genesis 27-29 ☐
Jan 22: Genesis 30-31 ☐
Jan 23: Genesis 32-34 ☐
Jan 24: Genesis 35-37 ☐
Jan 25: Genesis 38-40 ☐

[1142] Psalm 119:15-16

Jan 26: Genesis 41-42 ☐
Jan 27: Genesis 43-45 ☐
Jan 28: Genesis 46-47 ☐
Jan 29: Genesis 48-50 ☐
Jan 30: Exodus 1-3 ☐
Jan 31: Exodus 4-6 ☐
Feb 1: Exodus 7-9 ☐
Feb 2: Exodus 10-12 ☐
Feb 3: Exodus 13-15 ☐
Feb 4: Exodus 16-18 ☐
Feb 5: Exodus 19-21 ☐
Feb 6: Exodus 22-24 ☐
Feb 7: Exodus 25-27 ☐
Feb 8: Exodus 28-29 ☐
Feb 9: Exodus 30-32 ☐
Feb 10: Exodus 33-35 ☐
Feb 11: Exodus 36-38 ☐
Feb 12: Exodus 39-40 ☐
Feb 13: Leviticus 1-4 ☐
Feb 14: Leviticus 5-7 ☐
Feb 15: Leviticus 8-10 ☐
Feb 16: Leviticus 11-13 ☐
Feb 17: Leviticus 14-15 ☐
Feb 18: Leviticus 16-18 ☐
Feb 19: Leviticus 19-21 ☐
Feb 20: Leviticus 22-23 ☐
Feb 21: Leviticus 24-25 ☐
Feb 22: Leviticus 26-27 ☐
Feb 23: Numbers 1-2 ☐
Feb 24: Numbers 3-4 ☐
Feb 25: Numbers 5-6 ☐
Feb 26: Numbers 7 ☐
Feb 27: Numbers 8-10 ☐
Feb 28-29: Numbers 11-13 ☐
Mar 1: Numbers 14-15; Psalm 90 ☐
Mar 2: Numbers 16-17 ☐

Mar 3: Numbers 18-20 □
Mar 4: Numbers 21-22 □
Mar 5: Numbers 23-25 □
Mar 6: Numbers 26-27 □
Mar 7: Numbers 28-30 □
Mar 8: Numbers 31-32 □
Mar 9: Numbers 33-34 □
Mar 10: Numbers 35-36 □
Mar 11: Deuteronomy 1-2 □
Mar 12: Deuteronomy 3-4 □
Mar 13: Deuteronomy 5-7 □
Mar 14: Deuteronomy 8-10 □
Mar 15: Deuteronomy 11-13 □
Mar 16: Deuteronomy 14-16 □
Mar 17: Deuteronomy 17-20 □
Mar 18: Deuteronomy 21-23 □
Mar 19: Deuteronomy 24-27 □
Mar 20: Deuteronomy 28-29 □
Mar 21: Deuteronomy 30-31 □
Mar 22: Deuteronomy 32-34; Psalm 91 □
Mar 23: Joshua 1-4 □
Mar 24: Joshua 5-8 □
Mar 25: Joshua 9-11 □
Mar 26: Joshua 12-15 □
Mar 27: Joshua 16-18 □
Mar 28: Joshua 19-21 □
Mar 29: Joshua 22-24 □
Mar 30: Judges 1-2 □
Mar 31: Judges 3-5 □
Apr 1: Judges 6-7 □
Apr 2: Judges 8-9 □
Apr 3: Judges 10-12 □
Apr 4: Judges 13-15 □
Apr 5: Judges 16-18 □
Apr 6: Judges 19-21 □
Apr 7: Ruth □

Apr 8: 1 Samuel 1-3 ☐
Apr 9: 1 Samuel 4-8 ☐
Apr 10: 1 Samuel 9-12 ☐
Apr 11: 1 Samuel 13-14 ☐
Apr 12: 1 Samuel 15-17 ☐
Apr 13: 1 Samuel 18-20; Psalms 11, 59 ☐
Apr 14: 1 Samuel 21-24 ☐
Apr 15: Psalms 7, 27, 31, 34, 52 ☐
Apr 16: Psalms 56, 120, 140-142 ☐
Apr 17: 1 Samuel 25-27 ☐
Apr 18: Psalms 17, 35, 54, 63 ☐
Apr 19: 1 Samuel 28-31; Ps 18 ☐
Apr 20: Psalms 121, 123-125, 128-130 ☐
Apr 21: 2 Samuel 1-4 ☐
Apr 22: Psalms 6, 8-10, 14, 16, 19, 21 ☐
Apr 23: 1 Chronicles 1-2 ☐
Apr 24: Psalms 43-45, 49, 84-85, 87 ☐
Apr 25: 1 Chronicles 3-5 ☐
Apr 26: Psalms 73, 77-78 ☐
Apr 27: 1 Chronicles 6 ☐
Apr 28: Psalms 81, 88, 92-93 ☐
Apr 29: 1 Chronicles 7-10 ☐
Apr 30: Psalms 102-104 ☐
May 1: 2 Samuel 5:1-10; 1 Chronicles 11-12 ☐
May 2: Psalm 133 ☐
May 3: Psalms 106-107 ☐
May 4: 2 Samuel 5:11-6:23; 1 Chronicles 13-16 ☐
May 5: Psalms 1-2, 15, 22-24, 47, 68 ☐
May 6: Psalms 89, 96, 100-101, 105, 132 ☐
May 7: 2 Samuel 7; 1 Chronicles 17 ☐
May 8: Psalms 25, 29, 33, 36, 39 ☐
May 9: 2 Samuel 8-9; 1 Chronicles 18 ☐
May 10: Psalms 50, 53, 60, 75 ☐
May 11: 2 Samuel 10; 1 Chronicles 19; Psalm 20 ☐
May 12: Psalms 65-67, 69-70 ☐
May 13: 2 Samuel 11-12; 1 Chronicles 20 ☐

May 14: Psalm 32, 51, 86, 122 ☐
May 15: 2 Samuel 13-15 ☐
May 16: Psalm 3-4, 12-13, 28, 55 ☐
May 17: 2 Samuel 16-18 ☐
May 18: Psalms 26, 40, 58, 61-62, 64 ☐
May 19: 2 Samuel 19-21 ☐
May 20: Psalms 5, 38, 41-42 ☐
May 21: 2 Samuel 22-23; Psalm 57 ☐
May 22: Psalms 95, 97-99 ☐
May 23: 2 Samuel 24; 1 Chronicles 21-22; Psalm 30 ☐
May 24: Psalm 108-110 ☐
May 25: 1 Chronicles 23-25 ☐
May 26: Psalm 131, 138-139, 143-145 ☐
May 27: 1 Chronicles 26-29; Psalm 127 ☐
May 28: Psalms 111-118 ☐
May 29: 1 Kings 1-2; Psalms 37, 71, 94 ☐
May 30: Psalm 119:1-88 ☐
May 31: 1 Kings 3-4; 2 Chronicles 1; Psalm 72 ☐
Jun 1: Psalm 119:89-176 ☐
Jun 2: Song of Songs ☐
Jun 3: Proverbs 1-3 ☐
Jun 4: Proverbs 4-6 ☐
Jun 5: Proverbs 7-9 ☐
Jun 6: Proverbs 10-12 ☐
Jun 7: Proverbs 13-15 ☐
Jun 8: Proverbs 16-18 ☐
Jun 9: Proverbs 19-21 ☐
Jun 10: Proverbs 22-24 ☐
Jun 11: 1 Kings 5-6; 2 Chronicles 2-3 ☐
Jun 12: 1 Kings 7; 2 Chronicles 4 ☐
Jun 13: 1 Kings 8; 2 Chronicles 5 ☐
Jun 14: 2 Chronicles 6-7; Psalm 136 ☐
Jun 15: Psalms 134, 146-150 ☐
Jun 16: 1 King 9; 2 Chronicles 8 ☐
Jun 17: Proverbs 25-26 ☐
Jun 18: Proverbs 27-29 ☐

Jun 19: Ecclesiastes 1-6 □
Jun 20: Ecclesiastes 7-12 □
Jun 21: 1 Kings 10-11; 2 Chronicles 9 □
Jun 22: Proverbs 30-31 □
Jun 23: 1 Kings 12-14 □
Jun 24: 2 Chronicles 10-12 □
Jun 25: 1 Kings 15:1-24; 2 Chronicles 13-16 □
Jun 26: 1 Kings 15:25-16:34; 2 Chronicles 17 □
Jun 27: 1 Kings 17-19 □
Jun 28: 1 Kings 20-21 □
Jun 29: 1 Kings 22; 2 Chronicles 18 □
Jun 30: 2 Chronicles 19-23 □
Jul 1: Obadiah; Psalms 82-83 □
Jul 2: 2 Kings 1-4 □
Jul 3: 2 Kings 5-8 □
Jul 4: 2 Kings 9-11 □
Jul 5: 2 Kings 12-13; 2 Chronicles 24 □
Jul 6: 2 Kings 14; 2 Chronicles 25 □
Jul 7: Jonah □
Jul 8: 2 Kings 15; 2 Chronicles 26 □
Jul 9: Isaiah 1-4 □
Jul 10: Isaiah 5-8 □
Jul 11: Amos 1-5 □
Jul 12: Amos 6-9 □
Jul 13: 2 Chronicles 27; Isaiah 9-12 □
Jul 14: Micah □
Jul 15: 2 Chronicles 28; 2 Kings 16-17 □
Jul 16: Isaiah 13-17 □
Jul 17: Isaiah 18-22 □
Jul 18: Isaiah 23-27 □
Jul 19: 2 Kings 18:1-8; 2 Chronicles 29-31; Psalm 48 □
Jul 20: Hosea 1-7 □
Jul 21: Hosea 8-14 □
Jul 22: Isaiah 28-30 □
Jul 23: Isaiah 31-34 □
Jul 24: Isaiah 35-36 □

Jul 25: Isaiah 37-39; Psalm 76 □
Jul 26: Isaiah 40-43 □
Jul 27: Isaiah 44-48 □
Jul 28: 2 Kings 18:9-19:37; Psalms 46, 80, 135 □
Jul 29: Isaiah 49-53 □
Jul 30: Isaiah 54-58 □
Jul 31: Isaiah 59-63 □
Aug 1: Isaiah 64-66 □
Aug 2: 2 Kings 20-21 □
Aug 3: 2 Chronicles 32-33 □
Aug 4: Nahum □
Aug 5: 2 Kings 22-23; 2 Chronicles 34-35 □
Aug 6: Zephaniah □
Aug 7: Jeremiah 1-3 □
Aug 8: Jeremiah 4-6 □
Aug 9: Jeremiah 7-9 □
Aug 10: Jeremiah 10-13 □
Aug 11: Jeremiah 14-17 □
Aug 12: Jeremiah 18-22 □
Aug 13: Jeremiah 23-25 □
Aug 14: Jeremiah 26-29 □
Aug 15: Jeremiah 30-31 □
Aug 16: Jeremiah 32-34 □
Aug 17: Jeremiah 35-37 □
Aug 18: Jeremiah 38-40; Psalms 74, 79 □
Aug 19: 2 Kings 24-25; 2 Chronicles 36 □
Aug 20: Habakkuk □
Aug 21: Jeremiah 41-45 □
Aug 22: Jeremiah 46-48 □
Aug 23: Jeremiah 49-50 □
Aug 24: Jeremiah 51-52 □
Aug 25: Lamentations 1:1-3:36 □
Aug 26: Lamentations 3:37-5:22 □
Aug 27: Ezekiel 1-4 □
Aug 28: Ezekiel 5-8 □
Aug 29: Ezekiel 9-12 □

Aug 30: Ezekiel 13-15 ☐
Aug 31: Ezekiel 16-17 ☐
Sep 1: Ezekiel 18-19 ☐
Sep 2: Ezekiel 20-21 ☐
Sep 3: Ezekiel 22-23 ☐
Sep 4: Ezekiel 24-27 ☐
Sep 5: Ezekiel 28-31 ☐
Sep 6: Ezekiel 32-34 ☐
Sep 7: Ezekiel 35-37 ☐
Sep 8: Ezekiel 38-39 ☐
Sep 9: Ezekiel 40-41 ☐
Sep 10: Ezekiel 42-43 ☐
Sep 11: Ezekiel 44-45 ☐
Sep 12: Ezekiel 46-48 ☐
Sep 13: Joel ☐
Sep 14: Daniel 1-3 ☐
Sep 15: Daniel 4-6 ☐
Sep 16: Daniel 7-9 ☐
Sep 17: Daniel 10-12 ☐
Sep 18: Ezra 1-3 ☐
Sep 19: Ezra 4-6; Psalm 137 ☐
Sep 20: Haggai ☐
Sep 21: Zechariah 1-7 ☐
Sep 22: Zechariah 8-14 ☐
Sep 23: Esther 1-5 ☐
Sep 24: Esther 6-10 ☐
Sep 25: Ezra 7-10 ☐
Sep 26: Nehemiah 1-5 ☐
Sep 27: Nehemiah 6-7 ☐
Sep 28: Nehemiah 8-10 ☐
Sep 29: Nehemiah 11-13; Psalm 126 ☐
Sep 30: Malachi ☐
Oct 1: Luke 1; John 1:1-14 ☐
Oct 2: Matthew 1; Luke 2:1-38 ☐
Oct 3: Matthew 2; Luke 2:39-52 ☐
Oct 4: Matthew 3; Mark 1; Luke 3 ☐

Oct 5: Matthew 4; Luke 4-5; John 1:15-51 ☐
Oct 6: John 2-4 ☐
Oct 7: Mark 2 ☐
Oct 8: John 5 ☐
Oct 9: Matthew 12:1-21; Mark 3; Luke 6 ☐
Oct 10: Matthew 5-7 ☐
Oct 11: Matthew 8:1-13; Luke 7 ☐
Oct 12: Matthew 11 ☐
Oct 13: Matthew 12:22-50 ☐
Oct 14: Matthew 13; Luke 8 ☐
Oct 15: Matthew 8:14-34; Mark 4-5 ☐
Oct 16: Matthew 9-10 ☐
Oct 17: Matthew 14; Mark 6; Luke 9:1-17 ☐
Oct 18: John 6 ☐
Oct 19: Matthew 15; Mark 7 ☐
Oct 20: Matthew 16; Mark 8; Luke 9:18-27 ☐
Oct 21: Matthew 17; Mark 9; Luke 9:28-62 ☐
Oct 22: Matthew 18 ☐
Oct 23: John 7-8 ☐
Oct 24: John 9:1-10:21 ☐
Oct 25: Luke 10-11; John 10:22-42 ☐
Oct 26: Luke 12-13 ☐
Oct 27: Luke 14-15 ☐
Oct 28: Luke 16-17:10 ☐
Oct 29: John 11 ☐
Oct 30: Luke 17:11-18:14 ☐
Oct 31: Matthew 19; Mark 10 ☐
Nov 1: Matthew 20-21 ☐
Nov 2: Luke 18:15-19:48 ☐
Nov 3: Mark 11; John 12 ☐
Nov 4: Matthew 22; Mark 12 ☐
Nov 5: Matthew 23; Luke 20-21 ☐
Nov 6: Mark 13 ☐
Nov 7: Matthew 24 ☐
Nov 8: Matthew 25 ☐
Nov 9: Matthew 26; Mark 14 ☐

Nov 10: Luke 22; John 13 ☐
Nov 11: John 14-17 ☐
Nov 12: Matthew 27; Mark 15 ☐
Nov 13: Luke 23; John 18-19 ☐
Nov 14: Matthew 28; Mark 16 ☐
Nov 15: Luke 24; John 20-21 ☐
Nov 16: Acts 1-3 ☐
Nov 17: Acts 4-6 ☐
Nov 18: Acts 7-8 ☐
Nov 19: Acts 9-10 ☐
Nov 20: Acts 11-12 ☐
Nov 21: Acts 13-14 ☐
Nov 22: James ☐
Nov 23: Acts 15-16 ☐
Nov 24: Galatians 1-3 ☐
Nov 25: Galatians 4-6 ☐
Nov 26: Acts 17-18:18 ☐
Nov 27: 1 Thessalonians; 2 Thessalonians ☐
Nov 28: Acts 18:19-19:41 ☐
Nov 29: 1 Corinthians 1-4 ☐
Nov 30: 1 Corinthians 5-8 ☐
Dec 1: 1 Corinthians 9-11 ☐
Dec 2: 1 Corinthians 12-14 ☐
Dec 3: 1 Corinthians 15-16 ☐
Dec 4: 2 Corinthians 1-4 ☐
Dec 5: 2 Corinthians 5-9 ☐
Dec 6: 2 Corinthians 10-13 ☐
Dec 7: Acts 20:1-3; Romans 1-3 ☐
Dec 8: Romans 4-7 ☐
Dec 9: Romans 8-10 ☐
Dec 10: Romans 11-13 ☐
Dec 11: Romans 14-16 ☐
Dec 12: Acts 20:4-23:35 ☐
Dec 13: Acts 24-26 ☐
Dec 14: Acts 27-28 ☐
Dec 15: Colossians; Philemon ☐

Dec 16: Ephesians ☐
Dec 17: Philippians ☐
Dec 18: 1 Timothy ☐
Dec 19: Titus ☐
Dec 20: 1 Peter ☐
Dec 21: Hebrews 1-6 ☐
Dec 22: Hebrews 7-10 ☐
Dec 23: Hebrews 11-13 ☐
Dec 24: 2 Timothy ☐
Dec 25: 2 Peter; Jude ☐
Dec 26: 1 John ☐
Dec 27: 2 John; 3 John ☐
Dec 28: Revelation 1-5 ☐
Dec 29: Revelation 6-11 ☐
Dec 30: Revelation 12-18 ☐
Dec 31: Revelation 19-22 ☐

Gospel Fellowships Hymnal

FOR MANY believers there has been a lack of good resources to help them worship the Lord in private devotion or in public gatherings of the Lord's people. Many hymns and choruses that could be sung by memory and without instruments have been laid aside for more contemporary songs that have much musical accompaniment. The argument is not over styles of music or what is permissible in a worship setting but rather that a very powerful weapon of the Church has been lost. This occurs when we do not have many hymns and choruses that we can sing without instruments with a whole heart towards the Lord. Thus the burden here is to simply supply a resource of many old hymns, choruses and spiritual songs for *reading*, *meditation* and *singing* privately and corporately.[1143] We encourage the believers as they gather, to sing the choruses slowly and boldly to the Lord Himself.

Throughout the 2000 years of the Christian Church there have been many different modes of music used. We are not arguing for one specific style of music. This hymnal does not exclude the singing of more contemporary songs in meetings, this choice will be up to the discretion of brothers and sisters in each individual meeting. One interesting thought from the past, around 300 AD: "Augustine

---

[1143] Psalm 111:1-2

describes the singing at Alexandria under Athanasius as *more like speaking than singing*. Musical instruments were not used. The pipe, tabret, and harp were associated so intimately with the sensuous heathen cults, as well as with the wild revelries and shameless performances of the degenerate theatre and circus, that it is easy to understand the prejudice against their use in the Christian worship."[1144] In the time of Jesus singing *acapella* was normal and used much more than in our contemporary societies. The great benefit of an Assembly singing without instruments is that under persecution there is still an ability to easily worship the Lord in this fashion.

May God lead each group by His Spirit. This is simply a small resource that will benefit some. Even to be read aloud and meditated on they are a great help to encourage us along the pilgrim way.[1145]

From practical experience we have found that singing hymns very slowly and clearly allows the greatest time for meditation on the words so therefore each person can worship the Lord in Spirit and in truth.[1146] May we heed the Words in Ephesians: "Speaking to one another in psalms and hymns and spiritual songs, singing and making melody in your heart *to the Lord*."[1147] Sing to the Lord. Sing in a way where you direct the Words to God and give Him the glory.

Most of the hymns have been modernized in their wording to have younger generations participate, to help their understanding and to aid the understanding of those speaking other languages. Changes were made also to bring more attention to the work of Christ's blood shed for mankind. We even encourage brethren who are musically gifted to compose new tunes for these hymns so that a new generation can benefit greatly from the words of these precious hymns of the past.

We dedicate this hymnal to the Son of God, Jesus Christ. One day soon we will all worship the Lamb of God in heaven. *Amen.*

[1144] Ernest Edwin Ryden (1886-1981)

[1145] 1 Peter 1:17, 1 Peter 2:11

[1146] John 4:23

[1147] Ephesians 5:19

INDEX TO HYMNAL BY FIRST LINE

1. Jesus, I My Cross Have Taken................................395
2. If I Have Not Forsaken All.................................396
3. Holy, Holy, Holy...397
4. All Hail the Power of Jesus' Name!.......................398
5. One With You, O Son Eternal..............................399
6. Go to Dark Gethsemane....................................400
7. My Jesus I Love You 401
8. Shepherd of Tender Youth.................................402
9. Amazing Grace,How Sweet the Sound!.......................403
10. O Worship the King, All Glorious Above 403
11. O For a Thousand Tongues to Sing........................404
12. There is a Fountain Filled with Blood 405
13. Rock of Ages, Cleft for Me 406
14. Crown Him with Many Crowns..............................407
15. A Hundred Thousand Souls a Day..........................409
16. I Thirst, Wounded Lamb of God 410
17. Would Jesus Have the Sinner Die?........................411
18. Guide Me, Onward, Heavenly Redeemer.....................412
19. Father I Thank You for Guiding My Way...................413
20. Take My Life, and Let It Be 414
21. What a Friend We Have in Jesus..........................415
22. I'd Rather Have Jesus...................................416
23. Abide, O Dearest Jesus..................................416
24. We Praise You, Heavenly Father!.........................417
25. To God Be the Glory 418
26. Christian Hearts, in Love United........................418

27. Alas! And Did My Savior Bleed? 419
28. On a Hill Far Away.....................................420
29. Fill Me with Your Spirit, Lord.........................421
30. Jesus Christ, Our Blessed Savior 422
31. Abba, Father! We Approach You 423
32. Great is Your Faithfulness............................424
33. Pass Me Not, O Gentle Savior 424
34. When We Walk With the Lord............................425
35. Down at the Cross Where My Savior Died................426
36. I Gave My Life For You 427
37. O Soul, Are You Weary and Troubled?...................427
38. When This Passing World Is Done 428
39. What a Fellowship, What a Joy Divine 429
40. All to Jesus, I Surrender 429
41. I Have Decided to Follow Jesus........................430
42. I Stand Amazed in the Presence 431
43. We Lift Our Hearts, Dear Savior 432
44. Lord God, the Holy Spirit 432
45. Lord, Pour Your Spirit From on High...................433
46. When I Survey the Wondrous Cross......................434
47. Head of the Church, Your Body 434
48. Jesus, Your Head, Once Crowned with Thorns............435
49. Eternal Father in Heaven 436
50. O God, You Do Sustain Me.............................437
51. I Cry to You From Deepest Need........................438
52. Jesus, Your Blood and Righteousness...................440
53. Jesus Suffered In Our Place...........................441
54. Whether I Live or Whether I Die 441
55. The Savior Lives, no More to Die 442
56. Be Now My Vision, O Lord of My Heart! 443
57. Head of the Church Triumphant! 444
58. O God, We See You in the Lamb........................445
59. Lamb of God, Our Souls Adore You......................445
60. Jesus, Spotless Lamb of God 446
61. Behold the Lamb, Whose Precious Blood 447
62. All Fullness Resides in Jesus our Head 448
63. A Mighty Fortress is Our God..........................448
64. Here I Am Lord, Use Me Today..........................449

1

JESUS, I MY CROSS HAVE TAKEN,
All to leave and follow You.
Destitute, despised, forsaken,
You my all therefore will be.
Perish every fond ambition,
All I've sought or hoped or known.
Yet how rich is my condition!
God and Heaven are still mine own.

Let the world despise and leave me,
They have left my Savior, too.
Human hearts and looks deceive me;
You are not, like them, untrue.
And while You are smiling on me,
God of wisdom, love and might,
Foes may hate and friends disown me,
Show Your face and all is bright.

Go, then, earthly fame and treasure!
Come, disaster, scorn and pain!
In Your service, pain is pleasure;
With Your favor, loss is gain.
I have called You, *Abba, Father*;
Fixed on You my heart will be:
Storms may howl, and clouds may gather,
All must work for good to me.

Take, my soul, Your full salvation;
Rise over sin, and fear, and care;
Joy to find in every station
Something still to do or bear:
Think what Spirit dwells within you;
What a Father's smile is yours;
What a Savior died to win you,
child of heaven, frown no more!

Rush then on from grace to glory,
Armed by faith, and winged by prayer,
Heaven's eternal days before you,
God's own hand will guide you there.
Soon shall close your earthly mission,
Swift shall pass your pilgrim days;
Hope shall change to glad fruition,
Faith to sight, and prayer to praise.

2

IF I HAVE NOT FORSAKEN ALL
In answer to Your loving call;
If I've kept something back from You,
Lord, give me light, that I might see.

Lord, help me judge myself each day,
To walk this new and living way
I seek Your grace with all my heart,
To be made pure, just as You are.

If anything upon this earth
Attracts me with its sense of worth;
If money has a hold on me,
Lord, give me light, that I might see.

If all my life revolves round me
And thoughts of my own family;
If I am living selfishly,
Lord, give me light, that I might see.

Is there some good I should have done?
Is there some soul I should have won?
Have I hurt someone thoughtlessly?
Lord, give me light, that I might see.

If someone's failure has not brought

Concern and care within my heart;
If I've judged others inwardly,
Lord, give me light, that I might see.

If I have cared for men's applause
Or sought my own and shunned the cross;
If I have feared man's mockery,
Lord give me light, that I might see.

If I've not sought Your power in prayer
Because of earthly toils and care;
If I'm not longing after You,
Lord give me light, that I might see.

3

HOLY, HOLY, HOLY!
Lord God Almighty!
Early in the morning
our song shall rise to You;
Holy, holy, holy, merciful and mighty!
God in three Persons, blessed Trinity!

Holy, holy, holy!
All the saints adore You,
Casting down their golden crowns
around the glassy sea;
Cherubim and seraphim
falling down before You,
Who was, and is, and ever will be.

Holy, holy, holy!
though the darkness hide You,
Though the eye of sinful man
Your glory may not see;
Only You are holy;
there is none beside You,

Perfect in power, in love, and purity.

Holy, holy, holy!
Lord God Almighty!
All Your works shall praise Your Name,
in earth, and sky, and sea;
Holy, holy, holy;
merciful and mighty!
God in three Persons, blessed Trinity!

4

ALL HAIL THE POWER OF JESUS' NAME!
Let angels prostrate fall;
Bring forth the royal diadem,
and crown Him Lord of all.

Crown Him, you martyrs of your God,
who from His altar call;
Praise the Stem of Jesse's Rod,
and crown Him Lord of all.

You seed of Israel's chosen race,
you ransomed from the fall,
Hail Him who saves you by His grace,
and crown Him Lord of all.

Sinners, whose love can never forget
the price He paid for all,
Go spread your trophies at His feet,
and crown Him Lord of all.

Let every tribe and every tongue
before Him prostrate fall
And shout in universal song
the mighty Lord of all.

One day with all the heavenly host,
we at His feet will fall,
And join in everlasting song,
crown Him Lord of all.

5

ONE WITH YOU, O SON ETERNAL,
Joined by faith in spirit one,
Share we in Your death inclusive
And Your life, O God the Son.
One with You, holy Son beloved,
Part of You become through grace,
Heirs with You of our one Father,
We are Your Spirit's dwelling place.

One with You, Son of God incarnate,
Born with You, the Man of worth,
We, the members of Your body,
Tarry with You here on earth.
One with You, Son anointed,
Sharing too the Spirit's power,
We in full cooperation
Labor with You hour by hour.

One with You, Son of God forsaken,
Judgment and the curse has passed;
We to sin are dead forever,
Hell beneath our feet is cast.
One with You in resurrection,
Death can never us oppress;
We live in Your new creation,
Bearing fruits of righteousness.

One with You, Son of God ascended,
Seated with You on the throne,
Your authority we share eternally

Rule with You, servants you own.
One with You, Son of God returning,
Glorified with You we will be one day,
Forever to manifest Your beauty,
One with You forever to stay.

6

GO TO DARK GETHSEMANE,
You that feel the tempter's power;
Your Redeemer's conflict see,
watch with Him one bitter hour,
Turn not from His griefs away;
learn of Jesus Christ to pray.

Follow to the judgment hall,
beaten, bound, reviled, and maimed;
O the wormwood and the gall!
O the pains His soul sustained!
Shun not suffering, shame, or loss;
learn of Christ to bear the cross.

Calvary's mournful mountain climb;
there, adoring at His feet,
mark that miracle of time,
God's own sacrifice complete.
It is finished! hear Him cry;
learn of Jesus Christ to die.

Early hasten to the tomb
where they laid His breathless clay;
All is solitude and gloom.
Who has taken Him away?
Christ is risen! He meets our eyes;
Savior, help us so to rise.

7

MY JESUS, I LOVE YOU,
I know You are mine;
For You all the follies of sin I resign.
My gracious Redeemer,
my hand is to the plough;
If ever I loved You,
my Jesus, it's now.

I love You because
You have first loved me,
And purchased my pardon
on Calvary's tree.
I love You for wearing
the thorns as Your crown;
If ever I loved You,
my Jesus, it's now.

I'll love You in life,
I will love You in death,
And praise You as long
as You lend me the breath;
And say when the dew of death
forms on my brow,
If ever I loved You,
my Jesus, it's now.

In mansions of glory
and endless delight,
I'll ever adore You
in heaven so bright;
I'll sing with the glittering
crown on my brow;
If ever I loved You,
my Jesus, it's now.

8

SHEPHERD OF TENDER YOUTH,[1148]
Guiding in love and truth
Through devious ways;
Christ, our triumphant King,
We come Your Name to sing,
And here our children bring
To sing Your praise.

You are our holy Lord,
Christ the incarnate Word,
Healer of strife:
You did Yourself abase,
becoming sin's disgrace
That You might save our race,
And give us life.

Ever be near our side,
Our Shepherd and our Guide,
Our staff and song:
Jesus, the Christ of God,
Your love now shed abroad,
Lead us where You have trod;
Our faith make strong.

So now, until we die,
We lift Your Name on high,
And joyful sing:
In weakness make us strong
We to Your Church belong
Unite our hearts in songs
To Christ our King!

[1148] The oldest Christian hymn, Clement of Alexandria (A.D. 150-215)

9

AMAZING GRACE! HOW SWEET THE SOUND
that saved a wretch like me!
I once was lost, but now am found;
was blind, but now I see.

Twas grace that taught my heart to fear,
and grace my fears relieved;
how precious did that grace appear
the hour I first believed.

Through many dangers, toils, and snares,
I have already come;
Grace has brought me safe this far,
and grace will lead me home.

The Lord has promised good to me,
His Word my hope secures;
He will my shield and portion be,
as long as life endures.

Yes, when this flesh and heart will fail,
and mortal life will cease,
I will possess, within the veil,
a life of joy and peace.

When we've been there ten thousand years,
with endless days to come,
We've no less days to sing and praise
The glories of the Lamb.

10

O WORSHIP THE KING, ALL GLORIOUS ABOVE,
O gratefully sing His power and His love;
Our shield and defender, the Ancient of Days,
Full of great splendor, and girded with praise.

O tell of His might, O sing of His grace,
Whose robe is the light, whose dwelling is space,
His chariots of wrath the deep thunderclouds form,
And dark is His path on the wings of the storm.

Frail children of dust, and feeble as frail,
In You do we trust, nor find You to fail;
Your mercies how tender, how firm to the end,
Our Maker, Defender, Redeemer, and Friend.

11

O FOR A THOUSAND TONGUES TO SING
My great Redeemer's praise,
The glories of my God and King,
The triumphs of His grace!

My gracious Master and my God,
Assist me to proclaim,
To spread through all the earth abroad
The honors of Your Name.

Jesus! the Name that charms our fears,
That bids our sorrows cease;
It's music in the sinner's ears,
It's life, and health, and peace.

He breaks the power of canceled sin,
He sets the prisoner free;
His blood can make the foulest clean,
His blood availed for me.

He speaks, and, listening to His voice,
New life the dead receive,
The mournful, broken hearts rejoice,
The humble poor believe.

Hear HIm, you deaf; His praise, you dumb
Your loosened tongues employ
You blind, behold your Savior come,
And leap, you lame, for joy.

Glory to God, and praise and love
Be now and ever given,
By saints below and saints above,
The Church in earth and heaven.

I felt my Lord's atoning blood
Close to my soul applied;
Me, me He loved, the Son of God,
For me, for me He died!

Look to the Son and cry out,
Your God became like you;
Saved by faith, Christ died for you,
Justified by His blood.

See all your sins on Jesus laid:
The Lamb of God was slain,
A sacrifice for sin was made
For the soul of every man.

12

THERE IS A FOUNTAIN FILLED WITH BLOOD
drawn from Emmanuel's veins;
And sinners plunged beneath that flood
lose all their guilty stains.

The dying thief rejoiced to see
that fountain in his day;
And there have I, though vile as he,
washed all my sins away.
Dear dying Lamb, Your precious blood

shall never lose its power
Till all the ransomed Church of God
be saved, to sin no more.

Ever since, by faith, I saw the stream
Your flowing wounds supply,
Redeeming love has been my theme,
and shall be till I die.

Then in a nobler, sweeter song,
I'll sing Your power to save,
When this poor lisping, stammering tongue
lies silent in the grave.

13

ROCK OF AGES, CLEFT FOR ME,
Let me hide myself in You;
Let the water and the blood,
From Your wounded side which flowed,
Be of sin the double cure;
Save from wrath and make me pure.

Not the labor of my hands
Can fulfill Your Law's demands;
Could my zeal no respite know,
Could my tears forever flow,
All for sin could not atone;
You must save, and You alone.

Nothing in my hand I bring,
Simply to the cross I cling;
Naked, come to You for dress;
Helpless look to You for grace;
Foul, I to the fountain fly;
Wash me, Savior, or I die.
While I draw this fleeting breath,

When my eyes shall close in death,
When I soar through realms unknown,
See You on Your judgment throne,
Rock of Ages, cleft for me,
Let me hide myself in You.

14

CROWN HIM WITH MANY CROWNS,
the Lamb upon His throne.
Hark! How the heavenly anthem drowns
all music but its own.
Awake, my soul, and sing
of Him who died for you,
And hail Him as your matchless King
His love makes all things new.

Crown Him the Son of God,
before the worlds began,
And you who walk where He has walked,
crown Him the Son of Man;
Who every grief has known
each sorrow, every test,
And takes and bears them for His own,
that all in Him may rest.

Crown Him the Lord of life,
who triumphed over the grave,
And rose victorious in the strife
for those He came to save.
His glories now we sing,
who died, and rose on high,
Who died eternal life to bring,
and lives that death may die.

Crown Him the Lord of peace,
whose kingdom will not end.

From east to west and north to south,
All boundaries it transcends.
His reign shall know no end,
and round His nail pierced feet
The song of the redeemed ascends
before the mercy seat.

Crown Him the Lord of love,
behold His hands and side,
Those wounds, yet visible above,
in beauty glorified.
No angel in the sky
can fully bear that sight,
But downward bends his burning eye
at mysteries ever bright.

Crown Him the Lord of Heaven,
enthroned in worlds above,
Crown Him the King to whom is given
the wondrous Name of Love.
Crown Him with many crowns,
as thrones before Him fall;
Crown Him, you kings, with many crowns,
for He is King of all.

Crown Him the Lord of lords,
who over all does reign,
Who once on earth, the holy Word,
for ransomed sinners slain,
Now lives in realms of light,
where saints with angels sing
Their songs before Him day and night,
their God, Redeemer, King.

Crown Him the Lord of years,
the Architect of time,
Creator of the rolling spheres,
amazing in design.

All hail, Redeemer, hail!
For You have died for me;
Your praise and glory will not fail
for all eternity.

15

A HUNDRED THOUSAND SOULS A DAY
Are passing one by one away
In Christless guilt and gloom;
Without one ray of hope or light,
With future dark as endless night,
They are passing to their doom,
They are passing to their doom.

They are passing, passing fast away
In thousands day by day;
They are passing to their doom,
They are passing to their doom.

O Holy Spirit, Your people move,
Baptize their hearts with faith and love
And consecrate their gold.
At Jesus' feet their treasures pour,
And all their ranks unite once more,
As in the days of old,
As in the days of old.

The Master's coming now draws near;
The Son of Man will soon appear;
His kingdom is at hand.
Before that glorious day can be,
This Gospel of the kingdom we
Must preach in every land,
Must preach in every land.

Oh, let us then His coming haste,

Oh, let us end this awful waste
Of souls that never die.
A thousand millions still are lost;
A Savior's blood has paid the cost,
Oh, hear their dying cry,
Oh, hear their dying cry.

They are passing, passing, fast away,
A hundred thousand souls a day
In Christless guilt and gloom.
O Church of Christ, what will you say
When, in the awful judgment day,
They charge you with their doom,
They charge you with their doom?

16

I THIRST, O WOUNDED LAMB OF GOD,
To wash me in Your cleansing blood;
To dwell within Your wounds; then pain
Is sweet, and life or death is gain.

Take our hearts, and make them new
Forever closed to all but You:
Secure our hearts, and let us wear
Your seal of love forever there.

How blessed are they who still abide
Close sheltered by Your watchful side;
Who life and strength from You receive,
And with You move, and in You live.

What are our works but sin and death,
Until, with Spirit's quickening breath,
You breathe on us life from above;
O wondrous grace! O boundless love!

How can it be, O heavenly King,
That You should us to glory bring;
Make slaves the partners of Your throne,
Adorned with never-fading crowns?

To You our hearts and hands we give
Yours may we die, Yours may we live
Unloose our stammering tongues to tell
of Your love immense, unsearchable!

17

WOULD JESUS HAVE THE SINNER DIE?
Why hangs He then upon the tree?
What means that strange dying cry?
(*Sinners, He prays for you and me.*)
"*Forgive them, Father, O forgive,
They know not that by Me they live.*"

Jesus descended from above,
Our loss of Eden to retrieve,
Great God of universal love,
If all the world through You may live,
In us a quickening Spirit be,
And witness that You died for me,

You loving, all-atoning Lamb,
You—by Your painful agony,
Your bloody sweat, Your grief and shame,
Your cross and passion on the tree,
Your precious death and life, I pray,
Take all, take all my sins away,

O let me kiss Your bleeding feet,
And bathe and wash them with my tears!
The story of Your love repeat
In every drooping sinner's ears,

That all may hear the quickening sound,
Since I, even I, have mercy found,

O let Your love my heart constrain!
Your love for every sinner free,
That every fallen soul of man
May taste the grace that searched for me;
That all mankind with me may prove
Your sovereign everlasting love.

18

GUIDE ME ONWARD, HEAVENLY REDEEMER,
Pilgrim through this barren land.
I am weak, but You are mighty;
Guide me with Your powerful hand.
Bread of Heaven, Bread of Heaven,
You provide our every need;
You provide our every need.

Open now the crystal fountain,
Where the healing stream does flow;
Let the fire and cloudy pillar
Lead me all my journey through.
Strong Deliverer, strong Deliverer,
Be my refuge, strength and shield;
Be my refuge, strength and shield.

Lord, I trust Your mighty power,
Wondrous are Your works of old;
You redeemed your people from the bondage,
into which they had been sold.
You did conquer, You did conquer,
Sin, and Satan and the grave,
Sin, and Satan and the grave.

When I cross death's mighty river,

Bid my anxious fears subside;
Death of deaths, and hell's destruction,
Land me safe on heaven's side.
Songs of praises, songs of praises,
I will ever give to You;
I will ever give to You.

Thinking of my habitation,
Thinking of my heavenly home,
Fills my soul with holy longings:
Come, my Jesus, quickly come;
Vanity is all I see;
Lord, I long to be with You!
Lord, I long to be with You!

19

FATHER I THANK YOU FOR GUIDING MY WAY;
Father I thank You for caring each day;
Father You have done all things perfectly;
You always think of me lovingly.

Father, I thank You in midst of my pain:
Father, I thank You again and again.
Chastening is the best and holy *bread* for me;
Chastening will end my sin's misery.

Father, Your goodness fills each of Your deeds;
Father, Your chastening is what my soul needs.
Father, the outcome of the paths of pain
Can be but blessing and glorious gain.

Into Your hands I commit all, my Lord.
For I know suffering will bring rich reward.
I love the hand that is chastening me,
For it is training and healing me.

Firm shall my hold of Father's hand be;
Safe through the darkest night You will lead me.
Father then bring me home to the throne,
Through pain transform and grant me a crown.

Almighty Father, majestic and great,
Whom all the angels must serve and obey,
You send them out to Your child in need,
Showing Your might and assisting me.

So I will endure in distress and dark night.
Soon You will show me the bright morning light.
Countless the times You have poured out Your grace.
Father, my heart thanks You gratefully.

20

TAKE MY LIFE, AND LET IT BE
be consecrated, Lord, to You.
Take my moments and my days;
let them flow in ceaseless praise.
Take my hands, and let them move
at the impulse of Your love.
Take my feet, and let them be
swift and beautiful for You.

Take my voice, and let me sing
always, only, for my King.
Take my lips, and let them be
filled with messages from You.
Take my silver and my gold;
not a portion would I withhold.
Take my intellect, and use
every power as You will choose.

Take my will, and make it Yours;
it shall be no longer mine.

Take my heart, it is Your own;
it shall be Your royal throne.
Take my love, my Lord,
I pour at Your feet its treasure store.
Take myself, and I will be
ever, only, all for You.

21

WHAT A FRIEND WE HAVE IN JESUS,
all our sins and griefs to bear!
What a privilege to carry
everything to God in prayer!
O what peace we often forfeit,
O what needless pain we bear,
all because we do not carry
everything to God in prayer.

Have we trials and temptations?
Is there trouble anywhere?
We should never be discouraged;
take it to the Lord in prayer.
Can we find a friend so faithful
who will all our sorrows share?
Jesus knows our every weakness;
take it to the Lord in prayer.

Are we weak and heavy laden,
burdened with a load of care?
Precious Savior, still our refuge;
take it to the Lord in prayer.
Do your friends despise, forsake you?
Take it to the Lord in prayer!
In His arms He'll take and shield you;
you will find a comfort there.

22

I'D RATHER HAVE JESUS THAN SILVER OR GOLD;
I'd rather be His than have riches untold;
I'd rather have Jesus than houses or lands;
I'd rather be led by His nail-pierced hand

Than to be the king of a vast domain
And be held in sin's dread sway;
I'd rather have Jesus than anything
This world affords today.

I'd rather have Jesus than men's applause;
I'd rather be faithful to His dear cause;
I'd rather have Jesus than worldwide fame;
I'd rather be true to His holy Name

23

ABIDE, O DEAREST JESUS,
Among us with Your grace,
That satan may not harm us,
Nor we to sin give place.

Abide, O dear Redeemer,
Among us with Your Word,
Now and ever after
True peace and rest afford.

Abide with heavenly brightness
Among us, precious Light;
Your truth direct, and keep us
From error's gloomy night.

Abide with richest blessings
Among us, bounteous Lord;
Let us in grace and wisdom
Grow daily through Your Word.

Abide with Your protection
Our Shepherd and our King,
deliver from deception
And heavenly comfort bring.

Abide, O faithful Savior,
Among us with Your love;
Grant steadfastness, and help us
To reach our home above.

24

WE PRAISE YOU, HEAVENLY FATHER!
For the Son of Your love,
For Jesus Who died,
And is now gone above.

Hallelujah! Your's the glory.
Hallelujah! Amen.
Hallelujah! Your's the glory.
Revive us again.

We praise You, Heavenly Father!
For Your Spirit of light,
Who has shown us our Savior,
And scattered our night.

All glory and praise
To the Lamb that was slain,
Who has borne all our sins,
And has cleansed every stain.

All glory and praise
To the God of all grace,
Who has brought us, and sought us,
And guided our ways.

Revive us again;
Fill each heart with Your love;
May each soul be rekindled
With fire from above.

25

TO GOD BE THE GLORY,
great things He has done;
So loved He the world that He gave us His Son,
Who yielded His life an atonement for sin,
And opened the life gate that all may go in.

Praise the Lord, praise the Lord,
Let the earth hear His voice!
Praise the Lord, praise the Lord,
Let the people rejoice!
O come to the Father, through Jesus the Son,
And give Him the glory, great things He has done.

O perfect redemption, the purchase of blood,
To every believer the promise of God;
The vilest offender who truly believes,
That moment from Jesus a pardon receives.

Great things He has taught us,
great things He has done,
And great our rejoicing through Jesus the Son;
But purer, and higher, and greater will be
Our wonder, our transport, when Jesus we see.

26

CHRISTIAN HEARTS, IN LOVE UNITED,
Seek alone in Jesus rest;
Has He not your love excited?
Then let love each heart arrest;

Members on our Head depending
Lights reflecting Him, our Sun,
Brethren His commands attending,
We in Him, our Lord, are one.

Come, then, come, O Flock of Jesus,
Covenant with Him anew;
To Him who has conquered for us,
Pledge we love and service true;
And should our love's union holy
Firmly linked no more remain,
Wait you at His footstool lowly,
Till He draw it close again.

Grant, Lord, that with Your direction,
Love each other, we comply,
Aiming with holy, pure affection
Your love to exemplify;
Let our mutual love be glowing,
Then all men will find it true,
That we are from one Vine growing,
Living branches, part of You.

O that such may be our union,
As You with the Father are,
And not one of our communion
Walk unworthy of Your scars;
May our light with growing brightness,
From Your light reflected, shine
May our lives to men bear witness,
Of Your love and power divine.

27

ALAS! AND DID MY SAVIOR BLEED
And did my Sovereign die?
Would He devote that sacred Head

For such a worm as I?

At the cross, at the cross
Where I first saw the light,
And the burden of my heart rolled away,
It was there by faith I received my sight,
And now I rejoice all the day!

Your body slain, sweet Jesus, Yours—
And bathed in its own blood—
Your soul in anguish to it's core,
Beneath the wrath of God.

Was it for crimes that I had done
He groaned upon the tree?
Amazing pity! grace unknown!
And love beyond degree!

Well might the sun in darkness hide
And shut its glories in,
When Christ, the mighty Maker died,
for His creation's sin.

Thus might I hide my blushing face
While His dear cross appears,
Dissolve my heart in thankfulness,
And melt my eyes to tears.

But drops of grief can not repay
The debt of love I owe:
Here, Lord, I give my self away
It's all that I can do.

28

ON A HILL FAR AWAY
stood an old rugged cross,

The emblem of suffering and shame;
And I love that old cross
where the dearest and best
For a world of lost sinners was slain.

So I'll cherish the old rugged cross,
Till my trophies at last I lay down;
I will cling to the old rugged cross,
And exchange it some day for a crown.

O that old rugged cross,
so despised by the world,
Has a wondrous attraction for me;
For the dear Lamb of God
left His glory above
To bear it to dark Calvary.

In that old rugged cross,
stained with blood so divine,
A wondrous beauty I see,
It was on that old cross
Jesus suffered and died,
To pardon and sanctify me.

To the old rugged cross
I will ever be true;
Its shame and reproach gladly bear;
Then He'll call me someday
to my home far away,
Where His glory forever I'll share.

29

FILL ME WITH YOUR SPIRIT, LORD,
Fully save my longing soul;
Through the precious, cleansing blood
Purify and make me whole.

Come, O Spirit, seal me Yours,
Come, Your fullness now bestow;
Let Your glory in me shine,
Make me whiter than the snow.

Fill me with Your holy light,
I would have a single eye;
Make me perfect in Your sight,
It's Your will to sanctify.

Fill me with Your perfect love,
Nothing of self would I retain;
Losing all Your love to prove,
Lord, I count a happy gain.

Fill me with Your mighty power,
Father, Son, and Spirit, come;
In my soul the unction pour,
Make me ever all Your own.

Fill me with Your presence now,
Lord, Yourself in me reveal;
At Your feet I humbly bow
To receive the holy seal.

30

JESUS CHRIST, OUR BLESSED SAVIOR,
Turned away God's wrath forever;
By His bitter grief and woe
He saved us from the evil foe.

As His pledge of love undying
He, this precious food supplying,
Gives His body with the bread
And with the wine the blood He shed.

Praise the Father, who has given
Unto us the Bread from heaven
And with the blood of His dear Son,
Redeemed us from the wicked one.

If your heart this truth professes
And your mouth your sin confesses,
Saved from wrath your soul will be,
For Christ Himself will set you free.

31

ABBA, FATHER! WE APPROACH YOU
In our Savior's precious Name;
We, Your children, here assembled,
Now Your promised blessing claim;
From our sins His blood has washed us,
Now through Him our souls draw near,
As Your Holy Spirit taught us,
We Your holy Name revere.

Once as prodigals we wandered
In our folly far from You,
Your grace, over sin abounding,
Rescued us and made us new;
You Your prodigals have pardoned,
Kissed us with a Father's love,
You have called us out of darkness,
Ever to dwell with You above.

Clothed in garments of salvation,
At Your table is our place,
We along with you rejoicing,
In the riches of Your grace;
It is good, we hear You saying,
To rejoice though Blood was shed,
I have found My once lost children,

Now they live who once were dead.

Abba, Father! all adore You,
All rejoice in Heaven above,
While in us they learn the wonders
Of Your wisdom, grace, and love;
Soon before Your throne assembled,
All Your children shall proclaim,
Glory, everlasting glory,
Be to God and to the Lamb!

32

GREAT IS YOUR FAITHFULNESS,
O God, my Father;
there is no shadow of turning with You;
You change not, Your compassions, they fail not;
as You have been You'll forever be true.

Great is Your faithfulness! Great is Your faithfulness!
Morning by morning new mercies I see;
all I have needed Your hand has provided;
great is Your faithfulness, Lord unto me!

Pardon for sin and a peace that's enduring
Your own dear presence to cheer and to guide;
strength for today and bright hope for tomorrow,
blessings all mine, with ten thousand beside!

33

PASS ME NOT, O GENTLE SAVIOR,
Hear my humble cry;
While on others You are calling,
Do not pass me by.

Savior, Savior,

Hear my humble cry;
While on others You are calling,
Do not pass me by.
Let me at Your throne of mercy
Find a sweet relief,
Kneeling there in deep contrition;
Help my unbelief.

Trusting only in Your merit,
I would seek Your face;
Heal my wounded, broken spirit,
Save me by Your grace.

You the source of all my comfort,
You, the Song I sing,
Whom have I in earth or heaven?
Besides You, my God, my King?

34

WHEN WE WALK WITH THE LORD
in the light of His Word,
What a glory He sheds on our way!
While we do His good will,
He abides with us still,
And with all who will trust and obey.

Trust and obey, for there's no other way
To be happy in Jesus, but to trust and obey.

Every burden we bear,
Every sorrow we share,
Every labor He'll richly repay;
Every grief, every loss,
every tear, every cross,
Will be blessed if we trust and obey.

But we never can prove
the delights of His love
Until all on the altar we lay;
For the favor He shows,
for the joy He bestows,
Are for them who will trust and obey.

Then in fellowship sweet
we will sit at His feet.
Or we'll walk by His side in the way.
What He says we will do,
where He sends we will go;
Never fear, only trust and obey.

35

DOWN AT THE CROSS WHERE MY SAVIOR DIED,
Down where for cleansing from sin I cried,
There to my heart was the blood applied;
Glory to His Name!

Glory to His Name, Glory to His Name:
There to my heart was the blood applied;
Glory to His Name!

I am so wondrously saved from sin,
Jesus so sweetly abides within,
There at the cross where He took me in;
Glory to His Name!

Oh, precious fountain that saves from sin,
I am so glad I have entered in;
There Jesus saves me and keeps me clean;
Glory to His Name!

Come to this fountain so rich and sweet,
Cast your poor soul at the Savior's feet;

Plunge in today, and be made complete;
Glory to His Name!

36

I GAVE MY LIFE FOR YOU,
My precious blood I shed,
That you might ransomed be,
and raised up from the dead.

I gave, I gave My life for you,
What have you given for Me?

My Father's house of light,
My glory circled throne,
I left, for earthly night,
For wanderings sad and alone.

I suffered much for you,
More than your tongue can tell,
Of bitterest agony,
To rescue you from hell.

And I have brought to you,
Down from My home above,
Salvation full and free,
My pardon and My love.

37

O SOUL, ARE YOU WEARY AND TROUBLED?
No light in the darkness you see?
There's a light for a look at the Savior,
And life more abundant and free!

Turn your eyes upon Jesus,
Look full in His wonderful face,

And the things of earth will grow strangely dim,
In the light of His glory and grace.

Through death into life everlasting
He passed, and we follow Him there;
Over us sin has no more dominion—
For we are more than conquerors!

His Word shall not fail you—He promised;
Believe Him, and all will be well:
Then go to a world that is dying,
His perfect salvation to tell!

38

WHEN THIS PASSING WORLD IS DONE
When has sunk the glaring sun,
When we stand with Christ in glory,
Looking over life's finished story;
Then, Lord, shall I fully know --
Not till then -- how much I owe.

When I stand before the throne
Dressed in beauty not my own,
When I see You as You are,
Love You with unsinning heart;
Then, Lord, shall I fully know --
Not till then -- how much I owe.

Even on earth, as through a glass
Darkly, let Your glory pass;
Make forgiveness feel so sweet,
Make Your Spirit's help complete:
Even on earth, Lord, make me know
Something of how much I owe.

Chosen not for good in me,

From the coming wrath to flee,
Hidden in the Savior's side,
By the Spirit sanctified,
Teach me, Lord, on earth to show,
By my love, how much I owe.

39

WHAT A FELLOWSHIP, WHAT A JOY DIVINE,
Leaning on the everlasting arms;
What a blessedness, what a peace is mine,
Leaning on the everlasting arms.
Leaning, leaning, safe and secure from all alarms;
Leaning, leaning, leaning on the everlasting arms.

O how sweet to walk in this pilgrim way,
Leaning on the everlasting arms;
O how bright the path grows from day to day,
Leaning on the everlasting arms.

What have I to dread, what have I to fear,
Leaning on the everlasting arms;
I have blessed peace with my Lord so near,
Leaning on the everlasting arms.

40

ALL TO JESUS, I SURRENDER;
All to Him I freely give;
I will ever love and trust Him,
In His presence daily live.

I surrender all, I surrender all,
All to You, my blessed Savior,
I surrender all.

All to Jesus I surrender;

Humbly at His feet I bow,
Worldly pleasures all forsaken;
Take me, Jesus, take me now.

All to Jesus, I surrender;
Make me, Savior, Yours alone;
Let me feel the Holy Spirit,
Bearing witness from the Throne.

All to Jesus, I surrender;
Lord, I give myself to You;
Fill me with Your love and power;
All Your promises are true.

All to Jesus I surrender;
Now I feel the sacred flame.
O the joy of full salvation!
Glory, glory, to His Name!

41

I HAVE DECIDED TO FOLLOW JESUS;
I have decided to follow Jesus;
I have decided to follow Jesus;
No turning back, no turning back.

Though I may wonder, I still will follow;
Though I may wonder, I still will follow;
Though I may wonder, I still will follow;
No turning back, no turning back.

The world behind me, the cross before me;
The world behind me, the cross before me;
The world behind me, the cross before me;
No turning back, no turning back.

Though none go with me, still I will follow;

Though none go with me, still I will follow;
Though none go with me, still I will follow;
No turning back, no turning back.

42

I STAND AMAZED IN THE PRESENCE
of Jesus the Nazarene,
And wonder how He could love me,
A sinner, condemned, unclean.

How marvelous! How wonderful!
And my song shall ever be:
How marvelous! How wonderful!
Is my Savior's love for me!

For us it was in the garden
He prayed: *Not My will, but Yours.*
He had no tears for His own griefs,
But sweat drops of blood for ours.

In pity angels beheld Him,
And came from the world of light
To comfort Him in the sorrows
He bore for my soul that night.

He took my sins and my sorrows,
He made them His very own;
He bore the burden to Calvary,
And suffered and died alone.

When with the ransomed in glory
His face I at last shall see,
It will be my joy through the ages
To sing of His love for me.

43

WE LIFT OUR HEARTS, DEAR SAVIOR,
Redeemer and Creator,
for Your humility;
Your wondrous Name is holy,
and yet You came most lowly
as Elder of our Unity.

For us, the days we're living
a blessed taste are giving
of heaven here below;
for Your most gracious presence
exceeds the highest essence
of wonders we can see and know.

Dear Author of creation,
our Refuge and Salvation,
for all in grace You bled;
we take Your hands, nail-riven,
as pledge eternal given
be now and ever more our Head.

44

LORD GOD, THE HOLY SPIRIT,
In this accepted hour,
As on the day of Pentecost,
Descend in all Your power.

We meet with one accord
In our appointed place
And wait the promise of our Lord,
The Spirit of all grace.

Like mighty rushing wind
Upon the waves beneath,
Move with one impulse every mind;

One soul, one feeling breathe.

The young, the old inspire
With wisdom from above;
And give us hearts and tongues of fire,
To pray, and praise, and love.

Spirit of light, explore
And chase our gloom away,
With brightness shining more and more
Unto the perfect day.

Spirit of truth, be to us
In life and death, our Guide;
O Spirit of adoption, now
May we be sanctified!

45

LORD, POUR YOUR SPIRIT FROM ON HIGH,
And Your ordained servants bless;
Graces and gifts to each supply,
And clothe Your priests with righteousness.

Within Your temple when they stand,
To teach the truth as taught by You,
Savior, like stars in Your right hand,
Let Your Church's shepherds be true.

Wisdom, and zeal, and faith impart,
Firmness with meekness, from above,
To be broken by what breaks your heart,
And love the souls whom You do love.

To watch, and pray, and never faint,
By day and night their guard to keep,
To warn the sinner, cheer the saint,

To feed Your lambs, and tend Your sheep.

So, when their work is finished here,
May they in hope their charge resign;
So, when their Master shall appear,
May they with crowns of glory shine.

46

WHEN I SURVEY THE WONDROUS CROSS,
On which the Prince of glory died,
My richest gain I count but loss,
And pour contempt on all my pride.

Forbid it, Lord, that I should boast,
Save in the death of Christ my God!
All the vain things that charm me most,
I sacrifice them to His blood.

See from His head, His hands, His feet,
Sorrow and love flow mingled down!
Did ever such love and sorrow meet,
Or thorns compose so rich a crown?

Like a robe, His dying blood,
Spreads over His body on the tree;
And so, I am dead to all the world,
And all the world is dead to me.

Were the whole realm of nature mine,
That were a present far too small;
Love so amazing, so divine,
Demands my soul, my life, my all.

47

HEAD OF THE CHURCH, YOUR BODY,

O Christ, the great Salvation!
Sweet to the saints it is to think
Of all Your exaltation!
All powers to You are committed.
All power in earth and heaven;
To You a Name of widest fame
above all glory given.

With You believers raised,
With You on high are seated;
All guilty once, But cleared by You;
Redemption's toil completed.
And when You, Lord and Savior,
Will come again in glory,
There by Your side, Your spotless Bride.
Will crown the wondrous story.

At length—the final kingdom,
No bound, no end possessing:
When heaven and earth—God all in all,
Will fill with largest blessing.
All root of evil banished,
No breath of sin to wither,
On earth—on high—Nothing else but joy,
And blissful peace for ever!

48

JESUS, YOUR HEAD, ONCE CROWNED WITH THORNS,
Is crowned with glory now;
Heaven's royal crown adorns
The mighty Victor's brow.

O glorious light of courts above,
Joy of the saints below,
To us still manifest Your love,
That we its depths may know.

To us Your cross with all its shame,
With all its grace be given;
Though earth disowns Your lowly Name,
God honors it in heaven.
Who suffers with You, Lord, below,
Shall reign with You above;
Then let it be our joy to know
This way of peace and love.

To us Your cross is life and health;
It was shame and death to You;
Lord help us to deny ourselves,
Take up our crosses too.

49

ETERNAL FATHER IN HEAVEN[1149]
I call to You from deep within
Do not let me turn from You
Hold me in Your eternal truth
Until I reach my end.

O God, keep my heart and mouth
Watch over me, Lord, always
Do not let me part from You
Whether in anguish, fear or need
Keep me pure in joy.

To walk in Your strength in death
Through tribulation, martyrdom,
fear and need
Keep me in Your strength

[1149] This song was penned by Michael Sattler (1490-1527), a Catholic Priest who became an Anabaptist. Condemned as a heretic, the court stipulated that on his way to the stake, his tongue be progressively cut out, piece by piece. He was to have two pieces torn from his body by glowing tongs and burned five times with the tongs. Finally, he was bound with ropes to a ladder and pushed into the fire.

That I may never again be separated
From Your love, O God.

There are many who travel this path
On which stands the cup of suffering
And also much false doctrine
With which they try to turn us away
From Christ our Lord.

I lift up my soul to you, Lord
I hope in You in times of danger
Let me not become a disgrace
So that my enemies have the victory
Over me on this earth.

They have me here locked up
I wait, O God, from my heart
With great desire
If You would only stir
And save Your ones from prison.

Be comforted, you Christians
And always be joyous through Jesus Christ
He gives us love and faith
God comforts through His Holy Word
And we must trust in It.

I ask God and His Church
That He be today my guardian
For His Names's sake
My Father, let it be so
Through Jesus Christ, Amen.

50

O GOD, YOU DO SUSTAIN ME,
In grief and terrible pain

Heavenly Father I look to You plainly,
And comfort my distress.
O Lord let me find mercy
In bonds and prison bed
Men would seek to devour me
With guile and controversy
Save me from danger dread!

You will never forsake me
This firmly I believe
Your blood You have shed freely
And with it washed me.
In Him my trust is resting
In Christ, God's only Son
On Him I am now building
In tribulation trusting
God will me not disown!

To die and to be living
Until my end I see
To You my trust I'm giving
You will my helper be
My body, soul, and spirit
I commit, dear Lord, to You
Come soon, Lord, come and take me
From ruthless men do save me
Be honor ever to You. Amen.

51

I CRY TO YOU FROM DEEPEST NEED[1150]
O God, hear my call
Send your Holy Spirit to us
To Comfort our deepest despair
As you have done till now, Christ

[1150] This song comes from the seven Anabaptists martyred in Schwabich Gmund in 1528. Each of these seven Anabaptists composed this song while awaiting execution.

We rely on your command
But the heathen now want to kill us.

The flesh is weak, as you know
It fears the smallest pain
So fill us with your Spirit
We pray from our hearts
So that we may remain until the end
And go bravely into suffering
and not fear the pain.

The spirit is surely willing
To undergo suffering
Hear us, O Lord
Through Jesus Christ your beloved Son!
We pray also for our enemies
Who know not what they do
And think not of Your wrath.

We ask You, Father and Lord
As your loving children
Kindle the light through Jesus Christ
Even more in your little flock
That would be our heart's desire
That for which we hunger and thirst
And would bring us greatest joy.

You, Lord God, are my protection
We lift ourselves up to You
So it is but a small pain
If our lives be taken from us
You have prepared for us in eternity
So if here we suffer insult and blows
It will be for nothing.

Body, life, soul, and limbs
We have received from You
These we offer up to You

To praise and glorify Your Name
It is nothing but dust and ashes
We commend to You our spirit, O God
Take it into Your hands. Amen.

52

JESUS, YOUR BLOOD AND RIGHTEOUSNESS
My beauty are, my glorious dress;
When the world is aflame with judgement dread
With joy shall I lift up my head.

Bold shall I stand in Your great day;
Cleansed and redeemed, no debt to pay
By Your cross absolved I am.
From sin and fear, from guilt and shame.

The holy, meek, unspotted Lamb,
Who from the Father's bosom came,
Who died for me, even me to atone,
Now for my Lord and God I own.

Lord, I believe Your precious blood,
Which, at the mercy seat of God,
Forever does for sinners plead,
Even for my soul You did bleed.

When from the dust of death I rise
To claim my dwelling in the skies,
This then, shall be all my plea,
Jesus has lived, has died, for me.

To Jesus endless praises be,
His boundless mercy has for me—
For me a full atonement made,
An everlasting ransom paid.

53

JESUS SUFFERED IN OUR PLACE;
By a disgraceful death
He a full atonement made,
To save us from God's wrath;
And by His most precious blood
Brought us, sinners, near to God.

So that each afflicted soul
May repair, though filled with grief;
To the sick, not to the whole,
The Physician brings relief;
Fear not, therefore, but draw near;
Christ will calm your every fear.

But examine first your case,
Whether you be in the faith;
Do you long for pardoning grace?
Is your only hope His death?
Then, however your soul's oppressed,
Come, you are a worthy guest.

He who Jesus' mercy knows
Is from wrath and envy freed.
Love to each other shows
That we are His flock indeed;
Thus we may in all our ways
Show forth our Redeemer's praise.

54

WHETHER I LIVE OR WHETHER I DIE
May Christ be magnified in me
Whether I go to my Father on high
Let Christ be all that they see.

I am not afraid to die

I long to be away from this place
I'll take my wings, to His glory I'll fly
That I may behold His face.

To live is Christ and to die is gain
For the Kingdom dwells in my heart
No matter what I suffer, no matter the pain
From my Jesus I am never apart.

So let men do what ever they may
For I shall suffer for His sake
I will raise my hands to God and pray
For my soul is His and His to take.

So let us stand together as one
In the Gospel of Christ our Lord
And we shall stand till the day is done
With the Lamb and the blood and the Word.

Stand fast, my brothers, and do not yield
When the enemy comes in like a flood
We shall live or die on the battle-field
For we are covered by Emmanuel's blood.

55

THE SAVIOR LIVES, NO MORE TO DIE;
He lives, our Head, enthroned on high;
He lives triumphant over the grave;
He lives eternally to save.

He lives to still His people's fears;
He lives to wipe away their tears;
He went their mansions to prepare;
He comes to bring them safely there.

Then let our souls in Him rejoice,

And sing His praise with cheerful voice,
Our doubts and fears for ever gone,
For Christ is on the Father's throne.

The chief of sinners He receives;
His saints He loves and never leaves:
He will guard us safe from every ill,
And all His promises fulfill.

Abundant grace will He afford,
Till we are present with the Lord;
And prove what we have sung before,
That Jesus lives for evermore.

56

BE NOW MY VISION, O LORD OF MY HEART
Be nothing else to me, but what You are.
You're my best Thought, by day or by night
Waking or sleeping, Your presence my light.

Be now my wisdom, and be my true Word;
I ever with You, and You with me, Lord;
You my great Father, and I Your true son;
You in me dwelling, and I with You one.

Be now my battle shield, Sword for the fight;
Be now my Dignity, and my Delight;
You're my soul's Shelter, and You're my high Tower

Raise now me Heavenward, O Power of my power.

Riches I need not, nor man's empty praise,
You're my Inheritance now and always:
You and You only, first in my heart,
High King of Heaven, my Treasure You are.

High King of Heaven, my victory won,
May I reach Heaven's joys, O bright Heaven's Sun!
Heart of my own heart, whatever befall,
Still be my Vision, O Ruler of all.

57

HEAD OF THE CHURCH TRIUMPHANT!
We joyfully adore You;
Till You appear, Your members here
Would sing Your love and glory.
We lift our hearts and voices,
In blessed anticipation,
And cry aloud, and give to God
The praise of our salvation.

While in affliction's furnace
And passing through the fire,
The love we praise which tries our ways,
And ever brings us higher;
We lift our hearts exulting
In Your Almighty favor:
The love divine which made us Yours
Will keep us Yours for ever.

You guide and help Your people
Safely through temptation:
Nor will we fear, since You are near,
The fire of tribulation;
The world with sin and Satan,
Display their strength before us;
By You we shall break through them all,
And join the heavenly chorus.

By faith we see the glory
Of which You do assure us;
The world despise, for that high prize

Which You have set before us;
And may we, counted worthy
To meet the Son from heaven,
There see our Lord, by all adored,
To us in glory given.

58

O GOD, WE SEE YOU IN THE LAMB
To be our hope, our joy, our rest;
The glories that compose Your Name
Standing engaged to make us blessed.

So great and so good! So just and so wise!
You are our Father and our God,
For we are Yours by sacred ties,
Your sons and daughters—bought with blood.

Then, oh, to us this grace afford,
That far from You we never may move;
Our guard—the presence of the Lord;
Our joy—Thy perfect present love.

This gives us ever to rejoice,
Turning to light our darkest days;
And lifts on high each feeble voice,
While we have breath to pray or praise.

59

LAMB OF GOD, OUR SOULS ADORE YOU,
While upon Your face we gaze;
There the Father's love and glory
Shine in all their brightest rays;
Your almighty power and wisdom
All creation's works proclaim;
Heaven and earth alike confess You

As the ever great I AM.

Son of God, Your Father's bosom
Ever was Your dwelling-place;
His delight, in Him rejoicing,
One with Him in power and grace:
Oh, what wondrous love and mercy!
You did lay Your glory aside,
And for us did come from heaven,
As the Lamb of God to die.

Lamb of God, when we behold You
Lowly in the manger laid;
Wandering as a homeless Stranger,
In the world Your hands had made;
When we see You in the garden
In Your agony of blood,
At Your grace we are confounded,
Holy, spotless, Lamb of God.

When we see You, as the Victim,
Nailed to the accursed tree,
For our guilt and folly stricken,
All our judgment You bore for us,
Lord, we own with hearts adoring,
You have washed us in Thy blood:
Glory, glory everlasting,
Be to You, O Lamb of God!

60

JESUS, SPOTLESS LAMB OF GOD,
You have bought us with Your blood;
We are Yours, and Yours alone,
This we gladly, fully own.

Help us to confess Your Name,

Bear with joy the cross and shame;
Only seek to follow You,
Though reproach our portion be.

When we are to glory come,
And have reached our heavenly home,
Louder then each lip shall own,
We are Yours and Yours alone.

61

BEHOLD THE LAMB, WHOSE PRECIOUS BLOOD
Drawn from His riven side,
Had power to make our peace with God,
Nor lets one spot abide.

The dying thief beheld that Lamb
Expiring by his side,
And proved the value of the Name
Of Jesus crucified.

His soul, by virtue of the blood,
To paradise received,
Redemption's earliest trophy stood,
From sin and death retrieved.

We, too, the cleansing power have known
Of Christ's atoning blood,
By grace have learned His Name to own,
By which we're brought to God.

To Him, then, let our songs ascend,
Who stooped in grace so low:
To Christ, the Lamb, the sinner's Friend,
Let ceaseless praises flow.

62

ALL FULLNESS RESIDES IN JESUS OUR HEAD
And ever abides to answer all need:
The Father's good pleasure has laid up a store,
A plentiful treasure, to give to the poor.

Whatever distress awaits us below,
Such plentiful grace the Lord will bestow,
As still shall support us and silence our fear,
And nothing can hurt us while Jesus is near.

When sorrows attack us, or terrors draw near,
His love will not fail us, He will quiet our fear;
And when we are fainting and ready to fail,
He will give what is needed, and make us prevail.

We trust in His protection; we will lean on His might;
We are sure His direction will guide us aright:
We know who surrounds us, almighty to save;
And no one confounds us the Savior who have.

63

A MIGHTY FORTRESS IS OUR GOD,
a bulwark never failing;
Our helper He,
amid the flood of mortal ills prevailing:
For still our ancient foe
does seek to work us woe;
His craft and power are great,
and, armed with cruel hate,
On earth is not his equal.

Did we in our own strength confide,
our striving would be losing;
Were not the right Man on our side,
the Man of God's own choosing:

Do ask who that may be?
Christ Jesus, it is He;
The Great I AM, His Name,
from age to age the same,
And He must win the battle.

And though this world, with devils filled,
should threaten to undo us,
We will not fear, for God has willed
His truth to triumph through us:
The prince of darkness grim,
we tremble not for him;
His rage we can endure,
we know his doom is sure,
One little Word shall defeat him.

That Word above all earthly powers,
no thanks to them, abides;
The Spirit and the gifts are ours
through Him who with us sides:
Let goods and family go,
this mortal life also;
The body they may kill:
God's truth will abide still,
His kingdom is forever.

64

HERE I AM LORD, USE ME TODAY
I am nothing Lord but use me I pray
My contrite heart I ask to renew.
My heart's desire is to worship You.

Show me Your heart and open the door
Shine Your light that I may see more.
Of who I am and who I can be
To follow You for all eternity.

You have taken up residence inside of me
I can never repay You for setting me free.
I was simply a flower withering in the field
And now my desire is simply to yield.

You're my tomorrow, You're the Life that's in me
I am amazed just simply to be
Found in Your presence, clothed in Your love
A child of the King, my Father above.

I have found shelter in the arms of my King
To Your throne of mercy my poor heart I bring.
And there I find life, life more abundantly
My chains are broken, I am gloriously free.

Give life to my words that I share here on earth
May my heart follow You forever to serve
May revival break out in the hearts of all men
That You may be glorified on earth once again.

Gospel Fellowships Readings

THE IMPORTANCE of liturgy in the history of the Christian Church over the 2000 years cannot be underestimated. Some of the earliest hymns in the Church were chants or Scriptural truths read aloud in unison. To verbally proclaim in unison holy truths of God will have a great affect spiritually on the Assembly of believers to strengthen and unify them in the faith *once delivered to the saints.*[1151]

We are commended in the Scriptures to verbally proclaim our allegiance to the Son of God, confessing truths that we believe in our heart.[1152] Though modern day evangelicalism is mostly non-liturgical this was not so in the early days of Christianity.

The New Testament suggests that Christian worship incorporated singing of hymns and psalms,[1153] prayer,[1154] vocal thanksgiving,[1155] and instruction.[1156] In the Gospel of Luke, 1 Timothy,[1157] and Revelation[1158] we see preserved hymns that may have been used in the worship of the early Church.

[1151] Jude 1:3
[1152] Romans 10:9
[1153] Ephesians 5:19
[1154] 1 Corinthians 11:4-5
[1155] Ephesians 5:20, Hebrews 13:15
[1156] 1 Corinthians 14:26, Colossians 3:16
[1157] 1 Timothy 3:16
[1158] Revelation 5:9-10, Revelation 15:3-4

According to an old account of Christians, "On an appointed day they had been accustomed to meet before daybreak, and to recite a hymn antiphonally to Christ, as to a god." Then they would take an oath (*Latin. Sacramentum*) "to abstain from theft, robbery, adultery, and breach of faith."[1159]

In AD 200, Hippolytus compiled a document called the *Apostolic Tradition* which conveys many liturgical elements carrying over from the earliest days of the meetings of the Church. Liturgy was surrounded mostly by the celebration of the Lord's Supper (*Eucharist*). One recommendation is for a gathering of believers to speak one or more of these *readings* aloud in unison—or individually —for thanksgiving and declarations of faith. This can build more unified faith and can grant a sanctity to the time together as the body of Christ and the breaking of the bread.[1160]

This practice of reading Scripture out-loud in an Assembly or unified singing and reading of liturgy is not something that the Catholic church or other groups invented but rather it was a practice of the early Church.[1161] May God give us the grace to recapture this apostolic practice for the benefit of His body.

[1159] Pliny the Younger (A.D. 61-113)
[1160] 1 Corinthians 11:29
[1161] 1 Timothy 4:13, Ephesians 5:19

INDEX TO READINGS BY FIRST LINE

1. You Are Head and Savior of Your Body, the Church.............454
2. From the Sin of Unbelief...454
3. To the Lamb That Was Slain...455
4. I Believe in the One Only God..455
5. We Thank You, O Father, Lord of Heaven and Earth...........456
6. I Believe in the Name of the Only Begotten Son of God........456
7. We Wait in Faith for You..457
8. I Believe in the Holy Spirit, Who Proceeds From the Father..457
9. I Believe, That By My Own Reason and Strength.................458
10. In This Communion of Saints My Faith is Placed................458
11. Lord, Your Body Never Forsake..459
12. The Lamb, Who by Blood Our Salvation Obtained.............459
13. Preserve Us, Gracious Lord and God..................................459
14. Glory Be to Your Most Holy Priesthood............................460
15. Bless and Comfort us, Gracious Lord and God...................460
16. O Holy Spirit, Comforter Divine.......................................460
17. Say to Them That Are of a Fearful Heart............................461
18. O Savior of Our Race..461
19. Dear Desire of Every Nation, By Your All-sufficient Merit...462
20. Praise to You, O Lord, We Render.....................................462
21. Our Lord Said to His Disciples..462
22. Like Him We Then Shall Be..463
23. You Have Blessed Us With All Spiritual Blessings...............463
24. Hearts, That Once Were Taught to Own............................464
25. While the Foe Becomes More Daring.................................464
26. Send Your Servants Forth..464

27. Lord God, Son, You Are Savior of the World 465
28. By You Holy Incarnation and Birth 465
29. The Father of Glory Has Raised Christ From the Dead........466
30. Through His Own Blood He Entered in Once for All..........466
31. Fear Not, Says the Lord, I Am the First and the Last...........466
32. God Was Manifested in the Flesh.......................................467
33. For If We Died With Him...467
34. Worthy is the Lamb Who was Slain...................................467
35. We Give You Thanks, Holy Father....................................468

1

YOU ARE HEAD AND SAVIOR OF YOUR BODY, THE CHURCH.

Unite all the children of God in one spirit. Send faithful laborers into Your harvest. Give spirit and power to preach Your Word. Hinder all schisms and offenses. Put far from Your people all deceivers.[1162] Bring back all that have erred or that are deceived. Grant love and unity to all our congregations. Give to our shepherds and servant leaders soundness of doctrine and holiness of life, and preserve them. Teach us to bless them that curse us,[1163] and to do good to them that hate us.[1164] Have mercy on our slanderers and persecutors, and lay not this sin to their charge.[1165] *Hear us, gracious Son of God. Amen.*

2

FROM THE SIN OF UNBELIEF,

From all defilement of the flesh and spirit.[1166] From all self-righteousness. From every neglect of our duty. From all ingratitude and selfishness. From lukewarmness in our love to You[1167] and our

---

[1162] Matthew 7:15
[1163] Romans 12:14
[1164] Romans 12:21
[1165] Acts 7:60
[1166] 2 Corinthians 7:1
[1167] Revelation 2:4

neighbor. From indifference to Your meritorious life and death. *Deliver us, gracious heavenly Father. Amen.*

3

TO THE LAMB THAT WAS SLAIN,

And has redeemed us out of all nations of the earth. To the Lord Who purchased our souls for Himself. To that Friend who loved us, and washed us from our sins in His own blood.[1168] Who died for us once, that we might die to sin.[1169] Who rose for us, that we also might rise. Who ascended for us into heaven. To prepare a place for us.[1170] And to who are subjected the angels, and powers, and dominions. To Him be glory at all times, in the Church that waits for Him, and in that which is around Him.[1171] From everlasting to everlasting. *Amen.*

4

I BELIEVE IN THE ONE ONLY GOD, FATHER, SON, AND HOLY SPIRIT,

Who created all things by Jesus Christ,[1172] and was in Christ reconciling the world to Himself.[1173] I believe in God, the Father of our Lord Jesus Christ. Who has chosen us in Him before the foundation of the world.[1174] Who has delivered us from the power of darkness, and has translated us into the kingdom of His dear Son.[1175] Who has blessed us with all spiritual blessings in heavenly places in Christ.[1176] Who has made us to be partakers of the inheritance of the

---

[1168] Revelation 1:5
[1169] 1 Peter 2:24
[1170] John 14:3
[1171] Ephesians 3:21
[1172] Colossians 1:16
[1173] 2 Corinthians 5:19
[1174] Ephesians 1:4
[1175] Colossians 1:13
[1176] Ephesians 1:3

saints in light.[1177] To the praise of the glory of His grace. Where He has made us accepted in the Beloved.[1178] *This I truly believe. Amen.*

5

WE THANK YOU, O FATHER, LORD OF HEAVEN AND EARTH,

Because You have hid these things from the wise and intelligent, and have revealed them to children. Even so, Father; for so it seemed good in Your sight. Father, glorify Your Name.[1179] Our Father who are in heaven, hallowed be Your Name. Your kingdom come. Your will be done on earth, as it is in heaven. Give us this day our daily bread. And forgive us our trespasses, as we forgive them that trespass against us. And lead us not into temptation, but deliver us from evil.[1180] For Yours is the kingdom, and the power, and the glory, forever and ever. *Amen.*

6

I BELIEVE IN THE NAME OF THE ONLY BEGOTTEN SON OF GOD,

By whom are all things, and we through Him. I believe, that He was made flesh, and dwelt among us, and took on Him the form of a servant.[1181] By the overshadowing of the Holy Spirit, was conceived of the virgin Mary.[1182] As the children are partakers of flesh and blood, He also Himself likewise took part of the same.[1183] Was born of a woman. And being found in fashion as a man, was tempted in all points as we are, yet without sin.[1184] For He is the Lord, the Messenger of the covenant, whom we delight in. The Lord and His Spirit have sent Him to proclaim the acceptable year of the Lord.[1185]

[1177] Colossians 1:12
[1178] Ephesians 1:6
[1179] Matthew 11:25
[1180] Matthew 6:9-13
[1181] Philippians 2:7
[1182] Matthew 1:18-25
[1183] Hebrews 2:14
[1184] Hebrews 4:15
[1185] Luke 4:19

He spoke that which He did know, and testified that which He had seen. As many as receive Him, to them gave He power to become the sons of God.[1186] Behold the Lamb of God, which takes away the sin of the world.[1187] Suffered under Pontius Pilate, was crucified, dead and buried. Went also by the Spirit and preached to the spirits in prison.[1188] On the third day rose again from the dead, and with Him many bodies of the saints who slept. Ascended into heaven, and sits on the throne of the Father. Where from He will come, in like manner as He was seen going into heaven.[1189] *Amen.*

7

WE WAIT IN FAITH FOR YOU.

Soon—we implore You—come, Your glory let us see. The Lord will descend from heaven with a shout, with the voice of the archangel. And with the trumpet of God.[1190] To judge both the quick and the dead.[1191] This is my Lord, who redeemed me, a lost and undone human creature. Purchased and gained me from sin, from death, and from the power of the devil. Not with gold or silver, but with His holy, precious blood.[1192] And with His innocent suffering and dying. To the end that I should be His own. And in His kingdom live under Him and serve Him, in eternal righteousness, innocence, and happiness. Even as He, being risen from the dead, lives and reigns, world without end. *This I most certainly believe. Amen.*

8

I BELIEVE IN THE HOLY SPIRIT, WHO PROCEEDS FROM THE FATHER,

[1186] John 1:12
[1187] John 1:29
[1188] 1 Peter 3:19
[1189] Acts 1:11
[1190] 1 Thessalonians 4:16
[1191] 1 Peter 4:5
[1192] 1 Peter 1:19

And whom our Lord Jesus Christ sent, after He went away, that He should abide with us forever.[1193] That He should comfort us, as a mother comforts her children. That He should help our infirmities, and make intercession for us with groaning which cannot be uttered.[1194] That He should bear witness with our spirit, that we are the children of God, and teach us to cry, *Abba, Father*.[1195] That He should shed abroad in our hearts the love of God,[1196] and make our bodies His holy temple.[1197]   And that He should work all in all, dividing to every man severally as He will. To Him be glory in the Church, which is in Christ Jesus, the holy, universal Christian Church. In the communion of saints, at all times, and from eternity to eternity. *Amen.*

9

I BELIEVE, THAT BY MY OWN REASON AND STRENGTH,

I cannot believe in Jesus Christ my Lord, or come to Him. But that the Holy Spirit calls me by the Gospel, enlightens me with His gifts, sanctifies and preserves me in the true faith. Even as He calls, gathers, enlightens, and sanctifies the whole Church on earth,[1198] which He keeps by Jesus Christ in the only true faith. *This I assuredly believe. Amen.*

10

IN THIS COMMUNION OF SAINTS MY FAITH IS PLACED,

Upon my Lord and Savior Jesus Christ. Who died for me, and shed His blood on the cross for the remission of sins. And who has granted to me His body and blood in the Lord's Supper, as a pledge of grace. As the Scripture says. Our Lord Jesus Christ, the same night in which He was betrayed, took bread. And when He had given

---

[1193] John 14:16
[1194] Romans 8:26
[1195] Romans 8:15
[1196] Romans 5:5
[1197] 1 Corinthians 6:19
[1198] 1 Thessalonians 5:23-24

thanks, He broke it, and gave it to His disciples, and said. Take, eat this is My body which is given for you. This do in remembrance of Me. After the same manner also, our Lord Jesus Christ, when He had eaten. Took the cup, gave thanks, and gave it to them. Saying, drink all of you of it this is My blood, the blood of the New Testament. Which is shed for you, and for many, for the remission of sins. This do, as often as you drink it, in remembrance of Me.[1199] *Amen.*

11

LORD, YOUR BODY NEVER FORSAKE.

Never Your congregation leave. We to You our refuge take. Of Your fullness we receive.[1200] Every other help be gone. You are our support alone. For on Your supreme commands all the universe depends.[1201] *Amen.*

12

THE LAMB, WHO BY BLOOD OUR SALVATION OBTAINED,

Took on Him our curse,[1202] and death freely sustained. Is worthy of praises.[1203] Let with one accord all people say. *Amen. O praise the Lord.*

13

PRESERVE US, GRACIOUS LORD AND GOD.

From indifference to Your merits and death. From pride and self-complacency. From needless perplexity. From the unhappy desire of becoming great. From hypocrisy and fanaticism. From envy, hatred, and malice. From the deceitfulness of sin. From the murdering spirit and devices of satan. From the influence of the spirit of this world.

[1199] 1 Corinthians 11:23-25
[1200] John 1:16
[1201] Hebrews 1:3
[1202] Galatians 3:13
[1203] Psalm 145:3

Preserve us, gracious Lord and God. By all the merits of Your life. By Your human birth and circumcision. By Your obedience, diligence and faithfulness. By Your humility, meekness and patience. By Your extreme poverty. By Your Baptism, fasting and temptation. By Your griefs and sorrows. By Your prayers and tears. By Your having been despised and rejected. Bless and comfort us,[1204] gracious Lord and God. *Amen.*

14

GLORY BE TO YOUR MOST HOLY PRIESTHOOD,
Christ, Lamb of God. You were slain for us.[1205] Who by one offering has perfected for ever them that are sanctified.[1206] *Amen, Hallelujah.*

15

BLESS AND COMFORT US, GRACIOUS LORD AND GOD.
Lord God, Holy Spirit, abide with us for ever. I am the Resurrection and the Life, says the Lord. He that believes in Me—though he were dead—yet shall he live.[1207] And who ever lives and believes in Me will never die. Therefore, blessed are the dead who die in the Lord from now on. Yes, says the Spirit, that they may rest from their labors. O death, where is your sting? O grave, where is your victory? The sting of death is sin. And the strength of sin is the law. But thanks be to God, who gives us the victory through our Lord Jesus Christ.[1208] *Amen.*

16

O HOLY SPIRIT, COMFORTER DIVINE,

[1204] Isaiah 30:18
[1205] Revelation 5:12
[1206] Hebrews 10:14
[1207] John 11:25
[1208] 1 Corinthians 15:55-57

Giver of life and peace. Grant us Your abiding presence. Lord, make us to know our end, and the measure of our days, what it is.[1209] Let us know how frail we are. So teach us to number our days that we may get a heart of wisdom.[1210] Hear our prayer, O Lord, and give ear unto our cry.[1211] For we are strangers with You—sojourners—as all our fathers were.[1212] It is appointed to men once to die, and after this comes judgment.[1213] For we must all be made manifest before the judgment-seat of Christ. That each one may receive the things done in the body. According to what he has done, whether it be good or bad.[1214] What is your life? For you are a vapor that appears for a little time and then vanishes away.[1215] *Let it be so. Amen.*

17

SAY TO THEM THAT ARE OF A FEARFUL HEART,

Be strong and fear not.[1216] Behold your God will come and save you. He shall feed His Flock like a Shepherd. He shall gather the lambs with His arm. And carry them in His bosom.[1217] *Amen.*

18

O SAVIOR OF OUR RACE,

You are indeed welcome. Blessed Redeemer, fountain of grace, to this my longing heart! Therefore, rejoice in God, your Savior! For He that is mighty, has done great things. And holy is His Name.[1218] Through the tender mercy of our God, the Day-spring from on high

---

[1209] Psalm 39:4
[1210] Psalm 90:12
[1211] Psalm 143:1
[1212] 1 Chronicles 29:15
[1213] Hebrews 9:27
[1214] 2 Corinthians 5:10
[1215] James 4:14
[1216] Isaiah 35:4
[1217] Isaiah 40:11
[1218] Luke 1:49

has visited us. To give light to them that sit in darkness and in the shadow of death.[1219] To guide our feet in the way of peace. *Amen.*

19

DEAR DESIRE OF EVERY NATION, BY YOUR ALL-SUFFICIENT MERIT,

Joy of every longing heart. Raise us to Your glorious throne. You are blessed who dwell between the cherubim.[1220] And graciously regards them of low estate![1221] Praise the Lord, for He is good, and His mercy endures for ever.[1222] Grace be with you, and peace from God our Father, and from the Lord Jesus Christ. The God of all grace. Who has called us to His eternal glory by Christ Jesus. Make us perfect, establish, strengthen, and settle us! To Him be glory and power, from everlasting to everlasting.[1223] *Amen.*

20

PRAISE TO YOU, O LORD, WE GIVE,

For Your love in Jesus shown. May that love, so strong and tender. Bind us fast to Him alone. *Amen.*

21

OUR LORD SAID TO HIS DISCIPLES,

Let not your heart be troubled. Believe in God, believe also in Me. In My Father's house are many mansions; if it were not so, I would have told you. For I go to prepare a place for you. And if I go to prepare a place for you, I come again, and will receive you to Myself. That where I am, there you may be also.[1224] Even so come,

---

1219 Luke 1:79
1220 Isaiah 37:16
1221 Luke 1:48, Psalm 136:23
1222 Psalm 136:1
1223 1 Peter 5:10-11
1224 John 14:1-4

Lord Jesus. If we believe that Jesus died and rose again. Even so those also that have died in Jesus will God bring with Him. For the Lord Himself shall descend from heaven with a shout. With the voice of the archangel. And with the trumpet of God. And the dead in Christ shall rise first. Then we who are alive, that are left, shall together with them be caught up in the clouds, to meet the Lord in the air. And so will we ever be with the Lord. Therefore comfort one another with these words.[1225] *Amen.*

22

LIKE HIM WE THEN SHALL BE,

The Son of God has taken the throne, transformed and glorified. We too shall be revealed, and shine for we shall see Him as He is.[1226] In glory, like His own. And in His light abide. *Amen.*

23

YOU HAVE BLESSED US WITH ALL SPIRITUAL BLESSINGS,

In heavenly places in Christ.[1227] You have delivered us from the power of darkness, and have translated us into the kingdom of Your dear Son.[1228] In Him dwells all the fullness of the Godhead bodily.[1229] He is the true God, and eternal life.[1230] By Himself has He reconciled all things to Himself. Whether they are things on earth, or things in heaven.[1231] You who are the one God and Father of all. And who has adopted us as children in Jesus Christ—Your Son—in who we have redemption, even the forgiveness of our sins. Quicken us we beg You, who have been dead in trespasses and sins.[1232] For the sake

---

[1225] 1 Thessalonians 4:14-18
[1226] 1 John 3:2
[1227] Ephesians 1:3
[1228] Colossians 1:13
[1229] Colossians 2:9
[1230] 1 John 5:20
[1231] Colossians 1:20
[1232] Ephesians 2:1

of that great love where You have loved us. Make us to live in Christ our Lord. *Amen.*

24

HEARTS, THAT ONCE WERE TAUGHT TO OWN,

Idol gods of wood and stone. Now to light and life restored. Honor Jesus as their Lord. Behold, the darkness will cover the earth, and gross darkness the people. But the Lord shall arise over you, and His glory shall be seen over you.[1233] And the Gentiles shall come to your light, and kings to the brightness of your rising. Arise, shine. For your light is come, and the glory of the Lord is risen upon you.[1234] *Amen.*

25

WHILE THE FOE BECOMES MORE DARING,

While he *enters like a flood*,[1235] God the Savior is preparing means to spread His truth abroad. Every language soon shall tell the love of God. Bless our and all other Christian congregations gathered from among the heathen. Keep them as the apple of Your eye.[1236] Let them be a light to them who sit in darkness and in the region and shadow of death.[1237] Have mercy on Your ancient covenant people. Deliver them from their blindness. Oh that Ishmael might live before You![1238] Hear us, gracious Lord and God. *Amen.*

26

SEND YOUR SERVANTS FORTH,

[1233] Isaiah 60:2
[1234] Isaiah 60:1
[1235] Isaiah 59:19
[1236] Psalm 17:8
[1237] Matthew 4:16
[1238] Genesis 17:18

To call the Hebrews home. From west and east, from south and north. Let all the wanderers come. With Israel's great numbers sealed.[1239] Let all the nations meet. And show Your mystery fulfilled,[1240] Your family complete. *Amen.*

27

LORD GOD, SON, YOU ARE SAVIOR OF THE WORLD,

For as the children are partakers of flesh and blood. You did also Yourself likewise take part of the same, that through death You might destroy him that had the power of death—that is—the devil.[1241] You were in all things made like Your brethren, that You might be a merciful and faithful High Priest in things pertaining to God. To make reconciliation for the sins of the people.[1242] You were despised and rejected of men. A man of sorrows and acquainted with grief. You were wounded for our transgressions. You were bruised for our iniquities. The chastisement of our peace was upon You. And with Your stripes we are healed.[1243] *Amen.*

28

BY YOUR HOLY INCARNATION AND BIRTH.

Your early exile. Your pure and blameless childhood. Your willing obedience. Your humility, meekness, and patience. Your faithfulness in Your earthly calling. Your perfect life before God and man. Help us —O Christ—to dedicate both soul and body to Your service.[1244] Your tears and agony. Your crown of thorns and cross. Lead us to repentance for our sins.[1245] By Your willing sacrifice of Yourself even to death. Make known to us the mystery of Your love. Into Your open arms stretched out upon the cross. Receive us all. *Amen.*

[1239] Romans 11:26
[1240] Revelation 10:7
[1241] Hebrews 2:14
[1242] Hebrews 2:17
[1243] Isaiah 53:3-5
[1244] Romans 12:1-2
[1245] Acts 3:19

29

THE FATHER OF GLORY HAS RAISED CHRIST FROM THE DEAD,
And made Him to sit at His right hand in the heavenly places, far above all rule and authority and power and dominion and every name that is named. Not only in this world, but also in that which is to come. And He put all things in subjection under His feet. And gave Him to be head over all things to the Church—which is His body— the fullness of Him that fills all in all.[1246] Therefore with angels and archangels, and with all the company of heaven. We laud and magnify Your glorious Name. Evermore praising You. And saying, Holy, Holy, Holy, Lord God of Hosts, heaven and earth are full of Your glory. Glory be to You, O Lord Most High.[1247] *Amen.*

30

THROUGH HIS OWN BLOOD HE ENTERED IN ONCE FOR ALL,
Into the holy place, having obtained eternal redemption, now to appear before the face of God for us.[1248] Wherefore, also, He is able to save to the uttermost them that draw near to God through Him. Seeing He ever lives to make intercession for them.[1249] Who shall lay anything to the charge of God's elect? It is God that justifies. Who is he that condemns? It is Christ Jesus that died, yes, rather, that was raised from the dead. Who is at the right hand of God. Who also makes intercession for us.[1250] *Amen.*

31

FEAR NOT, SAYS THE LORD, I AM THE FIRST AND THE LAST,
And the living One. And I was dead, and behold, I am alive forevermore. And I have the keys of death and of Hades.[1251] He that

---

[1246] Ephesians 1:20-23
[1247] Revelation 4:8
[1248] Hebrews 9:12
[1249] Hebrews 7:25
[1250] Romans 8:33-34
[1251] Revelation 1:17-18

overcomes, I will give to him to sit down with Me in My throne. As I also overcame, and sat down with My Father in His throne.[1252] Thanks be to God, who gives us the victory through our Lord Jesus Christ.[1253] Beloved, now are we children of God, and it is not yet made manifest what we shall be. We know that, if He shall be manifested, we shall be like Him. For we shall see Him even as He is. And every one that has this hope set on Him purifies himself, even as he is pure.[1254] *Amen.*

32

GOD WAS MANIFESTED IN THE FLESH

Justified in the Spirit. Seen by angels. Preached among the Gentiles. Believed on in the world. Received up in glory.[1255] *Amen.*

33

FOR IF WE DIED WITH HIM,

We shall also live with Him. If we endure, we shall also reign with Him. If we deny Him, He also will deny us. If we are faithless, He remains faithful. He cannot deny Himself.[1256] *Amen.*

34

WORTHY IS THE LAMB WHO WAS SLAIN,

To receive power, and riches, and wisdom. And strength, and honor, and glory. And blessing, for ever and ever, Hallelujah! Blessing, and honor, and glory, and power, be to Him that sits on the throne, and to the Lamb, for ever and ever.[1257] *Amen.*

[1252] Revelation 3:21
[1253] 1 Corinthians 15:57
[1254] 1 John 3:2-3
[1255] 1 Timothy 3:16
[1256] 2 Timothy 2:11-13
[1257] Revelation 5:12

35

WE GIVE YOU THANKS, HOLY FATHER,[1258]

For Your holy Name, which You have caused to dwell in our hearts. And for the knowledge and faith and immortality that You have made known to us through Jesus your servant. To You be the glory forever. You, Almighty Master, created all things for Your Name's sake. And gave food and drink to humans to enjoy, so that they might give You thanks. But to us You have graciously given spiritual food and drink, and eternal life through Your servant. Above all we give thanks to You because You are Mighty. To You be the glory forever. Remember Your Church, Lord, to deliver it from all evil and to make it perfect in Your love. And from the four winds gather the Church that has been sanctified into Your kingdom. Which You have prepared for it. For Yours is the power and the glory forever. May grace come, and may this world pass away. Hosanna to the God of David. If anyone is holy, let him come. If anyone is not, let him repent. *Maranatha! Amen.*

[1258] Didache (A.D. 80-140)

Made in the USA
Lexington, KY
08 October 2013